The Durham Villages

David Simpson

The Northern Echo

Business Education Publishers Limited

© David Simpson and *The Northern Echo*

ISBN 1 901888 51 7
ISBN 978 1 901888 51 5

Cover Design Tim Murphy, Bradley O'Mahoney Creative Ltd.

Front cover: Shincliffe village. Photograph by David Simpson
Back cover: Shadforth village. Photograph by David Simpson

Published in Great Britain by
Business Education Publishers Limited
The Teleport
Doxford International
Sunderland
Tyne & Wear
SR3 3XD

Tel: 0191 5252410
Fax: 0191 5201815

British Cataloguing-in-Publications Data
A catalogue record for this book is available from the British Library

Printed in Great Britain by The Alden Group, Oxford

For my brother John

How to get to St. Aidan's College

⛫ University of Durham

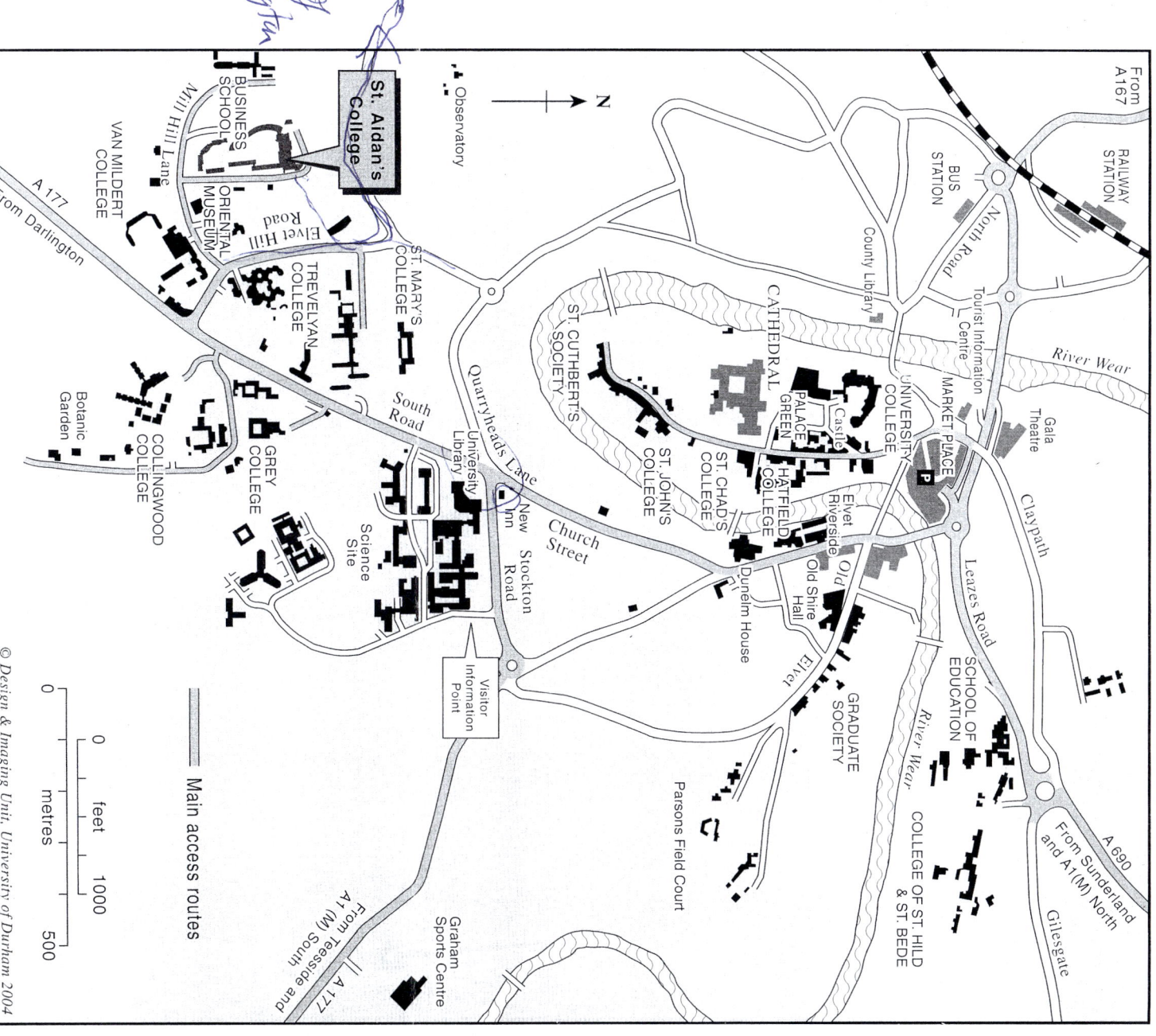

© Design & Imaging Unit, University of Durham 2004

Main access routes ▬

0 feet 1000
0 metres 500

Duke of Wellington

How to get to St. Aidan's College:

By Car

From the South and East

Drive north on the A1(M) and exit at Junction 61. Take the A177 signposted Bowburn and Peterlee. Follow the road, through Bowburn, for approximately three miles until you enter Durham on the Stockton Road. Turn left at the first roundabout and then left again at the New Inn traffic lights into South Road. Continue up the hill for half a mile. Take the first main right turn into Elvet Hill Road and then first left into Mill Hill Lane. Drive on until you see the signpost for St. Aidan's College on the right.

From the North and East

Drive south on the A1(M) and exit at Junction 62. Take the A690 to Durham. After three miles, at the first roundabout

take the second main exit which crosses under a pedestrian footbridge. You will see immediately in front of you a magnificent view of the Cathedral, Castle, and City. Turn left at the next roundabout into New Elvet and follow the road for approximately half a mile (bearing right into Church Street) to the New Inn traffic lights. Go straight ahead into South Road and then follow the instructions given above.

From the West

Drive on the A167 to the Cock of the North roundabout (junction with the A177). Take the Durham A177 exit into South Road, and follow it for approximately half a mile. Turn left just after the 30 mph signs into Elvet Hill Road, first left into Mill Hill Lane and then follow the instructions given above.

By Rail

Fourteen trains per day travel from London and Edinburgh to Durham. The journey takes less than three hours from London, one and a half hours from Edinburgh and forty-five minutes from York.

By Bus

There are several express coach services daily from most major cities.

By Air

The nearest airports are Newcastle upon Tyne and Teesside. Newcastle airport is linked to Durham by rail and Metro.

By Sea

European scheduled ferry services travel to and from Newcastle on a regular basis.

St. Aidan's Reception: 0191 334 5769

Mis Read.
Ragh House
Church St.
Beaumb...

Acknowledgements

Thanks to Anita Thompson, Jean Garland and all the staff of Durham Clayport local studies library. Thanks should also go to Darlington local studies library. Special thanks to Michael Richardson, June Crosby, George Nairn, John Kitching, Roy Lambeth, Bill Fawcett, David Williams, John Geddes, Barry Wood, Graham Cozens, Dorothy Meade, the late Gordon McKeag, Martin Roberts, John Richardson, Mr Wade, Mike Syers, Graham Robson, Jim Milburn, Dave Shotten, John Bones, Denis Dunlop, David Young, Jo Jones, Mitchells and Butler, Richard Hird, Mary Hawgood, John Lightley, Jean Stirk, Chris Fish, Clive Lawson, Gail Hudson, Jenny Lee and many, many others. In fact thanks to everyone who has phoned, written or taken me on a potted tour of one kind or another.

Thanks should also go to Petra Stanton, Chris Moran and Rob Greener for their work on the excellent maps that have accompanied Durham Memories from time to time. They have been skilfully and meticulously recreated from my inky sketches.

Photographs in this and the accompanying book are supplied from a number of sources including Michael Richardson (MR), George Nairn (GN), Gail Hudson (GH), June Crosby, the Fulling Mill Museum (FM), Roy Lambeth (RL) and Hamsteels Hall (HH). Photographs from the archives of The Northern Echo are marked (NE) and those taken by the author are marked (DS).

There are many old history books that have come to my assistance from time to time during my Durham Memories research. Where would I be for example without the nineteenth century histories of Robert Surtees and William Fordyce or the early twentieth century Victoria County History? And then of course there are the modern electronic sources that are such a gift for the historian of today. The invaluable 1881 census of Great Britain published on CD Rom by the Mormon Church is one worthy of mention but also tremendously useful are websites like Tomorrow's History, Keys to the Past and the Durham Mining Museum that have been such a great boon to local history research in our region. Thanks should also go to Peter Barron for inviting me to write the Durham Memories column but many thanks should go to Andrea Murphy, Moira Page, David Taylor and everyone at Business Education Publishers. Finally, a very, very special thanks should go to my long suffering wife Abi, who has put up with my obsession and has been left on more than one occasion, quite literally holding the baby.

Author Biography

David Simpson was born in Durham City in 1967 and is the author of thirteen books on North East history. He has worked for *The Northern Echo* newspaper since January 1994 and has been the author of the Durham Memories column since 2003. David's previous publications include *The Millennium History of North East England* hailed by the Prime Minister Tony Blair and *Northern Roots* which investigates the origins of people in Northern England. He has made many contributions to television and radio with appearances on Tyne Tees Television, Channel Four, BBC Radio 4, BBC Radio Newcastle, Radio Cleveland and other local programmes. He has given hundreds of talks across the North on various aspects of the region's history and in his spare time is an enthusiastic photographer and amateur actor treading the boards with local theatre groups. David lives with his wife, young daughter and two cats in Durham City.

Photograph by John Simpson

Contents

Preface

The villages featured in this book lie within a five or six mile radius of Durham City, with the occasional excursion beyond. All have been included in my Durham Memories feature that appears in *The Northern Echo* newspaper and the book is based on that column. It is one of two companion books and to complete the picture I recommend the accompanying title covering the City of Durham and its surrounding suburbs.

When I started writing the Durham Memories feature for *The Northern Echo* in January 2003 my initial focus was upon Durham City. It was an obvious choice since it has such a rich history with lots of legends, a famous cathedral and historic features galore. As a Durham City lad it was also a place with which I was very familiar.

My knowledge of the surrounding villages was, by contrast, a little more sketchy, although I did know one or two things about the area. I knew for example that there were architectural links between Pittington church and Durham Cathedral and that there were remnants of a fortified house at Ludworth. I knew that Bearpark was the site of a medieval manor, that Langley Park had a striking setting at the foot of the Browney valley and that there was a medieval hospital at Sherburn.

More than anything else I knew that many villages around Durham were mining settlements, but I knew little of the detail. It was not through lack of interest. These places are in my blood and I have a number of personal links to the surrounding villages. I went to school with people from villages like Sherburn and Bearpark and also have family connections with certain villages. I have relatives living in Sacriston, Brandon and High Shincliffe and my wife also has connections with surrounding villages. She grew up in Witton Gilbert before moving to Shincliffe and it was at Shincliffe that my daughter was christened.

My mother and father also have links to surrounding villages. My grandmother on Dad's side grew up in the little-known colliery village of Browney near Meadowfield. Browney is a tiny village named from the neighbouring river that will feature prominently in the history of many villages in this book. My grandmother's father was the Browney Colliery electrician and the family resided in Office Street in the village.

On my mother's side family history takes me into the neighbouring valley of the Deerness and the mining village of Esh Winning. Here my grandfather was born and raised. He belonged to one of many Irish families that settled in the neighbourhood during the nineteenth century and this Irish legacy, of which I am very proud, is one shared by many families in and around Durham City.

Although the Durham Memories column continued to focus on the city and its suburbs I made ever increasing visits to the surrounding places that lie within a five or six mile radius of the city. The only rule was that they should lie within the area covered by the north edition of *The Northern Echo* in which the Durham Memories column appears.

My eventual aim was to cover all of the villages in the Durham City area and it was a task that I had more or less completed by 2006. A huge task it has proved. My desire was to present an account of the history of each village showing how they came about and how they have developed and grown. Many of these villages are the home to *The Northern Echo* readers and I believed that residents would enjoy reading about the history of their home village, as well as other neighbouring villages, in the pages of their favourite newspaper.

As well as giving a history of each place I have also looked for interesting tales to tell. In this quest I have discovered a Victorian police murder at Sherburn, an outrageous strike at Ushaw Moor, and a tale of ghostly justice at Great Lumley. Such stories were always welcomed but I have never forgotten the history of the village itself. After all everywhere has a history so everywhere has a story to tell.

My view was that each village deserved a mention and this has been confirmed by the countless phone calls and correspondence that I have received from enthusiastic and often nostalgic readers.

It has been a particular joy to hear from those villagers now stranded across various parts of the world who have been sent copies of the articles from thoughtful friends and relatives back home in County Durham. Of course I am also grateful for the comments, corrections and contributions that have been provided by readers from time to time.

It has also been a real joy researching these articles, making the discoveries and acquiring the facts. I have found that some places are very old, while others are relatively new, but all are proud places with strong local identities.

Village by village I have worked my way through countless local and county histories, pored over old maps and photos and many a dusty directory. I have visited each place armed with camera to see what there is to see. In many places like Langley Park, Plawsworth, Kelloe and Esh Winning, to name a few, I have stopped and chatted to friendly locals to pick their brains for all that they could remember. I would like to thank all of those – and there were many – who shared their knowledge and pointed me in the direction of interesting features in almost every place I visited.

More often than not, as if by magic, I would pick someone in the street with a vast local knowledge of their home village. This was particularly notable in the case of Edmondsley where the chap I cornered just so happened to be the organiser for the local history society and took me on a tour. Then there was Witton Gilbert where a local man introduced me to an interesting collection of ancient stone carvings.

Apart from the friendliness and helpful nature of the locals, there were two other things that struck me about the land surrounding the City of Durham. One was the continuing growth and redevelopment that is taking place in many of the villages. Everywhere there are new, neat looking housing estates interspersed between older terraces.

The other thing that struck me was the wealth of lovely countryside that sits on the doorstep of many villages around Durham City. The scenery of Durham's surrounds is no longer scarred by the numerous collieries and monstrous pit heaps that were once everywhere to be seen. Coal mines were once the life and sole of this area and their closure brought hardship and an end to a way of life, but these places have survived and are being reborn.

The difference is that now it is rural scenery rather than pit heaps that predominate. It doesn't matter whether you are in the picturesque parkland of Croxdale, the limestone hills of Pittington and Quarrington, or the scenic valleys of Deerness or Browney, everywhere there is scenery and there are often wonderful views. Here and there we may even catch a glimpse of the distant Durham Cathedral, serving as a constant reminder that history is never very far away.

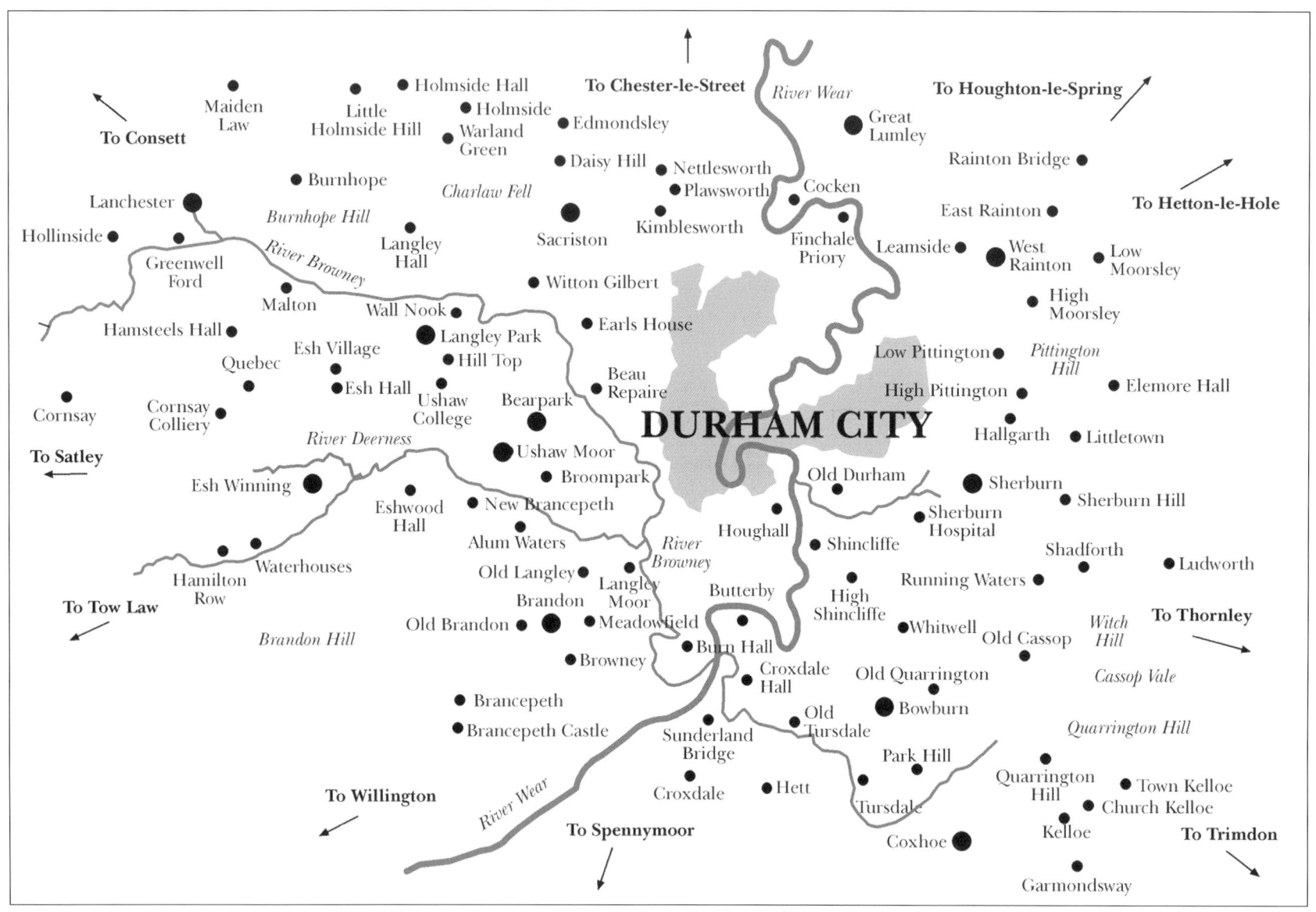

Durham Villages Map

Introduction
The Villages

Most of the villages covered in this book lie within the administrative boundaries of Durham City as they stand in 2006, but for geographical and historical purposes I will make a number of detours into the districts of Chester-le-Street and Derwentside where it seems necessary to complete the picture.

Villages like Sacriston, Edmondsley, Plawsworth and Kimblesworth all lie within the local government district of Chester-le-Street but are included here because they lie so close to Durham. In fact without their inclusion Witton Gilbert would be the only official Durham City village that I could include from the immediate north of the city.

The other major detour has been in the west where I travel up the course of the River Browney from Durham City. This takes us out towards the villages of Langley Park, Lanchester and even as far west as Satley where the Browney valley takes on a strong Pennine appearance. These villages are in the Derwentside district but are actually quite distant from the River Derwent. The River Browney is ultimately a tributary of the River Wear that it joins near Durham and the whole Browney valley will be covered in this book.

There are other good reasons for my occasional excursion across the boundaries. It would, for example, be rather artificial, to include places like Ushaw Moor and Esh Winning and then ignore Ushaw College and Old Esh village simply because they lie in Derwentside.

On the other hand there are some Durham villages that are right in the very heart of the city area that we will not be including here. Here I refer to those villages and settlements that have become absorbed by the city's suburbs. Pity Me, Framwellgate Moor and Carrville are the prime examples and all of these are covered in my accompanying book on Durham City itself. In truth the two books are intended as companion volumes that will complement each other. Indeed the stories and places in both the books are closely linked.

The Browney Valley near Wall Nook (DS)

The Northern and Eastern Villages

Immediately north of Durham City on the moorland hills to the east of the River Browney are the villages of Sacriston and Witton Gilbert that trace their origins back to medieval times. Sacriston is included here because of its historic links to Durham Cathedral but is now one of the largest former pit villages in the Durham city area. From Sacriston I head east to Kimblesworth which has some historic links with Pity Me and then on towards Plawsworth. This village is featured not only because it is interesting in its own right, but also because of the lovely neighbouring countryside in between the Great North Road and the River Wear. The scenery around Plawsworth forms a scenic backdrop to Finchale Priory and the northern fringe of Durham's Newton Hall estate.

The lovely riverside scenery around Plawsworth continues east from Finchale Priory across the river towards the farms of Cocken and the village of West Rainton. Here I will stray briefly into Chester-le-Street for a visit to Great Lumley in the closing chapter of the book.

West Rainton falls within Durham City and apart from a courtesy mention of East Rainton just over the boundary in Sunderland our coverage of the eastern villages is relatively straightforward. Here we feature the Raintons, the Pittingtons, Littletown, the Sherburns, the Quarringtons, the Cassops and the Kelloes.

It is a rather curious feature of such place-names in County Durham that they often occur in duplicate. Thus we have a Pittington and a High Pittington, a Sherburn and a Sherburn Hill, a Cassop and an Old Cassop, a Kelloe and a Town Kelloe.

St. Helen's Church, Kelloe (DS)

The villages to the east of the city lie amongst the magnesian limestone hills that rise to form distinct scenery hereabouts. Rolling hills typify this limestone district and can be rather attractive, with a softer, gentler appearance than the Pennines to the west. Of course, as everywhere in Durham, there is much evidence of former mining activity in this eastern district and many places clearly originated as pit villages, though there are no longer any collieries to see.

Significant features of this eastern area are the creamy stone outcrops of magnesian limestone or 'dolomite' that has been excavated hereabouts for centuries. The quarries are still very apparent in places today, particularly in the south eastern area and are often still active, forming deep craters with seemingly lunar landscapes that could easily swallow a whole village and have room left over. These quarries are rather extraordinary sights where heavy digger trucks look like nothing more than tiny childrens' toys lost at the bottom of enormous sand pits.

The Heugh at Quarrington Hill (DS)

It is remarkable that these quarries often go unnoticed on the ground even as we drive or walk within a few yards of them. Many are rather subtly hidden away amongst rolling hills but the scale of these quarries is very apparent in satellite photographs of County Durham. Here they show up as huge creamy blobs or blemishes that are by far the most prominent landscape feature on the aerial photographs of the county.

In this eastern and south eastern area our coverage of the villages does not stray beyond the boundaries of the administrative City of Durham. The Easington district to the east forms a quite distinct coastal area where there are many places worthy of mention but they are too numerous and too far beyond the boundaries of Durham City to be included here. Wheatley Hill, Wingate, Deaf Hill, Station Town and Thornley do not quite make it into the pages of this book, but will hopefully be covered in the memories column at some time in the future.

Nor have we headed south east towards the Trimdons, made famous in recent years as the northern home of the Prime Minister, Tony Blair. Here our limits are determined not only by administrative boundaries but by the practical limits of *The Northern Echo's* northern edition.

The Southern Villages

The boundaries that define our eastern limits also make the southerly coverage of this book quite clear cut. Shincliffe, High Shincliffe, Hett, Butterby, Bowburn, Croxdale and Coxhoe are clearly within our limits but Cornforth, Coxhoe's near neighbour unfortunately, is not, as it lies within the district of Sedgefield and is covered by a more southerly edition of *The Northern Echo*.

Hett and High Shincliffe do lie within our area of coverage however and both are situated on hill tops, but a large part of this southern area consists of a low lying vale formed by the meandering course of the River Wear. The vale divides the limestone quarry country to the east from the moorland foothills of Brancepeth, Brandon and the Deerness valley to the west.

Of the Durham villages in this southern area Shincliffe and the neighbouring scenery around Old Durham and Houghall form a particularly lovely area and it is here that we will begin our journey of the Durham villages in the first chapter. This is the closest we will get to the heart of Durham City and is a natural continuation from the accompanying city book.

The old chapel at Croxdale Hall (DS)

Equally appealing in this southern area is the lowland scenery around Croxdale. Away from the busy main road Croxdale has some wonderful but little-known parkland at Croxdale Hall. Also nearby is the magnificent mansion of Burn Hall and the lovely sylvan scenery of Butterby woods.

Croxdale, like Coxhoe lies at the southern limit of our boundaries and to its south lies Tudhoe and the town of Spennymoor – the headquarters for the separate administrative district of Sedgefield. Spennymoor owes its origins partly to mining but mostly to a nineteenth century ironworks and has a history all of its own. Unfortunately there is not the space to feature it here. In any case Spennymoor is a town, not a village. Nor will we visit Spennymoor's historic neighbour, the attractive and rather picturesque green village of Tudhoe that again lies outside the geographical and editorial limits of this book.

West of Croxdale, across the River Wear we enter yet another distinct region that will be covered in this book. At the south west of this area lies the historic Brancepeth Castle at the gateway to Weardale. This castle once dominated a vast tract of land that stretched for miles around. Near to the castle is the lovely but ever so tiny

village of Brancepeth. Both castle and village are included in this book.

Croxdale Hall (DS)

To the north of Brancepeth is the former mining village of Brandon and associated Brandon hill that once formed part of the Brancepeth estate. Brandon is covered in the book along with its near neighbours at Littleburn, Browney, Meadowfield and Langley Moor. In recent times Meadowfield has been associated with various administrative offices of Durham City council and thus has a strong modern link to that city.

Brancepeth Village (DS)

Meadowfield's neighbour, Langley Moor lies very close to the western suburbs of Durham City at Neville's Cross and significantly also lies at the junction of the Rivers Browney and Deerness. More than anything else, these two little rivers have dominated the hilly scenery and history of the land immediately west of Durham City.

The Deerness, the slightly smaller and generally more southerly of the two rises near Tow Law, and forms a significant valley that cuts its way towards Durham. The valley is home to the villages of Hamilton Row, Waterhouses, Esh Winning, Ushaw Moor, Broompark and New Brancepeth, all of which are featured in this book.

Brancepeth Castle (DS)

Here we will also pay a visit to the nearby College of Ushaw, a magnificent building that stands on a hill high above the valley. The college has an unexpectedly lengthy history that long predates that of Durham University with which it is now so closely associated. The college is a Roman Catholic institution and is the most outstanding reminder of the strong Roman Catholic links that the Deerness and Browney valleys have had for many centuries.

The Northern and Western Villages

The River Browney lies to the west and north west of Durham City and like the Deerness forms a valley that is home to a number of notable villages. At the end of its course the Browney forms a scenic western border to the Durham City suburbs of Neville's Cross and Crossgate Moor in a stretch of river that was once noted for its paper making mills. However we have featured this area more prominently in our accompanying book on Durham City. For the purposes of this book we are concerned more with the middle and upper sections of the valley from Bearpark and beyond.

Bearpark and the associated ruins of the manor house that belonged to the medieval park of Beau Repaire are of considerable interest here. The park dominated a vast section of the landscape and the ruins of the manor still lie on a bluff of land overlooking the River Browney. It was in this area that the Scots encamped prior to the Battle of Neville's Cross in 1346.

Nineteenth Century illustration showing the ruins of Beau Repaire

The River Browney near Langley Park (DS)

Also featured in this book is the village of Witton Gilbert that overlooks the Browney valley to the north. It is a village that can trace its history back to Bronze Age times, as exemplified by the ancient rock markings that occasionally turn up in its vicinity.

Unlike Sacriston, its neighbour to the north, Witton Gilbert lies just within the administrative district of Durham City but in order to explore the Browney valley we must by necessity stray into the neighbouring district of Derwentside to reach Langley Park, Witton's valley dwelling neighbour across the Browney to the west.

Derwentside is perhaps something of a misnomer for this particular area of Durham as the River Derwent is at least ten miles to the north. In fact the part of Derwentside that concerns us here might be more accurately called 'Browneyside'. It is an area that includes the village of Langley Park with its striking location at the bottom of the Browney valley. Around Langley Park we also turn our attention to the villages that lie on the hill tops between the Browney and Deerness. These include the

little villages of Cornsay Colliery, Quebec, Old Esh and the intriguing Catholic presbytery of Esh Laude.

We also head deeper into the Pennines towards Old Cornsay and Satley where the Browney more or less begins its course. This leaves only one more northerly excursion into the Browney's tributary valleys formed by the Smallhope and Alderdene Burns. Here lies Lanchester, a lovely village with a history tied to both the Browney valley and to the more north westerly sections of County Durham that lie outside the practical scope of this book. With a history dating back to Roman times Lanchester is an irresistible subject for this book and I make no apologies for straying so far north.

Beyond Lanchester we will draw the line but we will explore some of the historic houses and halls that surround the village before heading east to the neighbouring village of Burnhope at the top of the hill.

Langley Park nestles in the Browney valley (DS)

Lofty Burnhope with the Browney valley below offers some of the most wide ranging views in the County of Durham, as indeed does its eastern neighbour, Charlaw Fell. It is at the foot of Charlaw that we reach

Edmondsley and the little known village of Holmside as well as the much larger settlement called Sacriston just over on Charlaw's eastern flank.

Charlaw Fell near Edmondsley (DS)

Cottages at Little Holmside Hall (DS)

Villages in the City

There are a number of villages, farms and hamlets that won't be covered in this book but which are worth

mentioning briefly here. I refer to the places swallowed up by Durham's suburban growth. Such places are now regarded as part and parcel of the city and are covered in the accompanying book on the city.

Durham itself no doubt started life as a village, farmstead or little agricultural settlement of some kind or another. Indeed when the monks carrying St. Cuthbert's coffin settled at Durham in AD 995 and established their fledgling city, there already seems to have been some farming activity on the site.

Simeon of Durham, an eleventh Century historian records that the monks found that there was already a small, cultivated plain regularly ploughed and sown by farmers. The farming referred to here took place in the Anglo-Saxon period, but there had been agricultural development long before that time. Just south of Elvet at Maiden Castle is a probable Iron Age fort and here Celtic agriculturalists may have carried out farming nearby. Later, at neighbouring Old Durham there was an important Roman farm but the remnants of this site have now disappeared.

It is remarkable that some old farms with histories stretching back to medieval times survive right at the very heart of Durham City. Amongst them is the historic Kepier Farm which incorporates part of the medieval hospital of Kepier. Across the River Wear to the north of Kepier are two farmhouses called Frankland Farm and Frankland Park, where there are fine views of Durham Cathedral. It is known that Frankland Park was a deer park belonging to the Prince Bishops of Durham.

Other farmhouses close to the city centre include one at Crook Hall in the city's Sidegate while at Crossgate Moor we find the lovely Baxter Wood Farm on the banks of the River Browney, a stone's throw from Bearpark and Langley Moor. Other farms can be seen near the heart of

the city at Old Durham and at Houghall and these two places are covered in the Shincliffe chapter of this village book.

One of the most significant agricultural survivals from the medieval age is the farm called the Hallgarth that stands in the Elvet area of Durham City. Also once known as Elvet Hall Manor it was probably the most important farm in the whole of County Durham. It was the manor for the Priory of Durham Cathedral. This priory was centred upon the cathedral and its cloisters and was an extremely powerful landowner that controlled agriculture and land management across vast swathes of medieval Durham. The Priory and its offshoot at Finchale owned land at one time or another at places like Pittington, Bearpark, Sacriston, Shincliffe, Elemore, Coxhoe, Hett, Aldin Grange, Cocken and Rainton and thus played a very big part in the history of many of the Durham villages that are featured in this book.

Elvet Hall Manor, the home farm of the priory must have resembled a village itself at one time and its remains can still be seen just off Hallgarth Street in the city. It was originally a great complex of buildings and the surviving medieval tithe barn dates from the 1400s. It is one of the most remarkable medieval attractions of Durham City but unfortunately is not accessible to the public as it is now used by the staff of Durham prison.

Some of the developing suburbs of Durham City would have included farmhouses amongst their streets as they began to grow. In places these suburbs would have perhaps resembled villages or hamlets. For example the street of Claypath is known to have included farms along its course as did Gilesgate. In fact one part of Gilesgate that still closely resembles a village is Gilesgate Green, otherwise known as the 'Duckpond'.

There are however hints of other forgotten villages or hamlets hidden here and there amongst the city's suburbs. Near Framwellgate Moor we can for example still see a few older houses of the forgotten hamlet called Durham Moor. Situated on what was once the Great North Road this settlement included a pub called the Black Boy Inn and a small collection of cottages. There are still a couple of older, more distinct houses here overlooking the roundabout on the Sacriston road near Durham's New College but the pub has long since gone.

The former mining village of Framwellgate Moor is now a Durham suburb (DS)

Similarly at Moor End near Carrville we see a collection of houses around the Sportsman's Arms that still have a village-like appearance and not that far away at Dragonville is the historic Bay Horse pub, a surviving remnant of a settlement called West Sherburn. It is now stranded on the edge of a major retail development.

The largest villages to be swallowed up by the urban growth of the City of Durham were of course the former pit villages that have now become suburbs. These mining villages all developed in the early nineteenth century and included Framwellgate Moor and Pity Me in the north, Broomside and Carrville in the east and the long-lost village of New Durham which stood on the road opposite Durham's Sherburn Road Housing Estate.

Also of note were smaller pit villages like Brasside (that was subsequently relocated) and tiny colliery settlements of the early nineteenth century at Gilesgate Moor like Bell's Ville, Dragonville and Ernest Place. These last few often consisted of nothing more than a single street. Collieries serving these city colliery villages could be found at Carrville, Kepier, Framwellgate Moor, Brasside and Frankland.

In the nineteenth century places like Framwellgate Moor and Gilesgate Moor depended on coal mining for their survival, just as much as the surrounding villages like Sherburn, Bearpark or Brandon. There were also collieries at Aykley Heads, and Crook Hall right in the very heart of the city centre. In fact there was even a colliery at Elvet in the shadow of Durham Cathedral complete with a neighbouring pit terrace that housed the Elvet miners. However more about these places can be found in the accompanying book.

Village Place-Names

Many villages around Durham can trace their origins back to medieval times and beyond and even those that came into being as mining settlements in the nineteenth century often took their names from earlier settlements, farmhouses or neighbouring features. Place-names often reveal something about the origins of the first people who settled in these farms or villages and the place-names can also give clues to the nature of the landscape in times gone by.

Most place-names in England are Anglo-Saxon in origin and are most significantly exemplified by those ending in tun (ton) or ham that signify an enclosed farm, estate or a homestead. Around Durham City the tons and hams are quite rare but occasionally occur in farm names like Scripton and Nafferton near Brandon or hamlets like Malton near Lanchester. Quarrington and Pittington to the east of the city are both red herrings since these are not 'tuns' but duns. Dun is a quite separate Anglo-Saxon word that signifies a hill. Rainton however was a genuine 'tun' that belonged to someone called Raegnwald but seems to have developed in the later Anglo-Saxon period.

Rainton was the settlement belonging to Raegnwald (DS)

We know that Rainton belonged to Raegnwald because of an historical record that states this but often we have to look at the earliest recorded spelling of a place-name to understand its meaning or to find out the name of its historic owner or settler. By this means we learn that Coxhoe was the spur of land belonging to someone called

Cocc while Cocken was a stretch of river belonging to someone with a similar name. Pittington was the hill belonging to Pidda, Aldin Grange the ridge of Alda and Kimblesworth the enclosure of Cymel.

Most places in the Durham City area do seem to have names that are Anglo-Saxon in style but they generally refer to landscape features that suggest that the Durham area was a heavily wooded overgrown landscape with very little settlement in times gone by.

Place-names like Langley, of which there are two to the west of the city, mean the long clearing in the wood, since ley was an Anglo-Saxon word for a clearing. There are other occurrences of this in the west. Examples include Satley that may mean 'the hiding place clearing', and then there is the farm of Stockley – 'the log clearing' near Brancepeth which gave its name to a neighbouring beck. Near Esh Winning there is a Rowley meaning the rough clearing and near Brandon Hill a farm called Wooley. This last one could mean the wolf's clearing but early spellings point to it being wolf's law – the wolf's hill. North of Durham is Edmondsley, possibly meaning the shepherd's clearing while Lumley is the clearing of the pools. Close to Great Lumley is Leamside that means hillside at the clearings. Thornley, just outside the scope of the book was amongst the thorns, but Moorsley on a hill north of Pittington seems to be a corruption of Morulf's Law – the hill belonging to Morulf.

Indicators of thick woodland include the place-name Esh, meaning ash tree, Ushaw meaning the 'shaw' or copse of a man called Ulf or perhaps the wolf's wood. Witton Gilbert derives from the Anglo-Saxon Widu-Tun meaning the wood farm but the addition of the French name Gilbert came at a later date.

Broom or gorse seems to have been a common feature of the landscape in those distant days as it still is today. It gave rise to the name of Broompark (once known simply as Broom) as well as Broomside and the name Brandon that once literally meant Broom Hill.

The place-names Croxdale and Tursdale refer to little wooded valleys formed by the river or neighbouring streams but other places named from rivers and streams include Burnigill Farm near Brancepeth, Sleetburn (the alternative name for New Brancepeth), Burn Hall, Burnhope, Sherburn and of course Bowburn. Holywell near Brancepeth and Whitwell near Shincliffe are named from ancient wells.

Leamside – the name means hillside at the clearings (GH)

Stream names are of great interest in the Durham City area because according to the maps they undertake a major change in name here. Generally those on the north side of the city like the Millburn are called burns. Burn is an Anglo-Saxon word for a stream that was also adopted in Scotland. Streams to the south of the city and to the east are called becks in the Viking style that predominates in Yorkshire, Lincolnshire and the Lake District. The change in stream names around Durham City is most noticeable in the west between the valleys of the Deerness and Browney where we have a mixture of both styles of name and also around Pittington on the east side where again we have both becks and burns living side by side.

Viking influence in the place-names of old County Durham is generally rare, except in the south of the county along the Tees valley, but one or two creep into the area just south of the city. Tursdale is a possible example but Raisby and Butterby that both seem to end in the typical Viking fashion 'by' actually developed in a later period following the Norman conquest. Raisby, now best known for its quarrying activity has a name that seems to commemorate a donation in the 1100s of some land hereabouts to Sherburn Hospital by a man called Race Engaine.

Names that date from the period following the Norman Conquest include French place-names like Beau Repaire. This was the early name for what became Bearpark. Sacriston, once the home of the Durham Cathedral Sacristan also derives its name from a French word.

Some places acquired their present names in relatively modern times when mining settlements developed in these areas during the nineteenth century. The neighbouring medieval park of Beau Repaire probably provided the theme for naming nearby mining settlements like Bearpark, Broompark and Langley Park. Esh Winning and Kelloe Winning were named from the 'winning' or finding of coal.

Some mining settlements like Hamilton Row or Lymington took their name from the mine owning or land owning families while other places like New Brancepeth were named from the owner's estate. Others like High Pittington or Middle Rainton would simply take their name from a separate, but neighbouring village. Whatever their origin place-names remain today as a kind of archaeological remnant and record of the past.

Catholics and the Irish

We might associate Catholicism in the Durham villages with Irish immigrants who came to settle in the county during the nineteenth century mining boom but in truth the Catholic legacy in the county goes back to much earlier times.

Catholicism was once the established church in England and throughout medieval times English cathedrals like Durham and all the medieval parish churches across the land were Roman Catholic. It was the religious reforms instigated by Henry VIII in the Tudor period that brought about a break with the Pope in Rome and saw the establishment of the Church of England. Despite these changes there were many influential families in the north of England who remained loyal to the Pope – and often secretly so.

Durham was a hot bed of rebellious Catholicism and foremost amongst the Catholic families sympathetic to Catholicism were the Nevilles of Brancepeth Castle. There appears to have been much Catholic activity in the farms and villages that lay on and around the Brancepeth castle estate. Here priests would secretly hold mass, often ready to take refuge in little secret hiding holes should the Protestant authorities arrive to investigate.

There was much sympathy for the claims of the Catholic Mary Queen of Scots to the English throne and in 1569 the Nevilles were involved in a disastrous Catholic rebellion against Queen Elizabeth I. Known as the Rising of the North, it was plotted at Raby Castle but was focused upon Brancepeth. It ultimately aimed to oust Elizabeth in favour of the Scottish queen but in the event the rebels lost their nerve and fled. Despite the rebellion's half-hearted failure, this rising was not without its repercussions. Throughout Durham and other parts of the north, territory was confiscated from the rebels

including the vast lands belonging to the Nevilles who fled the country to avoid sentence of death. Many of the more lowly rebels were not so lucky and were sentenced to death. Over sixty were hanged in Durham City alone.

Many of the priests who continued to practice Catholicism in the Elizabethan period were executed for their activities. These priests were usually of English origin but arrived in the country under great secrecy from abroad after training at Catholic colleges like Douai in France. One such priest was John Boste, a northerner educated at Rheims. He was captured at Waterhouses in the Deerness Valley in 1593 and subsequently executed at Dryburn in Durham City in the presence of a large crowd.

Despite the dangers, there were still a number of notable Catholic families around in the Durham area during the 1600s. Notable amongst them were the Blakistons and Kennetts of Coxhoe, the Salvins of Croxdale, the Claxtons of Waterhouses and the Smythes of Esh village.

The cross at Esh village (DS)

By the late 1700s there was a greater tolerance of Catholics in England and we hear of the activities of a Father Ferdinand Asmall, a priest at Newhouse (between Esh and Waterhouses) who died in 1798 aged 103.

Much land at Esh was owned by the Catholic Smythe family and in 1798 part of their land at nearby Ushaw was sold for the establishment of a college. It would become a centre for the training of priests and was relocated here from Douai in France.

Also nearby and at around the same time a place of Catholic worship was established at what came to be known as Esh Laude just west of Esh village. Esh Laude still exists today and is one of the most beautiful stone buildings around. Three other places with strong links to Catholicism are Croxdale Hall, the nearby Burn Hall and the village of Tudhoe which all have associations with the Salvin family. The Salvins, who still live in the area today have been associated with Croxdale since the 1400s. In 1807 they incorporated a Gothic style Roman Catholic chapel into their hall at Croxdale. It was in 1926 that this family sold the magnificent Burn Hall to a Roman Catholic mission for training young boys as priests in foreign lands.

Although we can see that there was a very strong Catholic presence around Durham before the Irish arrived, the Irish gave the religion a firmer base in the nineteenth century. The new Irish communities in England would certainly keep Ushaw College busy in its training of priests. Many of these trainees would go on to serve the growing Irish communities, not just around Durham but in communities like Liverpool, Manchester and Tyneside.

In County Durham the Irish communities were a little more modest in size than those of the big northern cities but they are still more than worthy of mention. My grandma who was born in Penshaw but grew up in Durham referred to Durham villages like Sacriston, Brandon and Esh Winning as 'Paddy islands' because of their strong Irish links and like many towns and villages throughout Durham, these were significant locations for Irish settlement.

Ushaw College pictured in 1958 (NE)

In fact Grandma married a member of one such community. Her husband, my Granda Barney, hailed from Esh Winning but his family roots were across the sea in Catholic Monaghan.

Central and north west Durham, particularly Consett and the villages around Durham had significant Irish communities where perhaps at least eight per cent of the 19th century population could be of Irish origin.

Most Irish settlers arrived in Durham following the Irish Potato famine of 1845. Some arrived via Liverpool, others via Glasgow or the Cumberland ports. The 1840s, 50s and 60s were a period of rapid industrial development in England and the failure of the staple Irish potato crop lured many Irish to English industrial regions like the North East. Only Manchester, Liverpool, Glasgow and London were more significant than our region for their Irish populations.

Many Irishmen settled in the major towns of our region like Newcastle, Gateshead, Sunderland and Middlesbrough, finding menial jobs living by their wits as hawkers. Others were more fortunate, finding work in factories or shipyards. Another common occupation was in railway construction.

Irish navigators or navvies on the railways were once a familiar sight and some were involved in constructing railways in and around Durham City.

Coal mining is said to have been a major attraction for the Irish in Durham, but in truth Irishmen had little experience of this work in their homeland. Early Irish settlers generally avoided pit work and were more likely to be found working in newly opened iron works at places like Consett, Wolsingham, Witton Park or Tow Law. Such work was a more attractive proposition in the early days and here there were vacancies not so likely to be snapped up by the more experienced, indigenous pitmen.

As mining expanded and the supply of home bred miners was stretched to the limit, Irishmen became increasingly involved in colliery work. However a glance at records like the 1881 census shows that many were working at the colliery surface, often in neighbouring coke works. The term 'Coke drawer' or 'Coke filler' regularly appears in the occupations of the colliery Irishmen.

Irishmen and women added much colour and character to Durham's colliery villages. There is a wonderful description from a nineteenth century doctor who noted black-shawled Irish women in Sacriston squatting at doors smoking clay pipes. I have heard another account from a nun, who recalls a story of an Irish priest dragging a drunken Irishman from a Sacriston pub and booting him up the main street as punishment for beating his wife. I believe that he decided to improve his behaviour from that day on.

We may picture colliery pubs full of groups of Irishmen intermixed with Durham pitmen and men from many other parts of the country. Perhaps there would be a fiddler in the corner playing a jig. With imagination we can listen to the 'craic' or chatter of these colliery Celts. In

some cases we may have listened but not understood. Some new arrivals came from the Gaelic west of Ireland and spoke little or no English. It is known that a Gaelic speaking priest was employed at Sacriston during the nineteenth century for the benefit of some members of the congregation who flocked to the village's Catholic church.

Catholic churches sprung up everywhere to serve the Irish communities. Durham City's prominent church of St. Godric is an example. Erected in 1864 it served the huge Irish population of Framwellgate slum. This particular Irish community probably had more in common with Irish ghettos in Newcastle and Gateshead than the neighbouring terraces of Durham's colliery villages and iron towns. A few Irish miners resided in Framwellgate, but most were hawkers or agricultural labourers.

The Roman Catholic church of St. Bede at Sacriston (DS)

Drunkenness and outbreaks of violence were probably no more common amongst the Irish in Durham than amongst the natives. There is a record of a riot in Framwellgate involving around 50 Irishmen in 1865 but it seems to have been little more than a pub brawl that got out of hand and I have heard only scant details of sectarian rivalry between Catholic and Protestant Irish communities in places like Consett.

Because of their limited experience in mining, the employment of Irish blacklegs in collieries during strikes was rare. The major exception was in 1844 when the Marquess of Londonderry shipped in about 180 workers (without colliery experience) from Irish estates mostly in County Down to work in his Durham collieries like Rainton and Pittington. Few of these Irish were inclined to remain in the job and they had little impact breaking the strike.

It is probable that some Irish settlers were Protestants but most Irish in Durham appear to have been Catholic. In other parts of the country Irish arrivals often caused anti-Catholic resentment but in Durham the local tolerance of Irish Catholics may have had something to with the county's long-established Catholic links. And of course at Brandon, we have a village that by happy coincidence shares its name with an Irish saint. Perhaps it was features like these that attracted Irishmen like my grandfather's family to County Durham and made them feel so much at home.

The Mining Villages

Many of the villages around Durham have long histories and wherever possible we will give an account of these villages noting who has owned them or lived in them over the years. Occasionally these villages are typical English picture postcard places like Brancepeth, Shincliffe, Sunderland Bridge, Shadforth or Lanchester, but most of the villages featured in this book are in truth mining settlements that only developed in the early or mid nineteenth century.

Of course even the older agricultural villages were affected by the influence of coal mining over the years. Sherburn for example is a pit village built around an older agricultural core, while the old part of Brandon known as 'the village' is a former agricultural settlement. Even Witton Gilbert, an agricultural village that did not acquire a significant coal mine had streets that were built for miners who worked at neighbouring collieries. Occasionally miners would have moved into older villages like Witton Gilbert or perhaps the agricultural workers who lived in these villages would have changed their trade to the higher paid occupation of mining.

Historic view of the Victoria Pit, Sacriston on the edge of Charlaw

There has been mining around Durham City since medieval times. Mention is made of mining at places like Hett, Rainton, Coxhoe and Broompark at various times throughout the medieval era but it is likely that mining took place at many other neighbouring locations. There was also extensive mining in the 1600s and 1700s. For example, we hear mention of mining at Coxhoe in 1614, and at Plawsworth in 1647. During the 1730s mining is recorded at Whitwell near Shincliffe, at Old Quarrington and at Charlaw near Sacriston. Again it is likely that there were many other locations where mining was carried out. This is

reinforced by a glance at early nineteenth century maps of the Durham area. We see that the region is littered with the remnants of hundreds of little pits that were opened and abandoned at uncertain times in the past.

Until the nineteenth century most of the early collieries around Durham City would have been rather small scale affairs employing low numbers of people. Early pits would have been bell pits or simple drift mines. It was not until the 1820s and 1830s that the first of the larger collieries started to appear in the Durham City area. It was also from this period that the first colliery villages began to develop in the Durham City area to accommodate the miners. In fact many villages were built from scratch in previously unoccupied countryside.

The growth of coal-hungry industries was a significant factor stimulating this more intensive mining development. The emergence of steam locomotives in the 1830s facilitated the movement of large quantities of coal across the Durham landscape to the busy ports and burgeoning industrial areas of Tyneside, Wearside and Teesside.

Colliery railways brought significant mining growth to the Durham area. In those earliest days the railways were largely wooden wagonways operated by horse drawn wagons and were most prominent in the 1700s around Tyneside, north west Durham and around the Chester-le-Street and Washington area. Later most of the wooden wagonways were replaced by iron railways but at least one wooden wagonway is known to have existed in the Durham City area at Rainton in the early 1800s.

It was in the Rainton and neighbouring Pittington areas that some of the first nineteenth century collieries of the Durham City area were developed. They were established by the wealthy Marquess of Londonderry who was developing a new coal port called Seaham Harbour on the east Durham coast. He opened up the Adventure Pit, Plain Pit and Hazard Pit at Rainton between 1816 and 1818 and opened further pits at Pittington in the 1820s.

The dates of later colliery openings charter the growth of colliery railways in and around Durham.

In the 1830s a railway from Sunderland to Shincliffe resulted in the opening of collieries at Sherburn Hill, Whitwell and at Shincliffe. A similar railway of the same period called the Clarence Railway linked Teesside to Coxhoe and resulted in the opening of a collection of collieries there.

In the north, a line linked Sacriston's new colliery to Tyneside from 1839 and to a colliery at neighbouring Edmondsley the following year. There was further colliery development in the Sherburn area during the 1840s, perhaps associated with the construction of the nearby Leamside line, but it was the new railways that were built through the Deerness and Browney valleys to the west of the city that brought the next major period of growth.

In 1856 a new railway line was built linking Durham City to Bishop Auckland and this brought about the birth and growth of the colliery village of Brandon. Only two years later an offshoot of this railway was built through the adjacent Deerness Valley. The new railway was built by the Pease family of Darlington to serve their new colliery at Waterhouses. Other collieries would emerge in and around the Deerness valley during the following decade. Collieries soon opened at Esh Winning, Hamsteels, Cornsay Colliery, Ushaw Moor and New Brancepeth and all four of these mining villages were built from scratch.

Another offshoot of the 1856 line was the Lanchester branch of the North Eastern railway that passed through the Browney valley from 1862. Developed by the Consett Iron Company it was intended to enable the movement of coal and ore to Consett but also facilitated the opening of several new collieries during the 1870s. These included collieries at Bearpark, Langley Park, and Malton near Lanchester.

The iron companies had a huge impact on the growth of collieries during the second half of the nineteenth century. Bell Brothers (later acquired by Dorman Long) of Middlesbrough, for example, owned the colliery village called Browney near Langley Moor while Croxdale Colliery just across the river to the west was established by the Weardale Iron Company.

The lost mining village of Hamsteels

As each new colliery opened in previously empty fields, the brand new villages were often established by the colliery owners right on the doorstep of the mine.

Often the first development would be a 'sinkers row', consisting of primitive, temporary houses occupied by the itinerant sinkers whose short-lived work involved sinking or opening up the colliery before they moved on to their next job. By the time the colliery opened, the first colliery cottages had been built to house the pitmen who would extract the coal from the newly opened mine. The cottages were often very basic and this was also true for the slightly better quality homes that were often built for colliery officials.

A school would then be built to serve the community and this would often be endowed by the colliery owner. Pubs would quickly proliferate in these new villages as the new population moved in. Some kind of religious establishment was the next requirement but parish churches were often slow to arrive. They were usually beaten by the Methodist chapels that might even arrive a decade earlier. The Methodists usually appeared in three forms called Primitives, Wesleyans and New Connexion Methodists. Most of the larger colliery villages had at least one chapel of each kind.

Some villages had strong Roman Catholic communities formed by new Irish incomers who settled in the pit villages. We have already mentioned this legacy but of course most of the new miners in these brand new villages came from the County Durham neighbourhood. Many others came from neighbouring counties like Northumberland, Cumberland or Yorkshire. There were also large numbers of new miners from rural districts in the south. A significant number came from East Anglia where rural industries were in decline.

As well as the churches and obligatory school, other facilities might arrive in the mining villages at a later date as the communities developed. Such facilities might include a welfare institute and in the early decades of the twentieth century would even include a cinema or two.

By the mid twentieth century many collieries had already closed but some survived right through until the 1960s, 70s or 80s. Some colliery villages would disappear altogether along with the mines that sustained them but most have survived. However in most cases calling such places surviving pit villages can be slightly misleading as the original colliery villages have often been demolished and then rebuilt or relocated on an adjacent site. This is certainly the case with Esh Winning and Waterhouses and also Ushaw Moor.

Railway Street, Langley Park (NE)

The site of the original Ushaw Moor colliery village lies in fields to the west of the present village while the site of the first Waterhouses pit village lies hidden in woodland. Other villages with short-lived collieries have gone altogether and were never rebuilt again. Good examples are Houghall and Hamsteels. Traces of street guttering, a few doorsteps and the occasional house brick are all that remains of Houghall's pit village now lost amongst the trees of a woodland floor.

The older terraces of nineteenth century colliery villages rarely survive today and many of the villages that we describe in this book as pit villages often consist of post war houses. In cases where older pit terraces survive they are often terraces of a more notable kind. They often have a quite untypical quality or charm that has encouraged their preservation. The most notable examples are the attractive yellow stone houses that form the front street of the village formerly known as Croxdale Colliery and the rather beautiful former colliery terrace that forms the hamlet just outside Lanchester called Hollinside.

Hollinside Terrace near Lanchester (DS)

These charming colliery terraces are just a few of the many hidden and unexpected features that can be found in and around the villages that surround the historic city of Durham. I hope that by reading this book you will be encouraged to explore these places further.

Chapter One

Old Durham and the Shincliffes

Geographically Shincliffe is one of the closest villages to the city centre of Durham and its history is closely tied to the city. The rural area immediately south east of the city is steeped in heritage and includes the picturesque village of Shincliffe, the lost mining village of Houghall and the site of a Roman settlement called Old Durham.

The last of these, though never a village was one of the oldest settlements around. It was a Roman farm or villa and since many of the older villages in this book began their lives as farming settlements it seems as good a place as any to start our journey of the villages. In fact it is notable that the English word village ultimately derives from the Roman word villa.

Students of Durham's history are often drawn to the farmhouses of Old Durham that lie a mile to the east of Durham Cathedral. They are hidden away in quiet scenery between Gilesgate and the Houghall-Shincliffe area of the city that lies just across the river. The obvious question is how old is Old Durham?

Well, to put it into perspective we know that Durham City was first mentioned in the tenth century when monks carrying St. Cuthbert's coffin first settled there. By comparison, Old Durham's history goes back at least 900 years earlier to Roman times when it was the site of the villa that we have mentioned. It seems to have been abandoned when the Roman Empire collapsed around the end of the fifth century AD.

Old Durham Farm looking towards Durham Cathedral (DS)

The ancient Roman name for Old Durham is long since forgotten but at least we know that it really was a Roman site. Robert Surtees the Durham historian, could only speculate about Old Durham's origins when he recorded the site in his History of Durham in the nineteenth century. 'Induced by the easy command of water and rich surrounding pasturage' wrote Surtees, 'it may be easily conceived that Romans should fix their camp on this green semi-isle.' Surtees was by no means certain about Old Durham's Roman origins and speculated that neighbouring Maiden Castle just across the river to the west, could also be Roman. However, it is generally agreed that Maiden Castle dates from an earlier period.

In 1939, almost a century after Surtees wrote his speculative words, the land just south of Old Durham Farm was being quarried for sand when a man from Gilesgate called Jack Hay confirmed what Surtees and other historians had long assumed. Old Durham was indeed Roman.

Mr Hay discovered a small collection of broken Roman tiles, which aroused the interest of local archaeologists. The ever-expanding sand quarry was a threat to this ancient site, but a number of important discoveries were made. One person taking a keen interest was the Master of Sherburn Hospital, the appropriately named Canon Thomas Romans, who made detailed descriptions of the site's most important feature, a Roman bathhouse.

Old Durham was a civilian rather than a military site – a rare occurrence in the North. It was occupied in the second and fourth centuries but abandoned for a period during the third. It seems that it was originally a native farm occupied by ancient Britons who became Romanised. The presence of a villa suggests that important people lived here and it seems reasonable to assume that there was some connection with the pre-Roman site at Maiden Castle.

The Romans are thought to have diverted the course of the Old Durham Beck in the neighbourhood. This stream, known at times as the River Pitting, may originally have joined the Wear opposite Shincliffe Bridge but now joins the Wear further north, near the city's racecourse. The Roman redirection possibly enabled the stream to serve as a defensive ditch. In truth we do not know, but aerial photographs confirm the change in its course.

It is known that two Roman roads point to Durham City centre and these may be associated with Old Durham. One, an offshoot of Dere Street, passes through Brancepeth, Brandon and Langley Moor. The other, from Middleton St. George on the River Tees heads north via Sedgefield, continues through Coxhoe and Bowburn and then heads on to Shincliffe. The roads probably joined up at an unknown location near or within the present city centre, before continuing north to the Roman fort of Concangis at Chester-le-Street.

The discovery of Roman coins and pottery beneath Durham cathedral in the 1970s and 1980s gave further tantalising hints that there may have been Roman occupation in what would become Durham City.

The site of the Roman villa at Old Durham looking towards Shincliffe (DS)

Old Durham's story continued long after Roman times. From the 1200s it belonged to the rectors of St. Nicholas church in the Market Place, before passing to Kepier Hospital in the 1400s.

In 1569, a Londoner called John Heath purchased the land and a mansion house was built. Later, in 1642, Heath's great-great granddaughter and sole heir, Elizabeth married John Tempest, MP for Durham but they chose to live at Wynyard. In the following century the mansion at Old Durham was demolished, but substantial gardens that had been developed on a terraced slope were maintained and became a popular place of recreation for Durham City residents. They continued to be so until the early part of the twentieth century, but fell derelict after the Second World War.

Old Durham Gardens (DS)

The mansion and gardens at Old Durham stood immediately north of the present farm buildings, which date in part from the seventeenth century. The garden terrace survives, along with a gazebo but a garden house also survives. This house became a pub called the Pineapple Inn some time before 1837, but lost its licence in 1926 because of unruly behaviour. It is now a private residence.

The gardens underwent extensive restoration in the 1980s and 1990s but should in no way be confused with the Roman villa that stood well to the south of the farm near the north east side of the beck, close to a footbridge. There is no public access to this part of Old Durham and in any case nothing remains of the Roman site because of the extensive excavation of sand.

Just to the east of the Roman site stood Old Durham Colliery, on the north side of the beck almost opposite the Shincliffe Mill Boarding Kennels. This colliery opened in 1849 and was owned by the Marquess of Londonderry. He became the owner of the Old Durham estate through marriage to Frances Anne Tempest in 1819. His descendant, the seventh Marquess, sold the site to the Hopps family in the early twentieth century and it was a member of this family that sold part of the land to Durham City Council in 1985 for the restoration of the gardens.

Houghall

Houghall lies across the River Wear from Old Durham and covers a wider area than most people realise, stretching a mile from the north to the south. High Houghall Farm is at the southern extremity, while the agricultural college, near the A177, (which most people think of as Houghall), lies at the northern end. The College was founded in 1938 and merged with Peterlee's East Durham Community College in 1999.

Houghall Farm, a part of the college, is the site of the original Houghall manor. It lies half way between High Houghall and the main college building. The name Houghall derives from 'Heugh-Halh' meaning 'hill spur-water meadow' and neatly describes the setting of flat meadowland that is bordered by the thickly wooded hill spur of Houghall Wood.

In early times Houghall belonged to the Prince Bishops but passed to the monks of Durham Cathedral in the thirteenth century. The manor house was protected by a moat and was one of two houses in the neighbourhood that were defended in this way. Across the river to the south of High Houghall is Low Butterby that also had a moat.

The main house at Houghall was rebuilt in the Jacobean period but demolished in 1966. The present buildings are of a later date but a surviving barn is possibly medieval. The more southerly High Houghall Farm was probably sub-let from the main farm in the fifteenth century.

Durham monks farmed at Houghall throughout much of its history. They built flood defences along the river to protect the land and carried out fish farming in the ponds that can be seen near the manor house. This wetland was created from a redundant loop of the Wear that created an oxbow lake.

Houghall's oxbow loop was 8 feet deep in places but in 1961 it was filled in with material excavated during the building of Durham University's science department at Elvet. The ancient river-bed is now planted with trees.

Houghall's manor farm is reached from a lane just north of Shincliffe Bridge. This lane is popular with walkers and leads to the beautiful Hollinside and Great High Woods that crown the hill to the west of Houghall.

A sign-posted discovery trail highlights many features of local and natural history interest. They include a Victorian pump house at the beginning of the lane near Shincliffe Bridge. Dating from the 1840s, this building provided the first tap water to Durham City but was abandoned long before the end of the nineteenth century when water pollution from local collieries made its work impossible. Fortunately this rather impressive looking building has recently found a new role as a restaurant.

The old pump house at Houghall (DS)

The lane that leads from Shincliffe Bridge to Houghall Farm passing the old pump house runs along the northern bank of the River Wear. Nearby, the Discovery Trail marks the site of Shincliffe's first medieval bridge 100 yards upstream from the present bridge. After another 200 yards we reach the former site of a wooden Victorian bridge that carried a colliery wagonway to a pit near Burn Hall at Croxdale.

Of particular fascination, however is a small wooded area that stands on the site of Houghall Colliery. This colliery was sunk in 1840 and operated for 44 years, employing 241 men. It had its own village, a church, a school and 153 houses by 1870 but all have now gone.

The houses were demolished in the 1950s and virtually nothing other than rubble and bricks remain in this woodland site. The colliery houses have almost entirely disappeared except for the front doorsteps that remain on the woodland floor along with the outlines of village streets and guttering.

Joseph Love who also owned Bank Top colliery at High Shincliffe was owner of Houghall's mine and village and

some of the bricks that built the houses can occasionally be found imprinted with the word 'Love'.

The village school stood further west on the edge of Great High Wood in a field called 'Hospital Field' north of Houghall Farm. During the 1930s it served as an isolation hospital but was demolished in 1956.

The Hospital field is interesting because it includes the old course of the River Wear now marked with trees. The wet nature of the field makes growing conditions difficult for anything other than grass.

This part of Houghall also suffers from a natural phenomenon called a 'frost hollow' or 'frost pocket' caused by the wooded hills that surround them in a semi-circular fashion trapping pockets of cold air. In certain conditions it can become one of the coldest spots in England. Such a feature is no doubt an interesting topic of study for students at the neighbouring college.

Cross Street in the now lost mining village of Houghall

Shincliffe and High Shincliffe

Shincliffe is one of County Durham's most charming villages and its proximity to Durham City makes the village a sought after place to live. The village dates back to Anglo-Saxon times but the nearby village of High Shincliffe on the top of the bank consists of more recent housing developments. High Shincliffe rose from the ashes of a former mining settlement called Shincliffe Bank Top that was virtually deserted by the end of the nineteenth century.

Aerial view of Shincliffe village (NE)

Historically old Shincliffe has a close relationship with the city of Durham and lies within a bowl of fertile riverside land that forms an ancient plain surrounded by rolling hills. Woodland extends south from here to Butterby near Croxdale. Shincliffe's neighbours include the medieval Hospital of Sherburn and the lost Roman site of Old Durham.

A road of Roman origin also skirts the edge of the two Shincliffes and to the north lies the ancient hill fort of Maiden Castle. The whole view is crowned by the central tower of Durham Cathedral that peeps over the wooded hills in the distance.

Some of the intriguing features that surround Shincliffe may help to explain the village's ancient name. Early spellings like 'Scinneclif' point to the meaning 'haunted bank', since the Anglo-Saxon word 'Scinna' meant 'phantom or spectre'.

In truth nobody knows why Shincliffe was associated with ghosts, but it may be worth noting that in the thirteenth century Shincliffe Wood was described as 'the wood extending from Schynclyve to Trollesden'. This second place name is a medieval interpretation of Trellsden, the old name for Tursdale, about two and a half miles south of Shincliffe. It is tempting to think that there was a superstitious association with ghosts and trolls.

Since medieval times Shincliffe has had a close relationship with the City of Durham and particularly Durham Cathedral priory. In 1085, Bishop William St. Carileph, the builder of Durham Cathedral gave 'Syneclive', as it was then called, to the Prior and Convent of Durham.

A Shincliffe village scene (DS)

Shincliffe village seems to have been a focus for tensions between the bishops and priors in later years. In 1305, a prior claimed that one of the bishop's servants stole a horse from his Shincliffe stables and took it to Durham Castle without paying. Five years earlier, the bishop's guards had attacked the Prior as he crossed Shincliffe Bridge. It was only after King Edward I intervened that the tensions cooled.

A large tract of land north of Shincliffe was historically a park belonging to the Priors of Durham. It was first mentioned in the thirteenth century but was not enclosed until 1355. The park extended to the river and bordered the main road near Shincliffe Bridge. There is still a small wooded area called Shincliffe Park today. It is situated alongside Mill Lane on a road leading from Shincliffe to Sherburn Hospital.

Of fundamental importance to Shincliffe is its bridge. The Romans may have crossed the Wear near here but the exact course of the Roman Road is unknown between Shincliffe and Chester-le-Street. This can be rather frustrating because the road is so easily traced across other parts of County Durham.

The first medieval bridge at Shincliffe was in existence at least as early as 1200 but repairs were undertaken during the 1300s. By the end of the fourteenth century the bridge was in an irrecoverably ruinous state. This was despite revenue from certain lands being set aside for its upkeep. This situation prompted Bishop Hatfield in 1370 and Bishop Fordham in 1385 to launch enquiries into the maintenance of the bridge. It seemed that revenues were misapplied or embezzled, but no further action was taken.

It was eventually left to a later bishop called Walter Skirlaw, to replace the bridge at his own cost around 1400. Skirlaw could be described as Durham's 'Bishop of

Bridges' as he was also responsible for the construction of Yarm and Croft Bridges on the River Tees in the south of the county.

Shincliffe showing the Seven Stars public house (DS)

Skirlaw's bridge at Shincliffe lasted intact for three and a half centuries but in 1752 two northern arches of the Shincliffe Bridge were swept away during the severe floods of that year. Repairs were undertaken, but by the early nineteenth century the bridge was once again in need of attention.

The Durham architect and County Surveyor, Ignatius Bonomi believed that the old bridge was too narrow for its purpose and decided that a new bridge should be built on the Wear a few hundred yards to the east of the old one. Bonomi's bridge opened in 1826 and the old bridge was removed. Although Bonomi's Shincliffe Bridge has been widened it is still in use today, standing as a symbol of the ancient link between Shincliffe and Durham City.

The main street of old Shincliffe village is very picturesque. At the south end is the Seven Stars Inn, an early nineteenth century building and along the street are

several cottages of eighteenth and nineteenth century origin. These include the Manor House but the oldest house in the village appears to be Laxey Cottage, a seventeenth century building with an eighteenth century door frame.

Nearby, a lane leads off south from the main village street to a garden centre and a mansion called Shincliffe Hall. The first house on the site of this hall seems to have been built around 1771 by William Rudd who had been a Steward and Recorder of Durham from 1764-67. By the end of the eighteenth century Rudd's hall passed to John Thomas Hendry Hopper of Witton Castle and then to William Hutton of Cumberland.

The next owner of the house was John Prince, a Royal Navy captain who converted the property into Shincliffe Hall around 1829. Prince was born in Jamaica where his family owned a plantation. He was very wealthy and his possessions are thought to have included a painting by Rubens that is said to have hung on a wall in the hall.

Laxey Cottage, Shincliffe (DS)

Prince died in 1867 and the hall was subsequently bought in 1869 by the Dean and Chapter of Durham

Cathedral. It became the house of Richardson Peele the Dean and Chapter's Clerk, who became Mayor of Durham in 1889 but this was some years after Peele had left the hall.

Later owners of Shincliffe Hall included a government mines inspector called William Atkinson and a grain merchant called John Featherstone Ayton who owned the property at the beginning of the twentieth century. During the Second World War the hall housed land army girls and then became university accommodation which it remained until 2005 when it was bought as a private house.

Returning to the village, one of the most remarkable things about Shincliffe is that for most of its history it did not have a church. This might explain the popularity of John Wesley, the founder of Methodism, who preached at Shincliffe in 1780 while staying at the house of a Mr Parker in the village.

Wesley gave a sermon from Mr Parker's front door because the congregation was too large to fit inside the house. Wesley remarked: 'It seemed the whole village was ready to receive the truth.' A willow tree is said to have been planted on the site of Wesley's sermon and this apparently gave rise to the name of Willowtree Avenue. This avenue is the part of the A177 that links Shincliffe to High Shincliffe.

Sermons were something of a novelty in a village without a church but the absence of a place of worship was surprising considering Shincliffe's strong ecclesiastical links. The village had belonged to the Priors of Durham Cathedral in times gone by and was even reputed to be the birthplace of the sixteenth century Prince Bishop of Durham called William Sever. Nevertheless despite these ecclesiastical connections, the village was merely an outlying part of Durham City's St. Oswald's parish. The church of St. Oswald lies about a mile to the north west in the Elvet area of the city.

A rectory was built in Shincliffe village in 1800 and a chapel of ease opened in 1826, but Shincliffe's parish church was not built until 1851. Shincliffe's new church served an ever-increasing population attracted by Shincliffe's railways and collieries. From 1839, old Shincliffe village was home to Durham City's first railway station called Shincliffe Town located on the western terminus of a line from Sunderland. Several wagonways linked this line to neighbouring collieries. In 1844, a second station opened on a separate line (the Leamside line) at Shincliffe Bank Top. This building can still be seen near the main road as we head south to Bowburn.

Collieries were important for employment in the Shincliffe area. Whitwell Colliery, a mile south east of Shincliffe opened in 1837 and to the north east of Shincliffe, stood the Marquess of Londonderry's Old Durham Colliery of 1849 near Shincliffe Mill. All of these collieries were linked to a railway line from Sunderland.

Shincliffe Colliery itself opened in 1839 at Shincliffe Bank Top. A seam of coal, six feet thick was located and brought great joy to Mr William Bell JP of Ford Hall in Sunderland, who was the colliery's first owner. By the 1860s it was owned by Joseph Love, who was also owner of Houghall Colliery. Love was a former miner who married into wealth and became a coal owner with a reputation for harshness.

Shincliffe colliery was half a mile south of old Shincliffe village and a new mining village grew up next to the colliery that more than doubled the population of the Shincliffe area. The new colliery was linked to a railway that ran from Shincliffe to Sunderland constructed by the Sunderland Dock Company from 1831. Called the Sunderland and Durham Railway it ran through Ryhope, Murton, Hetton-le-Hole and Pittington before terminating at Sherburn House near Sherburn Hospital.

St. Mary's church, Shincliffe (DS)

The line was extended to old Shincliffe village when Shincliffe Colliery opened with a branch routed to Shincliffe Colliery itself. A colliery wagonway continued this line west from Old Shincliffe across a bridge to Houghall Colliery and then continued through a tunnel under the wooded hill of Hollinside to reach a pit near Burn Hall, Croxdale.

Some miners from Houghall initially resided in a street called Wood View in old Shincliffe village. It is near the road to Shincliffe Hall and Shincliffe garden centre but as we have noted Houghall had a colliery village of its own.

Old Shincliffe village became the site of Durham City's first railway station on 28 June, 1839. A more natural place for the city's station would have been at Old Elvet but the railway company couldn't find a route that was acceptable to landowners. So the line did not reach Old Elvet at this early stage. Shincliffe thus became the terminus for passengers and goods from Sunderland and East Durham. Some of the passengers were no doubt thirsty at the end of their journey and the Railway Tavern was built close to the station. It continued to serve customers until closure in the early 1990s.

The station in the old village was later called Shincliffe Town Station and was the first of two stations at Shincliffe. The second station was built nearer to Bank Top (or High Shincliffe) on the road to Bowburn. This station was located on the new line that opened in 1844. It became the main line from London to the north and is known today as the Leamside line. It was constructed by the Sunderland-born railway entrepreneur George Hudson. In its heyday it was called the Newcastle and Durham Junction Railway and became part of the North Eastern Railway in the early 1850s.

The railway station on the Leamside line at Shincliffe was called the Shincliffe York British Station, or Shincliffe Bank Top Station. The building is now a private house but served as a restaurant for a time.

Shincliffe Bank Top was a flourishing settlement but when the colliery closed in 1875 it became a virtual ghost town, an irony considering the original Shincliffe's ghostly links. It was around this time that Old Durham and Whitwell collieries also closed and Shincliffe's population plummeted from 2,123 in 1871 to 640 by 1891. Most of the 300 or so miners who worked at Shincliffe Colliery left to seek work elsewhere. It was unfortunate that a new Methodist Chapel had opened in the old village in 1874 and another had opened at Bank Top in 1875, just as the population was collapsing. Having waited so long for a church it seemed that there would now be too many places of worship in the area and not enough people.

It was also unfortunate that a school at Bank Foot had recently opened halfway between the two Shincliffe villages in 1870. It replaced the earlier school of the 1840s that stood near the colliery. Nevertheless, despite the population fall the new school remained open and served the two villages for 98 years until closure in 1968. In that year a new primary school opened at High Shincliffe. The old school is now a private residence.

Shincliffe School in 1969 (NE)

After the closure of the mines employment in the Shincliffe area during the last two decades of the nineteenth century was once again dominated by rural and agricultural trades as it had been in earlier times. Few miners remained, but the railways, two brickyards, a corn mill and a sawmill provided some employment.

Shincliffe Mill, east of Shincliffe, had been the site of a corn mill since the 1300s. It closed in 1900 and is now

the site of a cattery, boarding kennels and a garden nursery. The other mill in Shincliffe was the sawmill. Located south of Shincliffe on the road towards Bowburn behind the old Bank Top station, it closed in 1908.

Just south west of the sawmill was Shincliffe racecourse, Durham's racecourse from 1895. It replaced the previous city racecourse at Elvet but closed before the First World War. The remains of a concrete grandstand could be seen on the edge of the old race field until quite recently.

Shincliffe Bank Top's late nineteenth century problems contrast with the growth and prosperity of the two Shincliffes in the late twentieth century. The rural setting, charming houses of Old Shincliffe and the proximity to Durham City have made the area a popular place to live.

Accessibility to the main Stockton-to-Durham road is an added bonus, but this road had proved a problem as traffic increased during the twentieth century.

Vehicles originally passed through the old village, making an awkward dog-leg bend to do so. In the 1920s or 30s an old lane called Back Lane was improved and widened so that Shincliffe was bypassed on its eastern side. High Shincliffe received a similar bypass in the later decades of the century.

The first modern developments in Shincliffe took place in 1960 with the building of St. Mary's Close near the church. The layout received a planning award for its design. Other new estates followed at Bank Top village in the 1960s and that village came to be known as High Shincliffe. Amongst the residents of the new estate would be a family whose young son, Tony Blair, would go on to become Prime Minister. The Blairs resided in the Hill Meadows part of the village.

At the end of the 1960s *The Northern Echo's* property pages remarked that the price of houses in High Shincliffe

'may seem high – they reach the £4,500 to £6,000 mark – but they are of a better type and higher class of development.'

Hidden in amongst the estate houses that make up the modern village of High Shincliffe are a handful of older colliery houses. Surviving colliery terraces include Pond Street, Overman Street and Quality Street. Pond Street stood close to the site of the colliery pond. The houses in some of these older streets seem quite small today, but have a certain charm. They were probably the better quality pit houses of Bank Top village.

Also surviving from the old colliery village are some larger houses that formed the Front Street of Bank Top Colliery village. A continuation of the village street known as Avenue Street forms a gentle curve and was once part of the main road from Durham to Stockton.

Although the collieries have long since disappeared from Shincliffe, the loss of industry here is of little concern in the age of the motor car. Few residents now work in the parish and most are commuters with professional background that have brought new life to the area.

Shincliffe may have started life as the 'cliff of ghosts' and Bank Top may have become a ghost town for a short time, but the Shincliffes of today, far from being haunted by their history are places of prosperity that are proud of their past.

Whitwell and Whitwell Grange

Nothing remains of Whitwell pit village. It has been and gone and few have even heard of the place. Footpaths follow an old wagonway through the area, and if you visit today you find Whitwell Grange, Whitwell East Farm and Whitwell House, but no Whitwell village. Such farms existed in the neighbourhood long before the colliery developed in the 1830s, but they belong to Whitwell's agricultural history rather than the mining past. Whitwell was located a mile east of Shincliffe, but the site is now isolated from Shincliffe by the busy A1(M) motorway.

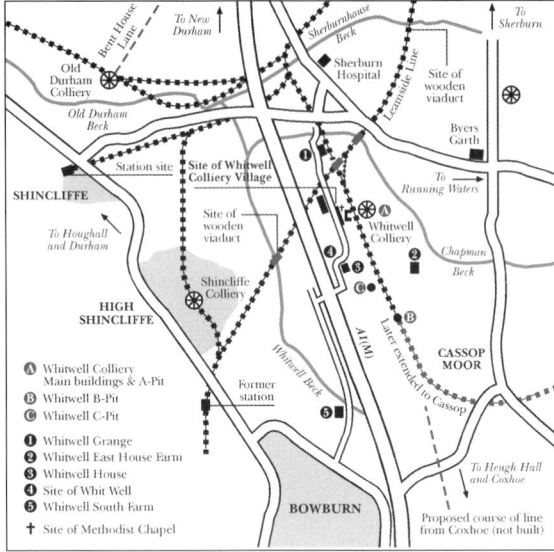

Map showing history of Shincliffe and Whitwell (NE)

The history of Whitwell goes back to Anglo-Saxon times and belonged, along with Sherburn and Shadforth, to the district of Quarringtonshire in times past. The name means 'white spring' and the Whit Well in question was situated on the north side of Whitwell House Farm. Wells were often trading places and the proximity of the Chapman Beck, on the east side of Whitwell, could be significant as Chapman was an old term for a trader.

In 1183, Whitwell belonged to a man called William but from about the 1200s it was held by the masters of Sherburn Hospital. The hospital still stands to the north.

Whitwell and its area were historically called Whitwell House and were extra-parochial. This meant that they did not belong to a parish and they had no church of their own. The other strange thing about Whitwell was that agricultural produce from here was apparently toll free at Durham market.

In the 1600s, Whitwell was held by the twice-widowed Thomasine, who was initially the wife of Ralph Lever, a Master of Sherburn Hospital. She later married Robert Warture, a gent, but he also passed away. When Thomasine died, Whitwell was sold to Thomas Bullock and then to Bullock's nephew, Thomas Brass of Flass, near Ushaw Moor.

In 1718, the Brasses sold Whitwell to John and Thomas Middleton, of Cleatlam and Isaac Teasdale, of Staindrop. These two families intermarried at a later date and in 1806, one of their number called, believe it or not, Middleton Teasdale, sold Whitwell to his aunt, Jane Bacon. When Jane died, she left Whitwell to her nephew, the Reverend Henry Wastell, who sold it to John Gregson of Durham City.

Between 1737 and 1739, a small land sale colliery was operated at Whitwell by Abraham Teasdale in conjunction with Ann Wilkinson. Land sale collieries were usually little pits where coal was sold for local consumption rather than exported via the coast. When Whitwell Colliery opened on a grander scale, almost exactly a century later, some old tools and a peculiar pump associated with the earlier mine were discovered.

The nineteenth century colliery at Whitwell opened in 1837. Its owners were Andrew White, Mr Robson and Mr Ogden. It was linked by wagonway to the new railway that ran from Shincliffe village to Sunderland and joined that line near Sherburn Hospital. From an early

date the colliery was also linked to the Leamside line that still passes through the area today. In those days the Leamside was the main east coast line.

Coal from Whitwell was shipped to Sunderland but it was also hoped to link the colliery to the Clarence Railway at Coxhoe. This would have allowed Whitwell's coal to be taken to Teesside and Hartlepool as well as to Sunderland. The intended branch from Coxhoe was approved by Parliament but never reached any further north than Heugh Hall Row at Old Quarrington on what is now the outskirts of Bowburn. Later, in the 1860s or 70s, Whitwell's wagonway was linked to Hartlepool via Cassop Moor.

Whitwell village was built next to Whitwell colliery and housed the miners. It was quite a small village of about 30 or 40 houses and had its own Primitive Methodist chapel. Its population in 1841 (including the farms) was 173.

The small population can be explained because Whitwell was not the only village built for the Whitwell miners.

One mile north, at Gilesgate Moor on the eastern outskirts of Durham City, a village of 700 souls called New Durham was built by the Whitwell Colliery owner, Andrew White. Fordyce, a Durham historian writing in the 1850s, stated that New Durham was built between 1836 and 1837 for the Whitwell miners. In reality, however, New Durham may have also served other collieries in the neighbourhood. This would explain why White built the village a mile north of Whitwell. There was good demand for houses in the colliery district of Gilesgate Moor and it brought in money from rent.

On the map, New Durham was much bigger than Whitwell, but the population figure of 700 probably included nearby pit rows like Teasdale Terrace near

A nineteenth century illustration showing Whitwell Colliery

Dragonville. Originally called Teasdale's Terrace, it is now overlooked by the huge Tesco supermarket at Dragonville. It was probably named after the Teasdale family who first worked coal at Whitwell.

Whitwell Colliery closed around 1874 and other collieries in the neighbourhood also closed around this time. New Durham was hard hit and by the 1920s most of this village was demolished. Two stone houses remain on what was once New Durham's front street opposite Durham's Sherburn Road housing estate. A shop occupies one old house, but another, now a private house, was once a pub. Now called Old Whitwell House it was once the Whitwell Inn and is a lasting reminder of the link between Gilesgate Moor and Whitwell.

Although New Durham was badly affected by pit closures in the late nineteenth century, Whitwell village seems to have faired better despite its proximity to Whitwell Colliery. The colliery closure of 1874 could have destroyed Whitwell, but two-thirds of the houses were still inhabited by the time of the 1881 census. By this time most miners at Whitwell had found work at Sherburn House Colliery, half a mile to the north east and they didn't mind the walk to work. Sherburn House Colliery kept Whitwell village alive for a number of years but when this colliery closed in 1935 Whitwell's days were numbered.

View of Durham Cathedral from High Shincliffe (DS)

Chapter Two

The Sherburns and Shadforth

The early history of Sherburn revolves around Sherburn Hospital which is one of the most historic and picturesque places in the Durham City area. The hospital has played an important role in the history of Durham City as well as Sherburn and the county at large. Now a care home for the elderly, it no longer looks after 'lepers' as it did in medieval times, but still stands in attractive scenery alongside the Sherburn House Beck, half way between the villages of Shincliffe and Sherburn.

The gateway at Sherburn Hospital (DS)

The chapel, Sherburn Hospital (DS)

Hugh Pudsey, the powerful Prince Bishop of Durham founded the hospital sometime between 1181 and 1184. It was placed under the rule of a steward and was a religious establishment. Pudsey dedicated the hospital to Christ, the Blessed Virgin as well as to Lazarus and his sisters, Martha and Mary.

The hospital housed 65 poor brethren or 'lepers' of both sexes who came from throughout the North of England. Their daily lives in the hospital were similar to that experienced by a monk or nun.

Lands throughout County Durham were granted to the hospital to raise finances for supporting the community. Early possessions belonging to the hospital included Ebchester near Consett, Whitton, near Stockton and Garmondsway near Kelloe. The churches of Bishopton, Grindon and Sockburn along with lands in Thorpe Thewles, Sheraton, Stillington, Cassop, Kelloe and Quarrington were also added to the hospital's possessions.

In addition to the lepers and steward there were three priests and four clerks in the hospital who slept in a chamber adjacent to the hospital's chapel. Each of the lepers had a daily allowance of a loaf and a gallon of ale

with meat supplied for three days in the week. Fish, cheese or butter were served on the remaining four. There would be extra helpings on festival days, including a fresh salmon on the feast day of St. Cuthbert and a goose at Michaelmas.

The lepers and poor brethren lived a strict daily routine and those who failed to comply were given a diet of bread and water as punishment. Despite the institution's benevolent beginnings, the hospital seems to have suffered a decline in standards by the 1400s. By this time the charitable work of the hospital was subject to abuse as some of the revenues from its extensive lands were being diverted into private hands to the detriment of the hospital's needy brethren. In an attempt to improve matters, Thomas Langley, the then Bishop of Durham, reorganised the institution and reduced the residents to 13 poor brethren and two lepers.

Like many other religious institutions medieval hospitals came under threat from closure during the dissolution of the monasteries in the 1500s. Fortunately, unlike Kepier Hospital in Durham City, Sherburn Hospital escaped closure and continued to look after the needs of the poor and needy well into the twentieth century.

The grounds of Sherburn Hospital (DS)

Sherburn Hospital pictured in 1780

It was in 1950 that the hospital became a care home for the elderly but it still retains links with the past. In fact the hospital charity still holds lands in Whitton and Ebchester.

The hospital as it exists today is built in a quadrangle around a large green and the whole place has the appearance of a rather beautiful old village. However, many of the present buildings only date from 1868. Only the hospital gateway and the chapel date back to medieval times, but even the chapel underwent significant restoration following fires in 1850, 1859 and 1864. Despite these nineteenth century restorations Sherburn Hospital is still a very historic building in a lovely rural setting.

Sherburn Village

The village of Sherburn lies to the east of Durham City and derives its name from the Anglo-Saxon words Scir-Burna meaning 'clear stream'. The stream in question is the Sherburn House Beck and it joins the Wear near Old Durham, a mile and-a-half to the west. Here it is called Old Durham Beck but was also known in the past as the River Pidding (or Pitting). It is not to be confused with the Pittington Beck that joins Sherburn House Beck near Sherburn Hospital.

Although Sherburn is named from a stream, the village is not close to water. In fact the oldest part of Sherburn village is a quarter of a mile from the nearest rivulet. A clue to this puzzle can be found in the medieval document called Boldon Buke compiled in 1183. It refers to two neighbouring villages called North Sherburn and South Sherburn and it seems the present Sherburn was originally North Sherburn.

South Sherburn was probably located alongside a stream and was probably the original. The Boldon Buke states that North and South Sherburn belonged to an ancient district called Quarringtonshire.

In 1183, a man called Ulkill held North Sherburn, while Christian the Plasterer (Cementarius) held South Sherburn. The plasterer was apparently exempt from rent as long as he provided services to the bishop. It is probable that this was the same Christian who built the nearby Pittington Church and the Galilee chapel at Durham Cathedral.

Records show there were five farmers and ten cottage dwellers living in the Sherburn area at the time. West Sherburn near Dragonville in the Gilesgate Moor area of Durham City and Sherburn Grange Farm near Belmont may have been among the farming settlements attached to the manor of Sherburn. Grange is usually a name for an outlying granary connected with an estate.

The exact location of South Sherburn village is uncertain but it appears to have become a deserted settlement. It was possibly located where Sherburn Hospital now stands. It is certainly known that in 1331, John Harpyn, Lord of Thornlaw (Thornley), sold the lands in the vill and territory of South Sherburn to the masters and leprous brethren of the hospital.

Today's village of Sherburn is often described as a former colliery village, but the village reveals rural origins that predate the days of mining. In fact, Sherburn's history dates back to prehistoric times. It is known for example that Neolithic axes have been found in and around the village and a Bronze Age burial was uncovered near Sherburn Grange just to the west.

There are a number of old houses clustered along the Front Street of Sherburn village and some of these date back to the seventeenth century. Remnants of a village green also give away Sherburn's rural roots. The most obvious reminder of the past is Sherburn Farm on the south side of Front Street near the green. Sherburn Farm and the neighbouring houses clearly predate the age of colliery development.

Sherburn Farm (DS)

However the feature of greatest antiquity in Sherburn is one created by nature, rather than man. It is the so-called 'Blue Stone' that stands near the roundabout at what was once the village crossroads. It is now sunken into the pavement near a baker's shop and a few years ago it was painted white for some unknown reason. It no longer displays the dark blue colour that gave it the name.

About 2ft high and of glacial origin, the Blue Stone has in the past been situated in more than one location in the village centre. The stone served many purposes, being used as a seat, a meeting point for miners and a pick-up point for horse-drawn wagons. According to one legend it was a meteorite that landed here centuries ago.

One prominent feature at the centre of Sherburn village that has now gone was Sherburn Hall. It was a gentleman's house resembling a little castle and was occupied over the centuries by well-known Durham families like the Tempests and Pembertons.

The last resident of the hall was a doctor who used the lower floor as a surgery. After he vacated the premises, the hall was used during the war for civil defence purposes and, like many old halls that were utilised in this way, it fell into ruin before it was finally demolished in 1952.

Historic view showing old houses associated with Sherburn Hall (MR)

It was back in the 1840s that coal mining came to Sherburn with the arrival of local railways. Large-scale collieries simply could not exist without a means of transporting coal to port and railways provided the answer.

Sherburn House Station (MR)

One of the earliest railways in the vicinity was the Sunderland Dock Railway that first opened in 1831. Starting at Sunderland, it reached old Shincliffe village in 1839 and a passenger station was built at the Shincliffe terminus. This was Durham City's first passenger terminal.

The new railway served pits around Shincliffe like Whitwell, Old Durham and Houghall on the south eastern outskirts of Durham City but it did not bring immediate colliery developments to Sherburn village. The line did however, initially terminate at Sherburn Hospital.

A railway station was built near the hospital in 1837 and was called Sherburn Station. This caused some confusion later on because it was one of two stations in the area named Sherburn Station. To clear up confusion the Sherburn Hospital station was renamed Sherburn House Station in 1874 and was rebuilt on an adjacent line in 1893.

The first big colliery in the Sherburn area opened in 1835 and was located at Sherburn Hill to the east of the village. Here a new mining village grew to serve the mine and was simply called Sherburn Hill. The village of Sherburn Hill is covered in a later part of this chapter.

At Sherburn itself there were two collieries but these opened slightly later than the one at Sherburn Hill. One was Sherburn House Colliery and the other was Sherburn Colliery. Both opened in 1844 and it was in that year that the main north-south passenger line from London to the north was opened. Sherburn Colliery was built alongside this line.

Although no longer the main line today, the 1844 railway is still in existence today and is now called the Leamside line. It runs along the western edge of Sherburn village and originally crossed Sherburn House Beck by means of a wooden viaduct just south of Sherburn.

Sherburn Colliery was built alongside the Leamside line, but it was a separate railway called the Lambton Railway that really served Sherburn Colliery. The Lambton Railway first opened in the 1700s as a wooden, horse-drawn railroad in the Penshaw area but was later rebuilt with iron.

The extension of the Lambton Railway to Sherburn Hill in the 1830s resulted in the opening of the colliery there and a further semi-circular extension south of Sherburn village resulted in the opening of Sherburn House and Sherburn Collieries. Coal from these two collieries was transported to Lambton Staithes on the River Wear near Penshaw.

The initial owner of the three Sherburn collieries was Lord Lambton, the Earl of Durham. Sherburn Colliery was itself called Lady Durham Pit after the earl's wife. Later in the century Lambton's colliery concerns became Lambton Collieries Ltd.

Lady Durham pit closed in 1919 and stood on the western side of Sherburn village near the Leamside line.

Industrial units now stand near this area close to Sherburn Sports Centre.

Sherburn House Colliery was half a mile south of the village. Its site lies opposite an isolated terrace of houses called Grand View. As might be expected, these homes enjoy good views of the surrounding countryside, but they came into being long after the colliery was established.

However in a small woodland copse opposite Grand View, there was a Victorian pit terrace that served the colliery and just behind it was the colliery itself. The terrace was removed about the time the colliery closed in 1935. Apart from this terrace there was never a colliery village called Sherburn House. Miners at this particular colliery came from the village of Whitwell near Shincliffe or from the other Sherburn villages.

Sherburn Hospital was one of the lessees of Sherburn House Colliery and was entitled to some of the royalties from the mine. It was agreed that coal from this colliery would be provided free to the hospital. In 1872 the hospital even built a gasworks in its own grounds utilising the coal gas from the colliery to light the building.

Historic view of Sherburn village (MR)

Collieries had a major impact on the growth of Sherburn village. From 1801 to 1891 the population of Sherburn Township which included Sherburn Hill, grew from 252 to 2,958. Mining was not the only industry in Sherburn by the mid-nineteenth century. Other industries included a water powered corn mill at Hallgarth Mill near Pittington and another mill on a beck south of the village near Sherburn House Colliery.

In the village itself was Parkinson's grease factory and to the south east, a magnesian limestone quarry. Lime kilns are shown alongside the quarry on an 1860s map, but although the quarry expanded later in the century it was disused by the 1920s. Other industries in Sherburn included a brick and tile works near Sherburn Hospital and another west of Sherburn near the village railway station.

We have already mentioned the station at nearby Sherburn Hospital, but there was another station in Sherburn village itself. Initially called Sherburn Station but later known as Sherburn Colliery Station, it was situated on what is now the Leamside line at the western end of the village.

Sherburn Colliery station closed to passengers in 1941 and to goods in 1959 and was subsequently demolished. The only surviving reminder of the station is a terrace called Sherburn Station that stands on the south side of Front Street at the western edge of the village.

This terrace was part of what was once a separate village called Sherburn Station. It consisted of the terrace we see today and two other terraces that stood parallel on the north side of Front Street. Wedged between the Leamside line to the west and the now removed Lambton Railway to the east, fields once separated this village from Sherburn itself.

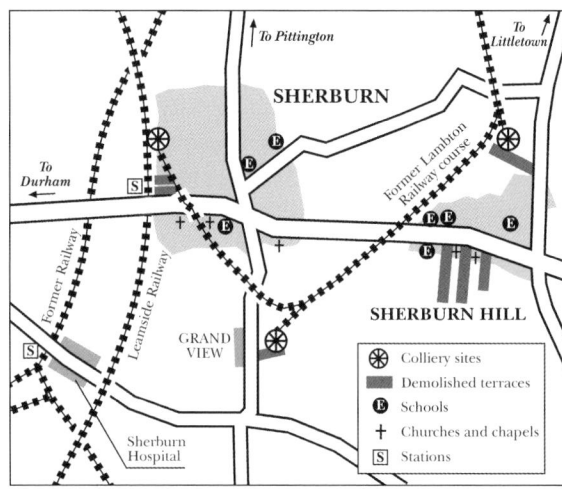

Map showing history of Sherburn (NE)

During the nineteenth century, the little village of Sherburn Station had two pubs called the Colliery Hotel and Station Hotel and was home to a Primitive Methodist chapel dating from 1862. This building has now gone, but older residents may remember that it was later Barnfather's Garage.

A Wesleyan Methodist Chapel of 1861 that stood at the eastern end of Sherburn village itself has also gone. The present Methodist chapel called the Parkinson Memorial Methodist Chapel opened in Sherburn's Hallgarth Street in 1964.

The most important place of worship in the village is the impressive parish church that lies to the west of the village centre. Built in 1872 it was designed by the Newcastle architects Austin and Johnson, who also constructed the Victorian buildings at Sherburn Hospital. A vicarage was built near the church in 1874 and can still be seen. Before 1872, Anglicans in Sherburn attended churches at

Shadforth or Pittington-Hallgarth, where many Sherburn residents of earlier times are buried.

Sherburn's first school was opened in 1804 by the local landholder Arthur Mowbray and rebuilt by Mrs Pemberton of Sherburn Hall in 1848. It stood on Front Street at the west end of the village close to where the parish church now stands. It was superseded by a school in Sherburn's Hallgarth Street in 1913 and by a secondary modern school in 1969.

Sherburn's pubs are the Cross Keys and Lambton Arms at the centre of the village and both appear in directories dating back to the 1850s.

The Lambton Arms was the scene of a rather dramatic nineteenth century murder that we will come to in a moment. Also nearby was once the Grey Horse, now a carpet shop, while to the west was the Forester's Arms. The Forester's was once the last building in the village as we headed to Sherburn Hill.

Other notable buildings located in the village included a Victorian reading room of 1850 and Sherburn House Welfare Hall of 1929. The reading room, endowed by Mr T.C. Thompson in 1850 is now a bakery shop. The Welfare Hall burned down in 1956.

Also of prominence in the village was the co-operative store established in 1899. It was a branch of Sherburn Hill co-operative society with the words Sherburn Hill on the shop sign. It must have confused the occasional visitor into thinking they had arrived at Sherburn Hill by mistake instead of Sherburn village. The building is now Sherburn Community Centre.

Since the 1950s, Sherburn village has seen the development of housing estates to the north and south of Front Street and one of the most recent is a small estate of private houses behind the Sherburn Station terrace.

The Sherburn Murder

On the evening of Friday 1 May, 1868, the village of Sherburn was in a state of shock. At about 6pm, an incident occurred in the centre of the village that would be engraved on the memories of those who witnessed it for the rest of their days. It all happened very quickly and ended with one man lying dead inside a pub, his body peppered with gunshot, while another lay dying outside the pub's doorway with a bullet in his head. He, too, lost his life later that day, but there was only one murder victim.

Sherburn's Lambton Arms, the site of a nineteenth century murder (DS)

The murder victim's name was John Cruickshank, a Scotsman and police officer who served the neighbouring village of Pittington just north of Sherburn. It was Cruickshank who lay dead on the floor of Sherburn's Lambton Arms. His murderer, a fellow policeman and also of Scottish origin, was David Paton, who served the village of Sherburn. The murder weapon, a Colt's six-chamber revolver, belonged to Paton, a former military man. This same weapon would be used to take his own life.

At 2pm that day Paton and Cruickshank had been in attendance at the office of Colonel White, the county's Chief Constable in Durham City. The meeting was an investigation into allegations of drunkenness against Paton.

Cruickshank had complained to Sergeant Caygill, Paton's senior officer about the Sherburn policeman's behaviour but the investigation could not prove the charge.

Paton was cleared but during the investigation the chief constable was made aware of a statement from Cruickshank that said Paton had been discharged from a police force in Scotland.

Home Office regulations forbade a police officer dismissed from one force from joining another so without hesitation, the chief constable discharged Paton from the force.

Paton greeted the dismissal with coolness and expressed no sign of anger. Straight after the investigation, the accuser Cruickshank departed for Pittington with a fellow officer called William Mackay who was a resident of Sherburn Hill.

The two of them proceeded up the steeply-sloping street of Gilesgate bank en route to their respective homes. On reaching New Durham, a pit village near Sherburn Road at Gilesgate Moor, the two men called into the home of Sergeant Caygill for a drink of water. When they departed from Caygill's house, they encountered Paton walking along the road and he calmly joined them.

Mackay and Cruickshank must have been wary of Paton's presence but were forbidden to talk any further about the investigation, so as the three men walked together it was not discussed. Even Paton did not mention the subject, although he did ask about some possible relatives of Cruickshank that he had known in a Scottish police force. Cruickshank said they were not related to him.

Other than this, the conversation between the three men seemed amiable enough. About half way between New Durham and Sherburn village, the walkers reached a bridge across the Shincliffe to Sunderland railway line. Here, Cruickshank intended to take a short cut home to Pittington but Paton told him that he had some important information to share and persuaded him to continue into Sherburn. Crossing another bridge, over the Leamside railway and entering Sherburn, they reached the village centre. Here, Mackay went on to talk to a friend he had spotted nearby.

Cruickshank told Paton he would wait near the Pittington Road while Paton collected the mysterious information from his house. Mackay and Cruickshank had not sensed any danger, because Paton remained calm all the time. In fact, when Mackay finished talking to his friend, he entered Paton's house to take a rest. As he did so, he saw Paton leaving by another door holding something behind his back that was presumably the information. Mackay then settled himself into a chair in the front room of Paton's house.

Coolly and without a word, Paton approached the waiting Cruickshank and revealed the weapon, unhesitatingly opening fire on the unfortunate man. A bullet hit Cruickshank in the groin and he staggered backwards into the nearby pub. Here sat the landlord's niece and two men, whose peace and quiet was suddenly interrupted.

Cruickshank sought safety behind a screen in the kitchen near the fire, but the witnesses said that Paton followed in quick pursuit. He fired the fatal shot into the cowering Cruickshank, with the bullet going between his ribs and into his heart. Just before the shot was fired, Harriet Thompson, the landlord's niece, said she overheard Cruickshank exclaim 'Oh dear; murder', but his last words were probably much stronger. Cruickshank died instantly and as he departed from this world, Paton immediately departed from the pub.

Nearby in Paton's house, the murderer's wife, Jessie had alerted Mackay that her husband had something in his hand. 'Something has happened, run after him' she cried, but it was too late. Mackay headed quickly towards the pub only in time to see Paton leaving the building.

Grave of Constable Cruickshank at Pittington churchyard (DS)

As Paton swung the gun round, Mackay must have feared for his life, but on this occasion the killer's intended victim was himself. With a single shot to the head Paton fell into Mackay's arms. He died later that evening.

An inquest was held in the pub the following day and a verdict of murder and suicide was agreed. Cruickshank's funeral immediately followed the inquest and his grave can still be seen in the churchyard of St. Laurence at Pittington. The headstone reads 'In memory of John Cruickshank, Police Constable at Pittington, a native of Grange, Banffshire, Scotland, who by the hands of his brother officer lost his life in the faithful performance of his duty at Sherburn on the 1 May, 1868 in the 31st year of his age.'

Two days later, Paton was buried nearby, but his grave is nowhere to be seen. Two widows and six children, four of them Cruickshank's would live to count the sorry cost.

Sherburn Hill

Sherburn Hill is situated to the east of Sherburn and south of Littletown. It is a quite separate village from Sherburn and the obvious distinguishing feature is that Sherburn Hill stands, rather unsurprisingly, on the top of a hill.

Heading east from Sherburn, we climb the hill to reach the village and after passing through less than half a mile of open countryside, the main road that formed the front street of one village becomes the front street of another. On reaching 'The Hill' as the village of Sherburn Hill is locally known, we can look back towards the west and are rewarded with excellent views of the distant Durham Cathedral and its surrounding countryside.

Climbing the hill gives a sense of leaving one part of County Durham behind and entering another. Administratively speaking, Sherburn Hill lies within Durham City, but you do feel you are now heading into the distinct region of eastern Durham.

At this point Durham City centre is 4 miles to the west and the coast is 7 miles east, but in geological terms, we really have entered eastern Durham. The hill we have climbed is part of the magnesian limestone escarpment. This limestone forms the local hills and rocks of the entire Durham coastline. Magnesian limestone is different to the limestone of the Pennines in the west of the county. It has a rich creamy coloured appearance that is apparent in former quarry sites at places like Pittington Hill to the north or Quarrington Hill to the south.

Magnesian limestone appears along the coast from Hartlepool to South Shields, where it creates the famous Marsden Rocks and is also found at Houghton-le-Spring, where the A690 cuts through it in a rather dramatic fashion. In the vicinity of Sherburn Hill the stone has been quarried for centuries along with sand.

One area that has been extensively quarried by the Sherburn Stone Company in recent times is Crime Rigg quarry just east of Sherburn Hill. Crime Rigg is the name of a farmhouse. It is also the name of the ridge or 'rigg' that lies between Sherburn Hill and the village of Shadforth.

Both the house and ridge at Crime Rigg are marked on the first Ordnance Survey map of the 1850s, but the explanation for the word crime in this particular place name has eluded me. It could be related to an old Celtic word 'crim' meaning crooked, but crooked ridge is a less appealing explanation than the image of some long forgotten crime that might have occurred here. Perhaps criminals were hanged here at one time.

Equally intriguing is the name of Cook's Hold Farm to the north of Sherburn Hill, near the old colliery site. I presume it was held by someone called Cook but maybe it was the unfortunate home of a Cuckold. It, too, appears on the first OS map.

When the first edition of the map appeared, the village of Sherburn Hill was already well developed and it was coal mining rather than quarrying that brought about its growth. Unlike Sherburn village, half a mile to the west, Sherburn Hill seems to have been entirely a product of

the coal mining age and does not display the older rural features of its neighbour.

The colliery at Sherburn Hill came before those at Sherburn village and for many years Sherburn Hill was the slightly larger settlement of the two. Most of the streets that made up the early mining village have been demolished, and because nearby Sherburn experienced considerable growth during the latter half of the twentieth century, Sherburn Hill is now only half the size of its neighbour, but is still a substantial village.

Sherburn Hill Colliery opened in 1835 in countryside half a mile north of the road that would become the village front street.

The pit heap at Sherburn Hill village (NE)

The Earl of Durham, who extended his Lambton Colliery Railway to Sherburn Hill, was the first owner of Sherburn Hill Colliery. His railway also served a nearby pit at Littletown just to the north, as well as several others along the railway's course. In 1914, Sherburn Hill Colliery was acquired by a Teesside industrialist called Sir Bernard Samuelson and from him it passed in 1923 to the Middlesbrough steel company of Dorman and Long.

Site of the Sherburn Hill pit heap after removal (NE)

In its time, Sherburn Hill colliery employed about 1,000 men, including some from Sherburn and Gilesgate Moor. The colliery closed in 1965 and was noted for having one of the largest pit heaps in the county, with a summit to rival the neighbouring hills for its views. The heap was lowered between 1969 and 1971 and the land reclaimed and re-landscaped. Today, there is no evidence to suggest a pit heap ever existed here. Since its closure in 1965, the actual colliery site has also reverted to countryside. Extensive woodland and a sawmill now occupy the spot that was once Sherburn Hill Colliery.

Little remains of the old pit village of Sherburn Hill and with the exception of Front Street, all the original colliery streets at Sherburn Hill have been demolished. Also a distant memory are Sherburn Hill's collection of nineteenth century pubs. These included the Blackbird Inn near Engine Row as well as the Oak Tree, Londonderry Arms, Commercial Inn, Crispin's Arms, Seven Stars and, as at Sherburn, a Lambton Arms. These pubs only survive as private houses or shops.

Alongside Front Street, the Primitive Methodists' Ebenezer Chapel was built in 1851 near Middle Row and was extended in 1901. Further west, along Front Street, the Wesleyan Chapel was built in 1857. Both chapels are still there but the latter is now a private house.

Sherburn Hill's first school was a colliery school for boys on the south side of Front Street built by the Earl of Durham in 1834. A national school for girls was built on the north side in 1845, but two new schools opened at the west end of the village in the later nineteenth century. One of these has been converted into two private houses and the other became a home for elderly people called The Chimneys.

In the early twentieth century, these schools were joined by another, now demolished school, on the south side of the road. The Sherburn Hill schools were superseded by the modern primary school at the east of the village.

Sherburn Hill pictured in the 1980s (NE)

Sherburn Hill Primary School stands near the site of a cinema of the 1920s called the Co-operative Picture Hall or Unity Theatre. The Co-operative Society's involvement in the showing of films in Sherburn Hill dated back to around 1906, when travelling showmen occasionally

visited the village to show silent movies. The purpose-built cinema opened around 1923 and initially seated 500 people. The cinema owner Wilfred Turnbull, owned cinemas at Bowburn and Thornley.

Sherburn Hill's cinema underwent major structural refurbishment in 1930 in the interests of safety, but closed in 1940. One major factor in the closure was the opening of the Majestic Cinema, in Gilesgate Moor's Sherburn Road in 1938. Many Sherburn Hill residents were happy to make the two and-a-half-mile trip down the bank to visit this larger venue.

Although the cinema has gone, Sherburn Hill's huge Co-operative store can still be seen in the centre of the village. It first opened in 1874 in a colliery house, but was superseded by a new store in 1877. This was replaced in 1913 by the impressive building that we still see today. By 1986 it had fallen out of use and was bought by a local businessman called John Marshall.

Marshall owned a small second-hand furniture business at the road ends in Gilesgate Moor Durham, but had bigger ambitions for the Sherburn Hill premises. Here the old Co-op became the first official store of his new company called Durham Pine. Later called DP Furniture Express, this company once had more than 70 stores throughout Britain. The impressive original building at Sherburn Hill, is full of character and has excellent far reaching views across the Durham countryside.

Apart from the former Co-op, the other notable building in the village is the community centre that stands next door. It was built as a welfare hall in 1926, but a mining institute was added in 1929. The building became a community centre following the closure of Sherburn Hill Colliery in the 1960s.

Ludworth

The villages of Shadforth and Ludworth lie half a mile apart in a pretty valley to the east of Durham City. The Shadforth Beck drains the valley which lies between two prominent hills. To the north is Sherburn Hill and to the south Witch Hill that separates Shadforth from the neighbouring Cassop Vale.

Shadforth and Ludworth are small villages by Durham standards, but their similarity ends there. Shadforth, the more westerly of the two, never had a colliery and is a throwback to a rural age with a tree-lined street of pretty cottages. Ludworth by contrast was a former mining village but now consists of post-war homes on the south side of the main road.

An old pit terrace lines the south side of Ludworth's main street but in truth, Ludworth's mining village was mostly on the north side of the road where there is now only woodland and a children's playground. The pit village was demolished after the war and was relocated across the road.

Ludworth's north side was home to a school, a Methodist chapel and to Ludworth Colliery from 1837. The colliery belonged to the Thornley Coal Company whose proprietors included John Gully, a champion boxer who lived in Durham City. The colliery shipped coals by rail to Hartlepool but after a succession of different owners it closed in 1931.

Despite its mining connections Ludworth was not entirely a product of the mining age. Its name goes back to Anglo-Saxon times and means either the enclosure of a man called Luda or the enclosure near a Loud Stream. A medieval village called Ludworth probably stood here, and from at least the 1400s there was a manor house.

Shadforth, Witch Hill and Silent Bank

The ruins of Ludworth Tower (NE)

While pit heaps and mining terraces dominated Ludworth and Sherburn Hill, Shadforth lived on as something of a rural oasis. The name of this village was first recorded in 1183 as Shaldeford but was called Shaldeforth by 1382. Its Anglo-Saxon name means Shallow Ford.

Shadforth's main street crosses the Shadforth Beck at the east end of the village by a minor bridge, but a ford may have existed here in earlier times. A floodgate is marked at this point on the 1860s map and a wind pump was built nearby that probably irrigated the local fields.

Less than a quarter of a mile east of here the road crosses the beck again where a ford existed as late as the 1950s. At the same distance to the east of Shadforth the beck becomes Sherburn Beck near the site of a nineteenth century corn mill called Sherburn East Mill and yet another ford existed at this point.

Shadforth's parish church of St. Cuthbert dates back no earlier than 1839 and is situated on the bank in Church Lane where the road leads up to Sherburn Hill. Here are mostly houses of the twentieth century that are in marked contrast to the older houses in the village centre. The exception on this bank is the old farmhouse called Crime Rigg – the last house in Shadforth as we head to Sherburn Hill.

Back in the heart of Shadforth village many houses are neat and rather sweet old farms and cottages. Here the main street is divided into 'North Side' and 'South Side' but the south side, which is the home of the pub and the village hall, has long been the focal point. South Side was home to a small school kept by a mistress in the nineteenth century that still operated in a modern form as late as the 1960s.

A family called Ludworth owned Ludworth during the 1200s and 1300s and they took their name from the place. Ludworth passed later to Thomas Holden who was wary of the Scottish raids that ravaged Durham at that time. In 1422 Holden obtained a licence to embattle his manor house. His fortification was built in the style of a pele tower, or tower house. Pele towers, (pronounced peel), can still often be found in Northumberland and the Borders but are something of a rarity in Durham so the ruins of Ludworth Tower that can still be seen are very important.

A single wall of Ludworth tower still stands, along with the foundations of a tight spiral staircase. In the 1850s. William Fordyce, the Durham historian, wrote: 'Considerable dilapidations have taken place during the last few years; and it is to be regretted that this relic of antiquity is not better protected from the injuries inflicted by the thoughtless population surrounding it'. Unfortunately, a large part of what Fordyce admired collapsed in 1890 but, the remaining enigmatic ruins of the tower can still be seen.

Shadforth Plough Inn (DS)

A tannery, post office and Methodist chapel were also situated on South Side during the nineteenth century. The chapel has long gone but stood near Shadforth Plough Inn which is the last survivor of the three Shadforth pubs. A private house now called the Old Saddle was once the Saddle Inn.

A Shadforth village scene (DS)

Shadforth Plough Inn incorporates the Witch Hill Restaurant, named from the hill that overlooks the valley to the south of the village. Now best known for a quarry alongside the A181, it is said that witches were once burned on the summit. It is one of the highest points for miles around.

The A181 is part of the old road from Durham to Hartlepool, called Silent Bank, also apparently called Sylum Bank or Signing Bank. It was possibly where pilgrims signed themselves with the cross on viewing Durham Cathedral for the first time. Alternatively it could be connected with the criminals seeking sanctuary or asylum at Durham Cathedral in medieval times.

Once the allocated time of sanctuary was up, they could stay and face punishment or be escorted along the road to Hartlepool from where they were permitted to leave the country.

The variant Silent Bank is less easy to explain, but intriguingly if traced along its original course, the road leads to Deaf Hill, near Trimdon. Silent Bank is known today as the site of the Three Horse Shoes public house. It is virtually all there is to be seen of the settlement called Running Waters. The pub is marked on nineteenth century maps when the settlement, noted for its quarry, was no bigger than today.

Running Waters may seem a slightly baffling name but the waters in question are most likely the Sherburn Beck and Chapman Beck that rise on either side of the A181. An old track way from Running Waters leads us back into Shadforth village half a mile to the north.

View of Durham City from Silent Bank near Witch Hill and Running Waters. Ushaw College can be seen at the top left of the photograph (DS)

Chapter Three

The Pittingtons and Littletown

Pittington is an appropriate name for a village that was once so dominated by pits but in truth the name goes back to Anglo-Saxon times when it was owned or inhabited by Pidda or Pytta. Originally called something like Pytta's don, the word don meant hill and referred to the magnesian limestone hill overlooking the village.

Cottages at Low Pittington village (DS)

In the nineteenth century, the historian William Fordyce mentioned bare rocks at the summit of Pittington hill and the steep sides 'covered with kitchen and flower gardens cultivated by local miners'. These gardens overlooked the plain in which the various Pittington villages were located.

The old farming village of Pittington, or Low Pittington sits at the very foot of Pittington hill and was known in earlier times as Piddington Towne. It was an important medieval settlement. High Pittington by comparison is a more recent mining village, whilst Hallgarth or Pittington-Hallgarth, known in earlier times as Kirkpiddington is also medieval.

Hallgarth is the most southerly of the three places but is a shrunken medieval village. It includes the earthworks of a manor house that belonged to the Priors of Durham Cathedral. The house was built around 1258 and in use until the sixteenth century. It should not be confused with Hallgarth Farmhouse, now known as Hallgarth Manor hotel. As far back as the Norman era Pittington belonged to the church of Durham and passed to Durham Cathedral's Dean and Chapter following the dissolution of the monasteries. At this time Hallgarth was granted on lease to Christopher Morland and by 1617 it had passed to his grandson Sir Henry Anderson.

In 1626 Hallgarth was leased to Ralph Simpson, a Gent who kept a horse for the service of King Charles I. Around 1675 Simpson's land passed through marriage to the Shipperdsons of Murton who moved into the manor house.

The most important historic building at Hallgarth is undoubtedly the medieval church of St. Laurence. It has been described by the architectural historian Nikolaus Pevsner as one of 'the most exciting pieces of architecture in the county'. This church was almost certainly built by Christian, the master architect of Hugh Pudsey, a powerful twelfth century Bishop of Durham. Pudsey's architect at Pittington church also built the Galilee Chapel at Durham Cathedral and there is a striking similarity between the two.

The interior of Pittington church resembles the Galilee Chapel of Durham Cathedral (NE)

In the nineteenth century, Hallgarth gained a great deal of notoriety when it was the scene of a brutal murder. It took place at Hallgarth water mill, which stood on a stream about half a mile south near the road to Sherburn.

On Sunday, 8 August, 1830, the mill owners were away visiting friends in Durham when around 6pm, one of the servants, a 19-year-old called Thomas Clarke, turned up at a house in Sherburn village to the south of the mill.

Clarke seemed distressed and claimed that six Irishmen had broken into the mill and ransacked the house for its money. Clarke claimed he had escaped, but not before the intruders had assaulted him with a poker and murdered a 19-year-old servant girl called Mary Ann Westropp.

On investigation, the girl's body was found in the mill kitchen with several wounds including a cut to her throat from ear to ear. Money appeared to have been stolen from the household and it seemed that a whitewashed tool was used to break into the drawers containing the money.

Clarke's room had recently been whitewashed and in the room was found a blunt piece of metal that was very likely the tool used in the robbery. Suspicions arose that Clarke was the murderer, particularly as there were no signs of an attack upon him. Moreover, Clarke and the girl had been seen together earlier that day by some residents in Sherburn. He was apparently overheard commenting on a 'saucy remark' that she had made to him.

Old photograph showing Hallgarth Mill which has now gone (MR)

Crowds turned out for Clarke's trial at Durham on 14 February, 1831 and, despite his plea of innocence, the young man was found guilty. On Monday, 28 February, he was hanged on the order of the judge. Clarke's last words were: 'Gentleman I am innocent, I am going to suffer for another man's crime'. The Hallgarth murder became the subject of a ballad first published in the *Durham Advertiser* shortly after Clarke's execution:

Eighteen hundred three times ten,
August the eighth that day
Let not that Sunday and that year
From memory pass away
At Hallgarth Mill near Pittington
Was done a murder foul
The female weak – the murderer strong
No pity for her soul.

Her skull was broke, her throat was cut,
Her struggle was soon o'er;
And down she fell, and fetched a sigh,
And weltered in her gore.

Her fellow servant, Thomas Clarke,
To Sherburn slowly sped,
And told a tale of strangers six
Had done the dreadful deed.

Now woe betide thee, Thomas Clarke!
For this thy coward lie;
A youth like thee for girl like her
Would fight till he did die.

'They've killed the lass', it was his tale,
'and nearly have killed me'
But when upon him folk did look,
No bruises could they see.

The Hallgarth murder is not the only murder associated with Pittington. In the previous chapter we have already mentioned the Pittington policeman murdered by a fellow officer at Sherburn. Also of interest is the victim of a separate, but quite mysterious murder who is said to be buried on the westerly back road linking Low Pittington with High Pittington.

The circumstances of this particular event may owe more to legend than fact as the road in question is Lady's Piece Lane. The story, of which there is admittedly very little detail, was perhaps created to explain the road's unusual name, but whether the inference was that the lady lies at peace or in pieces is open to question.

It is said that many years ago, the daughter of a family residing at Hallgarth Manor House used to regularly meet her lover in this lane, but one unfortunate day she failed to return home. Apparently murdered, her body was discovered and for some inexplicable reason, was buried under a stone alongside the road. The lane is still said to be haunted by her ghostly presence and in times past local villagers took care to avoid the lane at night. The actual identity of the girl remains a mystery.

Aerial view of Low Pittington village (NE)

It was in the early nineteenth century that the Pittingtons experienced extensive colliery developments that really brought about the growth of population in the district. Population figures for the area give some idea of the mining impact hereabouts. In 1801, 220 people lived in the area rising to 304 people by 1821. However it was the figures for 1831 and 1851 that were much higher at 1,632 and 2,530.

Old Pittington village or Low Pittington still has a rural feel and can't really be described as a pit village. It saw some population growth but most of the incoming population was focused upon the purpose built nineteenth century mining village called New Pittington or High Pittington as we know it today.

Several collieries surrounded the villages during the nineteenth century and Pittington Colliery was the first. Owned by the Marquess of Londonderry it opened around 1820. Four pits made up the colliery and they were interconnected by wagonways and railways.

The 1860s Ordnance Survey map shows an abundance of collieries, engines, boilers and railways around Pittington. William Fordyce, writing at this time described the volcanic appearance of the Pittington mines as they glowed at night. He also mentioned cottages or pit rows that formed a striking feature of the district. He noted that their doors were kept open allowing observation of 'handsome furniture contained within the majority of the houses'.

Fordyce noted that the local coal was known in the market as Stewart Wallsend from a reference to the Marquess of Londonderry's family name of Stewart and the coal's favourable similarity to a highly valued grade of Tyneside coal. The Pittington mines were some of the first major colliery developments in the Durham City area and Fordyce was clearly impressed. Fordyce also mentioned a railway 8 miles in length extending from Pittington to the Wear at Penshaw.

Two of the mines belonging to Pittington Colliery stood near High Pittington. One was Adolphus Pit of 1826, named after a son of the Marquess and close by was the Londonderry Pit of 1828. Both collieries were on the western side of the Coalford Beck and were connected by a short railway to the Sherburn House branch of the Lambton Railway. At the junction of the lines was yet another pit called the Buddle Pit. It was named from the Chief Agent of the Marquess. Although the Marquess of Londonderry dominated the Pittington pits the Lambton Railway's Sherburn House branch served Lord Lambton's collieries at Littletown, Sherburn and Sherburn Hill.

St. Laurence Church, Pittington (DS)

Pittington Colliery's fourth pit was the Marquess of Londonderry's Lady Seaham Pit. It was just north of Old Pittington on the Durham to Sunderland Railway of 1836. This particular railway terminated at Shincliffe and also served collieries at Broomside and Belmont. The Belmont Colliery dated from 1836 and was located just north of Belmont Hall (now called Ramside) and was very close to Pittington.

All of the mines around Pittington had closed by 1891 but Pittington miners could still find work at neighbouring collieries like Littletown, Moorsley and Elemore which lasted into the twentieth century.

New Pittington village was built for the Pittington miners but there were some amenities and houses used by the miners at Old Pittington as well.

Significantly, the old village was home to Pittington Station from 1836. Rebuilt in 1875, the station operated a passenger service until 1953. It finally closed as a goods station in 1960. The station and adjoining signal box (demolished in 1938) have now gone but a pathway runs north from Front Street to the Moorsley Road marking the course of the railway. Station Road and houses called Pittington Station Houses are the remaining clues to the railway past.

It might be assumed that Station Road was a nineteenth century street, but excavations have revealed that there were houses in this part of Pittington way back in medieval times. Of course it wouldn't have been known as Station Road in those days.

Several tradesmen and shops could be found in the Pittingtons in Victorian times of which the most prominent was High Pittington's Co-operative store of 1874 (rebuilt in 1897). In more recent times this developed into three separate shops.

Both Old and New Pittington had village schools including the nineteenth century National School in High Pittington's Wellington Street that later became a primary school. In 1933 another school was built in this village in Hallgarth Lane and it superseded the earlier school. It is now Pittington Primary School.

At Low Pittington, educational facilities existed at either end of the village in the nineteenth century. At the west end of Front Street was Pittington Literary, Scientific and

Map Legend:

- **S** — Schools/sites
- ▪━▪ — Former railways and wagonways
- ✳ — Colliery sites
- † — Churches and chapels
  - W – Wesleyan, P – Primitive, M – Modern
- (shaded) — Present built-up area
- 1 — Pittington station houses
- 2 — Pittington station (site)
- 3 — Site of smithy
- 4 — Blacksmith's Arms
- 5 — Site of Three Horseshoes
- 6 — Site of Belmont Tavern
- 7 — Duke of Wellington
- 8 — Bonny Pit Laddie (site)
- 9 — Bird in the Bush (site)

Map labels: To Rainton, Lady Seaham Pit, Belmont Colliery, 6, To High Moorsley and Hetton, LOW PITTINGTON, Stonebridge, Front St, High St, To Belmont and Durham, Shincliffe to Sunderland Railway, To Broomside Colliery, Lambton Railway, To Sherburn, Lady's Piece Lane, HIGH PITTINGTON, Wellington St, To Easington Lane, Elemore St, Adolphus Pit, Londonderry Pit, Buddle Pit, Site of Engine, Hallgarth Church, HALLGARTH, To Littletown

Reading Institute of 1842 holding about 400 volumes of books. In the 1850s it had about 60 members. Adjoining the library was a large room used as a parish school attended by 50 children.

At the eastern end of the village before the steep ascent up Pittington Hill is what is known as Pittington High Street. The name throws up images of a busy shopping street in a major town, but it is a quiet country lane that forms the main street in this little rural village. On the north side of this street the Marquess of Londonderry endowed a school in 1853 that was attended on average by 180 children.

After 1844 some Pittington pupils may have come from Ulster as in that year a nineteen week coal strike caused the Marquess to bring in many families from Northern Ireland to work the Pittington collieries. These people were replacements for striking miners and some may have stayed in the village.

The spiritual needs of Pittington were served by the church of St. Laurence at Hallgarth and two Victorian Methodist chapels in New Pittington. Wesleyan Methodists were located in Clayton Street and the Primitives in Dixon Street, but the current Methodist chapel in the village only dates from the 1960s.

Wellington Street and Elemore Street are the principal thoroughfares of New or High Pittington today and most houses in the Victorian village were originally clustered in an angle between them. Here were Clayton Street, Dixon Street and the slightly longer Londonderry Street, but modern houses now occupy the site.

Wellington Street and the Duke of Wellington pub commemorate the visit of this Duke to New Pittington in 1827 when the village was beginning to develop. The Duke visited with his friend the Marquess of

Durham Cathedral from Old Durham Farm (DS)

The site of the Roman farm at Old Durham looking towards Shincliffe (DS)

Gazebo at Old Durham Gardens (DS)

The village of Shincliffe (DS)

Laxey Cottage at Shincliffe (DS)

The chapel, Sherburn Hospital (DS)

The grounds of Sherburn Hospital (DS)

Sherburn Farm, Sherburn village (DS)

The village of Shadforth (DS)

St. Helen's church at Kelloe (DS)

The Browney valley (DS)

Langley Park (DS)

The ruins of Langley Hall (DS)

Wall Nook village (DS)

Hollinside Terrace near Lanchester (DS)

Lanchester village (DS)

Londonderry. Other pubs in High Pittington included the Bird in the Bush on the road to Littletown and the Bonnie Pit Laddie.

At old Pittington there was the Three Horse Shoes at the east of the village, shown on the 1860s map and the Blacksmiths Arms. The second of these is still there at the west end of the village near the corner of Station Road. A blacksmith's shop existed further along Station Road during the nineteenth and early twentieth century.

Historic photograph of the Duke of Wellington at High Pittington (MR)

Littletown

Littletown is a town only in name but stands close to the border of two cities. It is situated half way between Sherburn Hill and High Pittington and consists of little more than a street, an old chapel and a former pub. It is one of the smallest pit villages around and despite the word town in its name, it lies in pleasant open countryside that is far removed from an urban landscape. This is all the more surprising when we learn that it is only a mile south of the administrative boundary that separates two cities. The border of Durham City and

Sunderland lie to the north. The Littletown and Pittington areas are now popular with walkers and few traces can be seen of the mining that once dominated the surrounding land.

Littletown's early history is linked to the collection of villages called Pittington. These villages once formed a medieval administrative group called a township. Littletown was a part of this township and this may explain the name.

Littletown was originally called Suthton, a name that goes back to at least 1366. It means 'south farm' and was also known at one time as Suth Pittington. By 1581 it was called Little Pittington. The name was subsequently shortened to Littletown in 1613 but still only referred to a farm. The present village came later on a nearby site so it seems that the original Littletown wasn't even a village let alone a town.

Littletown is a tiny village (DS)

Since prehistoric times Littletown's livelihood was tied to the land, with agriculture and quarrying being important

activities. A prehistoric flint has been found as well as a couple of ancient grindstones made from local stone used in the making of flour.

Historic view of Littletown (GN)

There are feint remnants of medieval earthworks near Littletown Farm, but Littletown only really came to life in the nineteenth century when the colliery was established. John George Lambton, the First Earl of Durham, opened Littletown Colliery in 1831 and sunk two pits called Lord Lambton and Lady Alice Pits. Alice was the Earl's daughter, born in April 1831, the year the colliery was founded. A third pit, called Engine pit was sunk around 1833.

Lambton owned Sherburn Hill, Sherburn House and Sherburn Collieries, so in terms of mining Littletown was associated with the Sherburns rather than the Pittingtons where the Marquess of Londonderry owned the mines. Littletown remained under the Earl of Durham's ownership until 1896 when it was sold to Sir James Joicey's Lambton Collieries Ltd.

The Earl of Durham's Railway, called the Lambton Railway linked Littletown to coal staithes at Penshaw on the River Wear. Responsibility for the whole southern section of this railway fell to George Henry Hornsby who inhabited the nearby Littletown House in the early twentieth century. This building, across the main road from the village was previously home to a mining engineer called Thomas Crawford.

Littletown's colliery officials resided in Moor View cottages that can still be seen today. Here lived the colliery manager, under manager, a coachman and a gardener. In front of this row stands an old Wesleyan Chapel of 1858 that was the only chapel in the village. It fell out of use in 1979 and narrowly escaped demolition three years later. It is now owned by a timber business.

One of the most famous men connected with Littletown was Peter Lee (1864-1935) whose first job was at Littletown Colliery. He worked here in the 1870s when he was only ten. Here he worked as a pony driver but later went on to work at mines in Haswell, Pittington, Elemore and Brandon. He also had a spell working at mines in the United States.

Lee, who was of part gypsy descent became an important union leader and a local councillor. He was the first leader of Britain's first all Labour County Council which assembled at Durham in 1909. The town of Peterlee built in 1948, near the Durham coast, is named in his honour.

Littletown never grew to the extent of High Pittington or Sherburn Hill and consisted of Moor View Cottages and four little terraces in a quadrangle that is now the village green. All of the old terraces have now gone and most of the present population in the village live in Plantation Avenue that stands on the site of a terrace called Long Street.

At the corner of Plantation Avenue and the main Pittington to Haswell road stands the former Duke of York pub. This was Littletown's second pub. The first was the Moor Hen that existed nearby in the nineteenth century. The Moor Hen's last publican was Matthew Hepburn who became publican of the newly opened Duke of York around 1894. Hepburn was related to Wheldon Hepburn, the colliery manager of the time. The Duke of York operated as a pub until quite recently but became Littletown Lodge guest house a few years ago.

The miners' leader, Peter Lee (NE)

Historic view of the now demolished Heather View at Littletown (NE)

Just along the main road to the south of the pub stood an isolated terrace called Heather View. It was built in the later nineteenth century and was separated from the pub by The Earl of Durham's Colliery School of 1874. You might think that glorious heather moorland could be seen across the road from Heather View but for most of its life this terrace looked straight out onto the monstrous Sherburn Hill Pit heap that stood just across the road from the school.

The pit heap was precariously close to the school in the light of the disaster that beset the Welsh village of Aberfan in October 1966, when a pit heap collapsed onto a school killing 116 children.

Sherburn Hill Colliery closed in 1967 and the heap was removed in 1969-70 in the interests of safety and scenery. It was just as much a feature of Littletown's landscape as it was for Sherburn Hill and filled the countryside on the east side of the road that linked the two villages.

After a heavy snowfall the heap resembled an Alpine mountain and its height was such that views stretched out to sea from the summit. Ironically after the heap was removed, Heather View and the school did not live long enough to really enjoy their newly uninterrupted view of the surrounding countryside as both were demolished during the 1970s.

Littletown Colliery Institute of 1907 was also pulled down during this decade of demolition. It was situated near the pub, and once housed a reading room and billiard tables. The words Lambton Collieries Littletown Colliery Institute were inscribed above the door.

By this time Littletown's Front Street had been pulled down and all that remained were better quality houses in Moor View Cottages and Plantation Avenue along with the pub and former Wesleyan chapel. By this stage most of the local miners in Littletown worked at Sherburn Hill so the closure of that colliery in 1965 had a huge impact on Littletown. Littletown Colliery itself had closed many years before back in 1914.

During the sixties and seventies Littletown wasn't perceived as a particularly desirable place to live. 'Littletown isn't a pretty place' wrote *The Northern Echo* reporter on a visit in 1967, further remarking that people in neighbouring villages referred to it as the lost city.

However, after demolitions, the attraction of what remained was increasingly clear. Despite its lack of amenities Littletown's rural setting has become increasingly apparent and there were even plans for building 30 new houses opposite the Duke of York. Nothing came of this development and quaint little Littletown, with its extensive village green remains little to this day.

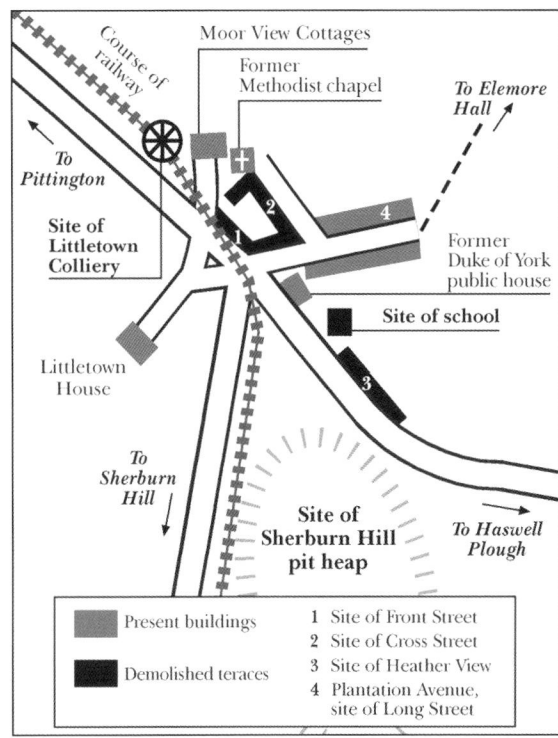

Map showing history of Littletown (NE)

Elemore Hall

The estate of Elemore Hall near Littletown originally belonged to the neighbouring settlements of Little Haswell and Haswell Grange and was given along with them by Hugh Pudsey, Bishop of Durham to the priory of Finchale sometime before 1190. The name Elemore may mean the moor of Ella or perhaps the moor of Elms but most of the surrounding area today is dominated by coniferous woodland that was planted to enhance the grounds of the Georgian estate.

Historic photograph of Elemore Hall (MR)

After the dissolution of the monasteries Elemore passed from Finchale Priory into the hands of Bartram Anderson of Newcastle around 1553. Anderson was some time mayor and Sheriff of Newcastle and was clearly a man of influence. It was he who probably built the first stone manor house between 1553 and 1557. Built in the shape of an E or U, parts of the house were later incorporated into the present Georgian building. The original house consisted of around 20 rooms and by 1600 they included a hall, kitchen, parlours, workhouse, milk house and butchery.

Elemore was first referred to as a hall around 1587 but the present hall dates from the Georgian period and was built at the centre of the country estate. It ceased to be a private mansion in 1947 when it was sold to Durham County Council and has since that time served as a special school.

Elemore was historically the seat of families called Hall and Baker and it was William Hall who acquired the property from Bartram Anderson's grandson for £4,600 in 1631. William's son, Sir Alexander Hall, a merchant and Alderman of Newcastle divided the property between his two sisters but gave the greater part to his cousin Nicholas Hall, the Rector of Loughborough.

During Parliamentary uprisings in the 1600s Nicholas was ejected from Loughborough and came to settle at Elemore. The property passed to his son Thomas and then to his granddaughter who married Thomas Conyers, a Durham City MP. It was through this line that the house came to be the property of the Baker family who had been connected with Crook Hall near Leadgate since the 1630s.

Old photograph showing gamekeepers at Elemore Hall (MR)

The Baker family's history is made complex by a succession of family heads called George. One such George married an Elizabeth Conyers in the 1700s and their son, yet another George, inherited Elemore Hall after other lines of descent and inheritance passed away. An alum mine at Boulby on the Cleveland coast and a colliery at Biddick near Washington were also part of his inheritance.

This particular George had a reputation for extravagant dress, dancing and gambling on the horses, but his wife

Judith Routh of Dinsdale, described as 'a beautiful young lady with a handsome fortune', is thought to have brought some stability to his financial affairs. Judith's mother was a member of the Milbanke family of Halnaby in Yorkshire and it is said that a famous member of this family called Anna Isabella Milbanke was born at Elemore in 1792. Anna was the wife of the poet Lord Byron, but some sources give her birthplace as London.

When Judith and George married in 1749 they initially chose to live in the Chester-le-Street area but George employed the Helmsley architect Robert Shout to set about rebuilding Elemore Hall as a luxurious family home. Rebuilt in brick and stone, but keeping the general E-shape, the house was completed in 1753 and encompassed what has been described as 'an uncomfortable mixture of Baroque and Palladian architectural styles'. A walled garden and a pond were also added to the property.

Old photograph showing staff at Elemore Hall (MR)

Judith and George's son had a daughter called Elizabeth and a son called George, who inherited Elemore after the death of his father in 1774. This George was a typical country squire, principally known in sporting circles for

his passion for hunting and cock fighting. He was apparently regarded as 'one of the best gentleman riders in England'.

A memoir records a conversation between this George and Robert Surtees, the famed Durham historian. Baker was said to have asked 'I Wonder Mr Surtees why you should spend so much money and time over a history of Durham?' Surtees retorted 'I wonder Mr Baker why you spend so much money and time in following a pack of hounds after a poor hare?' It was during this particular George Baker's residence at Elemore that Elemore colliery was opened up in the neighbourhood just to the north east.

Established in 1825 by the Hetton Coal Company, the history of Elemore Colliery really belongs to the nearby village of Easington Lane but it was established on land leased from Baker. The two shafts in the colliery were named George and Isabella after members of the family. However when Baker died in 1837 he left only a daughter, Isabella, as his heir.

George was thus the last in the line of the George Bakers at Elemore. He wished to commemorate this notable fact on his headstone with a rather immodest inscription that read: 'Here lies the last of the George Bakers of Elemore Hall, and though he may not be the last George Baker, he will be succeeded by no one of more gentlemanly sport who will live longer in the hearts of the poor and unfortunate to whom he was constant benefactor and the kindest friend.'

In 1844 George's heir, Isabella married her cousin Henry Tower, the son of Elizabeth Baker and by virtue of this double connection with the family George changed his name to Baker Baker. The family were subsequently called Conyers Baker Baker and retained their links with Elemore until the sale of the hall in 1947. Today they reside at Sedbury Hall near Scotch Corner in North Yorkshire.

Chapter Four

Cassop, Kelloe, Quarrington and Coxhoe

Cassop, Kelloe and Quarrington lie amongst the Magnesian limestone hills to the south east of Durham. It is in an area long noted for its quarrying and is now bordered on its western side by the A1(M) motorway. Here close to this busy road lie the former mining villages of Coxhoe and Bowburn and it is at this point that the limestone escarpment rises smoothly and suddenly on the eastern side of the motorway.

With the exception of Kelloe, much of this area lay within an ancient district called Quarringtonshire. This district extended north to take in Sherburn and Whitwell, but in this chapter we are concerned with the area stretching from Cassop in the north to Kelloe in the south and then west towards Coxhoe and Bowburn.

In the northern part of this area is Old Cassop, one of two Cassops that are quite distinct places. The other is New Cassop, once called Cassop Colliery. It is the larger of the two villages and is now simply called Cassop. It lies on the top of a hill near the village of Quarrington Hill.

Old Cassop village (DS)

Old Cassop is a farming village with a history stretching back to medieval times. It lies on the southern slopes of the hill that rises up from Cassop Vale towards Running Waters and Silent Bank. The village is an agricultural settlement with a rural character and includes Cassop Farm, Hillcroft and Pilmore Farm amongst its buildings. The whole village was designated a special conservation area in 1981.

Farm buildings at Old Cassop (DS)

Old Cassop is separated from Quarrington Hill and New Cassop by the attractive low lying area of noted natural beauty called Cassop Vale. This vale forms a nature reserve and is designated a Site of Special Scientific Interest. In times gone by it was apparently the Cat's 'Op', or vale frequented by wild cats that gave Cassop its name. It was part of a hunting park used by the Prince Bishops but is better known today for its wild flowers.

Cassop Vale is an extremely rare habitat of magnesian limestone grassland that also includes marshland and a woodland fringe. A Victorian mine called Cassop Vale Colliery once stood in the vale but another stood to the east on Cassop Moor.

Cassop Moor (NE)

A larger colliery simply called Cassop Colliery stood near New Cassop, but all the collieries of Cassop and Quarrington Hill had ceased operating by the end of the nineteenth century. In the twentieth century the main industry has been limestone quarrying and in recent years care has been taken to ensure that Cassop Vale and the local environment are not adversely affected by this activity.

Quarrington and Quarrington Hill

Scars of quarrying can be seen to the north and west of Quarrington Hill in amongst attractive countryside, as quarrying has long been a feature of this landscape. It has been this way since the days when the quern stones that gave Quarrington its ancient name were excavated.

During the twentieth century the activity has become more and more intensive and in the 1960s, villagers at Quarrington Hill regularly complained of dust clouds from the quarries that rose in clouds from 'pyramid-like piles'.

Quarringtonshire was the name of the ancient district that included Quarrington, Sherburn, Shadforth, Cassop and Tursdale. It was named in Anglo-Saxon times but the district's history could be much older and may trace its origins back to a tribal region of Celtic origin.

The shire was named from Quarrington, (Querningdon) a place-name that means 'quern stone hill'. Querns were millstones used in grinding corn and it seems that the local stone was used in their manufacture.

The actual hill at Quarrington Hill covers a wide area and rises near the A1(M) motorway at Bowburn. At this point it forms a prominent hill spur or 'heugh' near a farm called Heugh Hall. On the south side of the Heugh at Heugh Hall Row, is a terrace of isolated houses, and nearby, a little village called Old Quarrington that resembles an overgrown farmstead.

Old Quarrington and Heugh Hall Row can be reached from the south end of Bowburn via Crow Trees Lane, which passes beneath the motorway to reach the two settlements. Old Quarrington should not be confused with the village of Quarrington Hill, the much larger, former mining village, on the hilltop a mile to the east.

Although the term Quarringtonshire was still used for the area during the medieval period, it was always part of Durham. The shire was simply a district in the Palatinate of Durham and was not a shire in the sense of a modern county.

Early families associated with medieval Quarringtonshire included the Baliols, Rothburys and Salvins, but during the 1500s Quarrington manor was leased by the Bishop of Durham to a man called John Raket.

The manor of Quarrington was probably centred upon Old Quarrington, but the Baliols are thought to have owned a moated mansion called Standalone in the Tursdale area to the west of Coxhoe. Unfortunately, the site has long since gone.

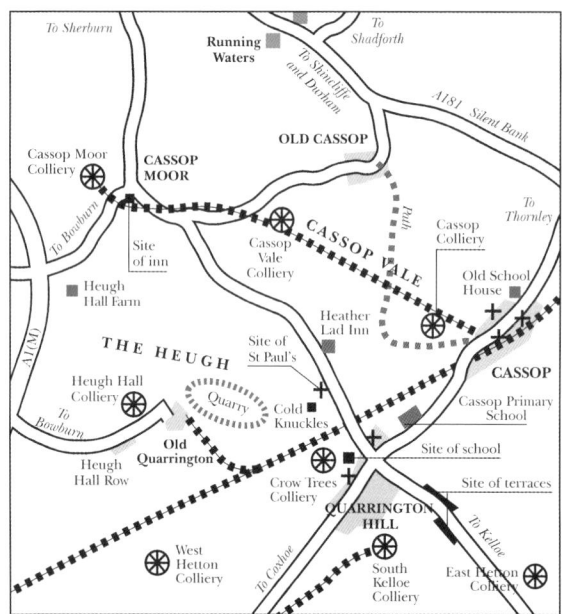

Map showing history of the Quarrington Hill area (NE)

For most of its history Quarrington was a quiet rural district and there were few events of note to puncture the peace. So, when two major military encampments came to the top of Quarrington Hill in the seventeenth and eighteenth centuries it must have been something of a disruption to the local people.

In April 1644, during the English Civil War, a huge Scottish army commanded by the Earl of Leven encamped on Quarrington Hill for seven days before heading south to fight alongside English Parliamentarian troops at Marston Moor near York. The Scots would play a significant part in the victory over the Royalists on that famous Yorkshire battleground.

Almost exactly 103 years later, in April 1747, an army was once again encamped on Quarrington Hill. This time they were English troops consisting of a large detachment of soldiers commanded by the Duke of Cumberland who encamped there for several weeks. The army set up their temporary home on the hill after returning from a particularly brutal Scottish campaign.

Here, the troops celebrated their recent victory in Scotland where they had crushed the Jacobites at the Battle of Culloden earlier in the month. Local historians record that traces of huts belonging to the English army could still be seen on Quarrington Hill as late as the 1850s.

In 1801 Quarrington was still a largely agricultural area that was home to little more than a hundred people. Things changed with the arrival of wagonways and collieries in the 1830s. Not that Quarrington was unfamiliar with coal mining. Back in 1777, a Quarrington Colliery opened somewhere near Old Quarrington and although production was probably not on the scale of the nineteenth century collieries, the colliery did include a Newcomen engine. It was a stationary engine used to pump water from the mine and suggests that the colliery was of some significance.

In 1825, William Hedley opened Crow Trees Colliery near the site of what became the mining village of Quarrington Hill. Crow Trees did not become a major colliery until 1834 when it began shipping coals on the Clarence Railway. It was probably during this period that South Kelloe Colliery opened on the southern fringe of Quarrington Hill. This mine was linked to the Clarence Railway by a separate wagonway to Coxhoe.

Like Quarrington Hill, Old Quarrington was affected by the colliery developments. Here William Hedley opened Heugh Hall Colliery in 1840. It was linked by incline to the collieries at Crow Trees and Cassop. From there wagonways shipped the coal to Hartlepool. From 1840, Heugh Hall Row and Old Quarrington probably housed a mix of miners and agricultural labourers.

The history of the Cassops and the Quarringtons are closely connected and their names are linked in the civil parish called Cassop-cum-Quarrington. Strangely, this particular parish does not include the village of Quarrington Hill, which is technically a part of Kelloe, but it does, include Old Quarrington.

The village of Cassop lies on the top of the hill just up the road from Quarrington Hill and is the 'New Cassop' of the nineteenth century. It has no direct link to the Old Cassop in the vale to the north.

Of the three Cassop Collieries which served the area from the 1830s onwards it was the one simply called Cassop that served New Cassop village. This village developed along with Quarrington Hill in the 1830s when wagonways linked local coal mines to recently arrived railways. Housing was provided for the miners and pubs, chapels and schools were built to serve the population.

Spiritual needs were served by two Methodist chapels at New Cassop and two at Quarrington Hill. New Cassop's wooden Wesleyan Chapel of 1842 was the earliest. It stood at the west of the village and was joined later in the century by a Primitive Methodist chapel at the east end. Both have now gone.

At Quarrington Hill, the chapels survive. One is the Primitive Chapel of 1886, still bearing its inscription. The other, in Church Street, dates from the early twentieth century.

The now demolished church of St. Paul, Quarrington Hill (NE)

Quarrington Hill's Church Street is named from the Anglican parish church that served both villages. This was St. Paul's Church, and it stood in a windy location at the top of the slopes just north of Quarrington Hill. Built in 1868, it was described as an unpretending building of Norman style and in the nineteenth century stood near a small terrace of houses called Cold Knuckles.

St. Paul's fell redundant in the late twentieth century due to dwindling attendances and was demolished, despite protests, in 1995. Only the cemetery remains. Cassop and Quarrington Hill are now served by churches at Bowburn and Kelloe.

Old school house at Cassop village (DS)

Victorian schools existed in Quarrington Hill and Cassop, but they were superseded by a new school in 1912 that is now Cassop Primary School. The earlier school at the east end of Cassop was demolished after the war and a modern Methodist Chapel dating from 1960 now stands on the site. Only the school house of this early school remains and is arguably the most attractive house in Cassop.

Quarrington Hill School stood just north of the village near Crow Trees Colliery. Its site seems to have become a cinema in the early 1900s, but this was later demolished. The present Cassop Primary School of 1912 serves Cassop and Quarrington Hill and lies halfway between the two villages. Being on a hill, it has a rather windy location and a wind turbine stands nearby. The turbine, erected in 1999, made Cassop Primary the first wind-powered school in the UK.

Throughout the nineteenth century, many pubs were built in the two villages to quench the thirsts of hardworking miners. According to Fordyce, writing in the 1850s, there were several colliery rows at New Cassop, with eight public houses and a few shops. Pubs at New Cassop included the Cassop Inn, Black Bull and Victoria. The Victoria is now the only inn in the village.

At Quarrington Hill, there were also several pubs, including The Crow Trees Colliery Inn, The Good Intent, Cross Keys and Black Boy. Also there in the nineteenth century was the Half Moon at the corner of Front Street and Church Street. It still serves Quarrington Hill's residents today. Today most houses in Cassop and Quarrington Hill date from the twentieth century as most of the Victorian pit terraces were demolished.

Church Street leads north to the Heather Lad Inn near the site of St. Paul's Church. The inn is located in wonderful open countryside, beyond Quarrington Hill. On a sunny day, it is worth walking along the road to take in the surrounding views on the edge of the limestone escarpment.

When *The Northern Echo's* John North column visited the Heather Lad in February 1975, it had no gas, no water supply and had to generate its own electricity. The generator had failed at the time of the visit and although it was working when John North returned in 1983, little else had changed.

Before we leave Quarrington Hill we must make mention of a notable house in the village that goes by the name Aston Villa. The house was named in 1913 by a Sunderland Football Club supporter called Albert Gillett who later went on to run a bus company in the village. Sunderland Football Club were having a very successful season at the time and when his beloved team reached the FA Cup final, Albert confidently promised his house would be named after the FA Cup winners. Unfortunately for Albert, the Birmingham side called Aston Villa were the victors. Albert, who apparently hoped to call his home Sunderland House kept his

promise and to this day the property in Quarrington Hill's Front Street is called Aston Villa.

Aston Villa, Quarrington Hill (NE)

Kelloe

The village of Kelloe lies south of Quarrington Hill and traces its history back to medieval times. Its earliest recorded name was Kelf-Law, meaning calf hill, but a possible alternative name, 'bare hill', deriving from Caluh Law, has been suggested. Law is an Anglo-Saxon word for a hill and the law in question is further east between Kelloe and Trimdon.

There were two medieval settlements at Kelloe, both of which shrank in size, perhaps because they were economically unviable or maybe because of a plague. The early settlements were called Town Kelloe, now a tiny farming village and Church Kelloe, the home of Kelloe church. Although Town Kelloe still exists, virtually nothing remains of Church Kelloe other than the church.

Just south of Church Kelloe there stood, during the nineteenth century yet another village. It was called East

Hetton and like the ancient village of Church Kelloe it has also vanished.

Rather confusingly Kelloe was also the name the locals gave to East Hetton. It is now remembered as Old Kelloe even though it dated from no earlier than the 1830s. The present village called Kelloe only came into being during the second half of the twentieth century and like East Hetton served as the mining village for East Hetton Colliery. This colliery closed in 1983 and its site stands to the north of Kelloe. The land here is currently undergoing reclamation.

Present day Kelloe incorporates the site of Church Kelloe on its western fringe. Here is a remnant of the old vicarage alongside the historic parish church. This wonderful old church, dedicated to St. Helen, was the focal point of Kelloe's early history, but was important to a much wider area. It was once the parish church for Coxhoe, Quarrington, Cassop, Tursdale, Thornley, Wheatley Hill, Wingate and Trimdon Grange as well as for Kelloe itself.

St. Helen's Church, Kelloe (DS)

Records relating to these villages can be found in and around the church, including graves and a memorial to

74 men and boys who lost their lives in the Trimdon Grange Colliery disaster of 1882. Inside the church there is a memorial to the locally-born poet Elizabeth Barrett Browning, who was baptised in the church, but the building's most cherished monument is the ancient St. Helen's Cross.

The Church tower, St. Helen's Kelloe (DS)

Kelloe Cross has been described by the architectural historian Nikolaus Pevsner as 'the best piece of medieval sculpture in County Durham'. It probably dates from the twelfth century, but was only discovered in 1856, embedded into the chancel wall in six separate pieces.

The pieces were assembled together and now stand near the altar. They depict St. Helena (St. Helen), the mother of the Roman Emperor Constantine the Great, who was a Christian convert. According to legend, the whereabouts of the true cross of Christ was revealed to Helena by an angel. This angel is depicted on Kelloe's cross holding a scroll while Helena is shown holding a spade with which she intends to find the cross.

Kelloe church dates to Norman times and from 1181 was closely associated with Sherburn Hospital. Much revenue raised from agricultural activity in Kelloe parish was used to run the hospital. Sherburn Hospital was founded by the Prince Bishop, Hugh Pudsey (1153-1195), but Kelloe is known to have produced a Prince Bishop of its very own. His name was Richard Kellaw and he reigned as Bishop of Durham from 1311 to 1316. He was probably born in a manor house at Town Kelloe, where the present farmhouse called Kelloe Hall now stands.

Bishop Kellaw was described as a placid character, who was ill-equipped to deal with the ravages of the Scots who troubled Durham at the time. During his reign he generally resided at Bishop Middleham Castle near Sedgefield. This castle is about three miles south of Kelloe and its earthworks can still be seen. It was there that Kellaw died in 1316. It was fortunate for Kellaw that during his turbulent reign, his much tougher brother, Patrick, was able to lead the forces of Durham against the invading Scots.

The Kellaws were an influential family who owned much land around Kelloe in medieval times. One of the first mentioned family members was Alexander Kellaw, benefactor of Sherburn Hospital in the 1200s, but the Kellaws still owned land here until the early 1400s when Joan Kellaw sold Kelloe to the Fossour family.

The ancient St. Helen's Cross, Kelloe Church (DS)

The Fossours held Kelloe until 1782 when they sold it to the Tempests. Through the Tempests it passed by marriage to the Marquess of Londonderry in the nineteenth century. Kelloe Hall at Town Kelloe was the birthplace of one of the Marquess of Londonderry's daughters.

The wealth of characters associated with Town Kelloe is matched by a list of notable vicars at Church Kelloe. They included Thomas of Canterbury, who was temporarily ex-communicated by the Pope in 1314 for failing to pay his Peter's Pence. He eventually paid up and was awarded absolution. In 1485, another vicar called Roger Morland, took in a murderer called James Manfield, who turned up at Kelloe church after wandering the Durham countryside. He had axed to death the chaplain of Wycliffe in the Teesdale village of Ovington and then fled north, where he stumbled into Kelloe. The vicar escorted him to Durham Cathedral where he was awarded sanctuary.

The seal of Bishop Kellaw

Another notable incumbent of Kelloe was John Lively, known as 'the vicar of Kellow who had seven daughters, but never a fellow'. Lively built a three-storey vicarage near the church in the 1600s, but only the ground-floor remains. Around the time of the Civil War, the vicar's eldest daughter married a local Roundhead called Anthony Busby of Cassop. Lively, who was later vicar of Gainford on Tees, once met Oliver Cromwell on a visit to Durham and presented him with the gift of burnt wine and shortbread. What Cromwell thought of the gesture is not recorded.

Vicars and local landowners may have dominated Kelloe's rather rural history for hundreds of years, but things changed in the early nineteenth century with the arrival of coal mines and wagonways. In 1836, the brand new village called East Hetton came into being at Kelloe with the opening of the neighbouring East Hetton Colliery.

At around the same time, the West Hetton Colliery was opened at Coxhoe. A collection of cottages called West Hetton Houses was built for the miners there but this settlement was swallowed up by the rapid growth of Coxhoe in subsequent years.

East Hetton, by contrast was a village in its own right. It consisted of about 300 houses in eight colliery terraces. By the 1860s it had a grocers, a drapers, a butcher and pubs called The Red Lion, Bradyll Arms, Newcastle Arms, Grey Hound, Mason's Arms and Turk's Head.

At Church Kelloe there was an additional pub called the Davy Lamp. Alongside was a little settlement of wooden cottages that was likewise called Davy Lamp. It was built for sinkers, or labourers who first opened up the East Hetton colliery. A Davy Lamp pub can still be seen here today but it is not the original.

The village of Town Kelloe showing Kelloe Hall (DS)

In the 1860s the Kelloe area still needed a school so in 1873, the Marquess of Londonderry, who owned land at Town Kelloe, built a national school there. There had been a school in Kelloe back in the 1700s, but it served a largely agricultural community and little is known about the establishment. A new school came to East Hetton in 1877 when the Coxhoe School Board opened a school that could hold about 400 pupils after it was extended in 1892. The schools were attended by the children of local farmers and quarrymen, as well as those of miners.

East Hetton village was home to a Wesleyan and Primitive Methodist Chapel as well as an Institute, but all the streets and features of the village have disappeared forever. Most of the colliery village was demolished in the decades following the Second World War due to poor quality housing. Empty fields now occupy the village site.

Locals always defiantly referred to East Hetton as Kelloe but it was popularly known as Canaan during the nineteenth century. Named from the ancient Biblical lands and city it was possibly an ironic nickname. The nickname was sufficiently well known to be remarked upon by William Fordyce in his 1850s History of Durham.

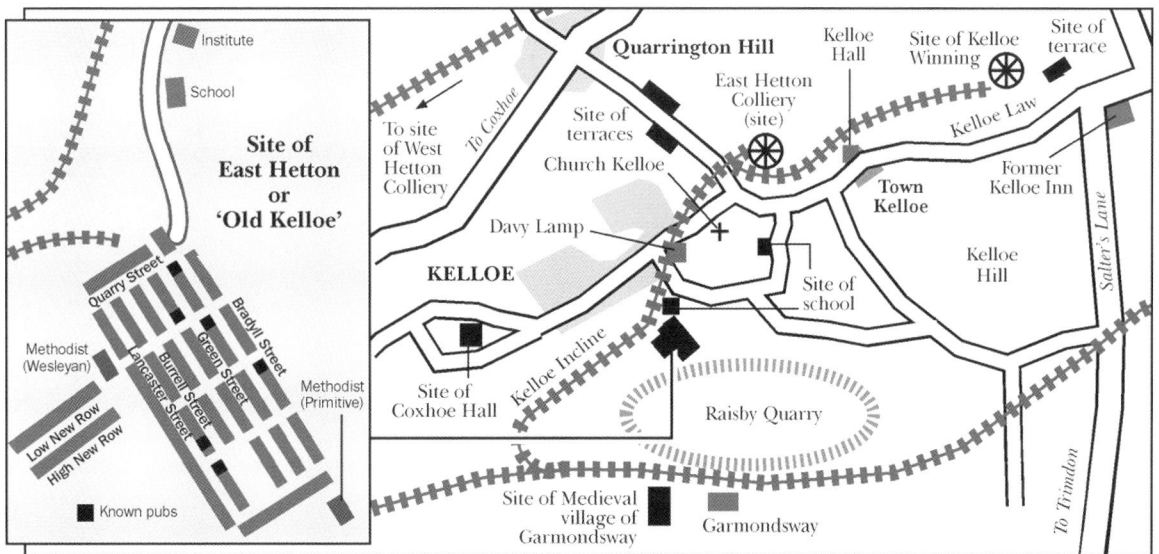

Map showing history of Kelloe and East Hetton (NE)

It is not surprising that the locals rejected the name East Hetton as it must have caused much confusion with Hetton-le-Hole, where the famous Hetton Colliery had opened in the 1820s. This colliery was the first to significantly penetrate below the magnesian limestone of eastern Durham and was principally famed for Stephenson's Hetton Colliery Railway of 1822. Hetton-le-Hole was a good seven miles north of Kelloe but there was a loose connection between the two places in the shape of a military gentleman called Colonel Bradyll.

In 1833 Bradyll opened what he called South Hetton Colliery just to the south of Hetton-le-Hole and this gave rise to the mining village of South Hetton. Bradyll retained the Hetton theme at Coxhoe, where he opened West Hetton Colliery in 1836. Calling places Hetton was probably a kind of branding exercise. In the coal market, Hetton coal had a good reputation and some coal owners

would have considered the branding of their product a more important issue than the naming of a village.

It seems likely that Bradyll was also involved with Kelloe's East Hetton Colliery, as Bradyll was the name of a terrace and a pub in East Hetton village. However, neither East nor West Hetton Colliery were connected to the Hetton Colliery Railway. Both shipped their coals on separate lines to Hartlepool.

East Hetton Colliery wasn't the only mine in the Kelloe area. A smaller nineteenth century mining settlement and little colliery called Kelloe Winning could also be found about two miles east of Kelloe, near Trimdon. It was a tiny hamlet with a single terrace and was established when the Kelloe wagonway was extended there in the 1860s. This wagonway ran close to the Kelloe Inn on Salters Lane. The lane is now the B1278 and stands close to a hill called Kelloe Law. Kelloe Inn was renamed The Wingate

Arms in the late nineteenth century and is now a private house. Kelloe Winning terrace has also long since gone.

Memorial to the Trimdon mining disaster at Kelloe (DS)

Coxhoe

Coxhoe is situated on the lower-lying land that borders the edge of the magnesian limestone hills that rise suddenly to its east. It is on a Roman road and in places the main road through the village may follow this ancient route.

The old road headed south from Hadrian's Wall and, at Coxhoe, avoided the neighbouring hills. In 1742, a turnpike road was built from Durham to Stockton, on a similar course through the area and more or less follows the main street of today.

There doesn't seem to have been a Roman settlement at Coxhoe, but there were Iron Age enclosures to the east close to where an Anglo-Saxon settlement came into being at the 'hoh', or hill spur, belonging to someone called Cocc.

Coxhoe's medieval village was not located on the Roman road, but was situated to the east of the present village, near Kelloe, in the area known until the 1950s as the site of Coxhoe Hall. The old village stood near East House Farm, but was abandoned in the 1500s due to plague or for economic reasons. The feint earthworks of houses can still be seen and this was one of two deserted medieval villages in the vicinity. The other was Garmondsway, a lost village to the south of Kelloe, near Garmondsway East Farm.

The similar, but larger medieval earthworks of Garmondsway village exist near the back road from Coxhoe to Trimdon. Garmondsway was the place where King Canute, the Danish ruler of England, commenced a barefoot walking pilgrimage to St. Cuthbert's shrine at Durham City in 1020 AD. It was a genuine event, but the story that neighbouring Trimdon came about from Canute trimming his hair and donning a cloak like a monk seems to be a legend.

Garmondsway stands near another lost village, called Raisby, in what appears to be one of the northernmost Danish-style place names in Durham. It survives only in the name of a farm close to the huge Raisby quarry and once belonged to someone called Race Engaine. However this particular fellow owned the land here at least two centuries after the Viking period. It seems that Engaine donated land here to Sherburn Hospital during the 1100s.

Medieval Coxhoe included a corn mill on the Coxhoe Beck, south of East House Farm. From 1235, this mill and most of the village belonged to the monks of Finchale Priory. It was given to them by Walter Audre and his wife, Constantina, in return for burial at the priory. Other lands were given to Sherburn Hospital during the 1200s.

Thirteenth century Coxhoe landowners included Peter the Farmer and Richard De Coxhoe. In the fourteenth century, a landowner called John Denum first mined coal hereabouts. From 1380 to 1617, Coxhoe was owned by the Blakistons, a Catholic family of Norton, near Stockton who owned a manor house in the village that was described as ruinous by 1418.

In 1621 Coxhoe passed through marriage to another Catholic family, called the Kennetts of Kent. In the Civil War, Sir William Kennett, of Coxhoe, supported the Royalists and he and his sons, Samuel and Major John Kennett, fought at Marston Moor in 1644. Samuel was killed in battle but John survived as heir to the estate. For his involvement in the war, the victorious Roundheads fined him £80, but this was promptly raised to £300 when John objected.

In 1714, the estate passed through a Kennett marriage to a Scottish lord, the fifth Earl of Seaforth, who fled to France after taking part in the unsuccessful Jacobite rising of 1715. The manor was looked after by a steward and then sold to John Burdon who built a grand hall on the site of the manor house about 1725.

The grand new hall was Coxhoe Hall, a three-storey house of 14 bedrooms surrounded by a park, four gatehouses and an avenue through the trees that joined the main road to the west. Part of the avenue is the present day Coxhoe street called The Avenue, and is now lined with houses rather than trees.

In the early 1700s, there does not appear to have been a substantial village at Coxhoe, but ten houses called Coxhoe Square (now demolished) were built for estate workers near the hall in the late eighteenth century. It was during this century in the 1750s, that Coxhoe passed to the Swinburn family, and then to John Foster and Thomas Cooke in the 1790s.

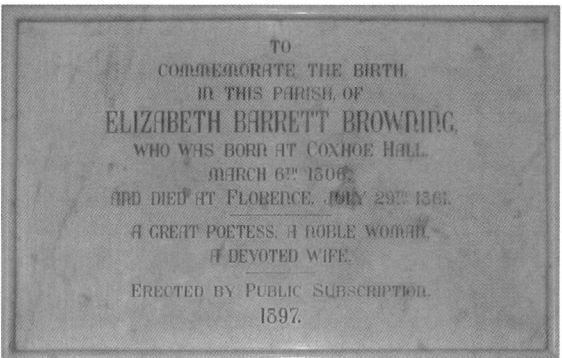

Memorial to Elizabeth Barrett Browning at Kelloe church (DS)

In 1795 some sugar plantation owners called Mr and Mrs Edward Barrett returned to England from the West Indies with their daughter, Mrs Elizabeth Moulton. They came to live at Coxhoe Hall but leased the property and did not own it. They came to the North East because Mr Barrett was a friend of the wealthy Newcastle merchant, Graham Clark, whose daughter Mary married Mrs Moulton's son Edward. Edward and Mary moved to Coxhoe Hall and here, on 6 March, 1806, Mary gave birth to Elizabeth Barrett Moulton Barrett, better known in her later life as the famed poet, Elizabeth Barrett Browning.

Historic view showing Coxhoe Hall (NE)

Elizabeth was baptised at Kelloe church, in February 1808, along with her younger brother Edward (born 1807), but the family moved from Coxhoe in 1809 after purchasing a Herefordshire estate called Hope End. Never returning, they had chosen their moment of departure well. In the decades that followed, much of the open countryside surrounding Coxhoe Hall was transformed into a landscape of collieries, railways, coke ovens and quarries.

Coxhoe Hall came up for sale in 1817 and was purchased by Anthony Wilkinson of Crossgate, a member of an influential Durham City family. It was subsequently acquired by Thomas Wood, a mining engineer in 1850. The Woods held the property until the 1930s and later members of the family included John Wood, who was a Justice of the Peace and High Sheriff of Durham.

In 1938, the hall was offered for sale again and was purchased this time by the East Hetton Colliery Company that mined the estate for coal. The hall

remained empty, but from 1939, British troops used it as a barracks. Later, Italian and German prisoners of war were kept here. After the war, the hall passed to the National Coal Board but increasingly fell into ruin. It was eventually condemned, owing to mine subsidence, and was demolished in August 1952.

It was mostly rural trades that dominated Coxhoe before the nineteenth century but there was some industrial activity here in early times. A corn mill operated on Coxhoe Beck south of Coxhoe Wood from at least 1235 and a mill operated on or near the site until closure during or just after the 1890s. The mill buildings remained standing after it was abandoned and were not demolished until 1965.

Elizabeth Barrett Browning

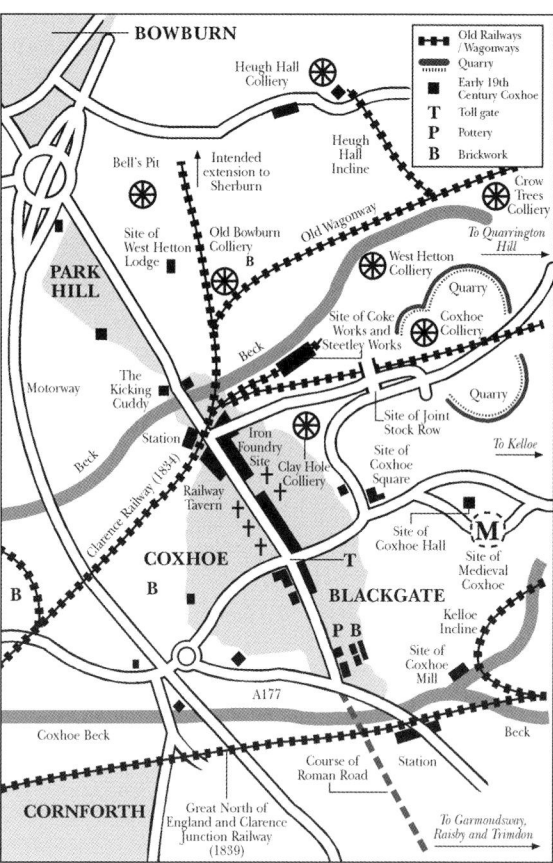

Map showing history of Coxhoe (NE)

Mining and quarrying at Coxhoe had medieval roots, with lime quarrying mentioned in 1495 in the accounts of Durham Cathedral. John Denum (or Denham) was mining coal at Coxhoe in 1327 and mining also took place here during 1695 and 1769. Back in those days it was always on a small scale. Good transport links were important for industrial development and the construction in 1742 of the turnpike road that replaced the earlier Roman road through the area may have further encouraged mining activity.

Road maintenance was funded through tolls and a tollgate called Blackgate Bar was erected at the Coxhoe crossroads. The crossroads is the one at the bottom of the Avenue in what is now the centre of Coxhoe. In the nineteenth century, the houses that developed south of this toll were called Blackgate but would become part of Coxhoe's colliery village.

Close to Blackgate was a pottery established by the Lammas family on the east side of the turnpike road some time before 1769. Here, a hamlet called Coxhoe Pottery developed and was one of two eighteenth century settlements at Coxhoe, the other being a collection of estate workers' houses called Coxhoe Square near Coxhoe Hall.

Other than this, there were only a few scattered farms and a pub on the turnpike road called the Blue Bell, mentioned in 1791. In fact, according to the census of 1801 the total number of buildings in the whole Coxhoe area amounted to no more than 27 houses and a population of 117. It had only risen to 154 people by 1831.

Before 1817, an additional pottery called Cornforth Pottery opened across the road from the earlier establishment and a brickworks opened alongside the original pottery. In the 1850s, they were joined by a clay pipe works belonging to William Row of Yarm, but this business closed in the 1860s.

Other brickworks opening at Coxhoe included Mr Field's works at Cow Close near Cornforth Lane, about 1850, Mr Goodyear's near the Coxhoe-Tursdale boundary, in 1864, and Mr Barker's brickworks of 1873 near what is now the Kicking Cuddy Inn.

These industries were attracted by the rich clay deposits at the foot of Coxhoe's limestone escarpment. It was,

however, the collieries that had the biggest impact on Coxhoe's population growth.

Aerial view of Coxhoe village (NE)

The arrival of the railways brought large scale collieries and it was only then that the mining village of Coxhoe really came into being. In the 1820s, the Pease family, who were famous railway entrepreneurs from Darlington discussed bringing a railway to the Coxhoe and Quarrington mines but nothing happened. However, the railway engineer William Hedley, best known as the inventor of the Puffing Billy locomotive, opened Crowtrees colliery near Quarrington Hill in 1825. A colliery called Bell's Pit also opened in 1827 near what is now Park Hill housing estate. The mines were no doubt opened in response to the news of a forthcoming railway. The Bell's Pit owner was John Bell of Crowtrees, a farm near what is now Bowburn motorway services. The mine seems to have ceased operating before the railway arrived.

Coxhoe's first railway was the Clarence Railway and arrived in 1833 linking Coxhoe to Stockton and Port Clarence on the banks of the River Tees. The railway was named after the Duke of Clarence, who would later become King William IV. It was intended that the line

would be extended north to Sherburn with a separate branch from Ferryhill to Durham, but it never reached beyond Coxhoe.

Initially, coal was hauled along the line from Coxhoe to Teesside by horses but there was also a horse drawn passenger service operating on the line from 1835. Soon after, William Hedley introduced steam locomotives for coal while some locomotives conveyed passengers from 1838.

At Coxhoe, the line crossed the main street by a level crossing near the Blue Bell Inn at what soon became the north end of the growing colliery village. The inn served as a booking office and was renamed the Railway Tavern when a station was built nearby. The tavern was rebuilt in 1897 and although no longer a pub, the building still stands near the former station.

New collieries opened at Coxhoe as a result of the railway, including Coxhoe Colliery (1835), West Hetton Colliery (1837) and Clay Hole Colliery (1839). The last of these was otherwise known as Clarence Hetton.

In 1839, the Clarence Railway's coal monopoly at Coxhoe was challenged on two fronts. Firstly, an inclined railway was built uphill through Quarrington linking Coxhoe's collieries to wagonways at Cassop. These wagonways were ultimately linked to the rival Hartlepool Dock Railway.

West Hetton and Crowtrees Colliery found it financially beneficial to switch to this route as did two other new collieries, namely the first Bowburn Colliery (opened by Ralph Ward Jackson in 1840) and the Heugh Hall Colliery opened by Hedley in 1841. These two collieries were located on land just north east of the Kicking Cuddy pub.

The Clarence Railway's second challenge came in 1839 from a rival line called the Great North of England

Clarence and Hartlepool Junction Railway that opened just south of Coxhoe. It was linked to the coal port of Hartlepool via Trimdon and it intended to take trade away from the Clarence line.

At the south end of Coxhoe village, near the beck, the village's main street crossed the line by means of a new bridge and here in 1846 the line opened a new, rival railway station called Coxhoe Bridge Station.

Historic view of Coxhoe Bridge station

Coxhoe now had two railway stations on two separate lines and by 1841 they were serving a population of 3,904 people in Coxhoe village and no doubt many others from the surrounding area who needed to catch a train.

So by 1841, Coxhoe had two railways, two stations, several wagonways and at least six coal mines. By that year, there were 816 houses in the village. Most residents had arrived in the late 1830s, when the railways and collieries opened.

About 30 pubs now existed along the main street through the village serving the thirsty miners. They included Tyneside Inn, West Hetton Inn, the Old Red Lion, The Bunch of Grapes and The Oddfellows Arms.

Early public houses in Coxhoe did not include the Kicking Cuddy at the north end of the village. This was initially a private house, called Clarence Villa, that became the Clarence Villa Hotel in 1870. Kicking Cuddy was a nickname arising from donkey or 'cuddy' races. The races were run from a nearby colliery manager's house called West Hetton Lodge. The Clarence Hotel was at the finish line.

In the 1840s and 1850s, there was no parish church in Coxhoe as the village was divided between Kelloe and Bishop Middleham. However, the Methodists, who were always keen to challenge the miners' drinking culture, set up meeting houses in the village and had a strong following.

Wesleyan Methodists built a chapel in 1840 at Wesley Place in a building that was later a music hall and a butchers. Primitive Methodists occupied cottages in

Foundry Row by the 1830s. Both denominations were respectively relocated to new sites in 1865 and 1871.

St. Mary's, which is Coxhoe's Anglican parish church, was not built until 1867, and by this time there was already a Catholic chapel in the village. Coxhoe's Catholic community was previously served by a Sedgefield priest, and later by one at Trimdon, until the Catholic chapel was erected at Foundry Row in 1866. The present St. Joseph's Church superseded it in 1966.

Coxhoe's National School, later a Church of England school, opened in 1871, but closed in 1955. An institute opened in the village in 1910, but was replaced by a larger building in 1932. There were three cinemas in the village – opening in 1909, 1914 and 1932. One cinema later became the Gem Café. The other two were bingo halls by the 1960s.

The crossroads at Coxhoe (NE)

Basic Cottages at Coxhoe are a reminder of the limestone works (DS)

Most of the old streets and stone houses in Coxhoe's early mining village have been demolished over the years. They included several streets forming a hamlet called West Hetton Houses that served West Hetton Colliery. They were at the north end of the village behind what is now Commercial Road East. The oldest houses in Coxhoe today are in Blackgate and the old pottery area at the south end of the village.

Coxhoe's collieries were extensively worked and all had closed by 1881. The last to close was Coxhoe Colliery, a mine served in part by miners from a nearby terrace called Joint Stock Row. This street was completely demolished by the time of the 1890s map.

Redundant miners found work at neighbouring collieries like Tursdale, West Cornforth and Kelloe (East Hetton) and remained in the village, but the 1870s had seen particular hardship, with the closure of Coxhoe Coke Works and Coxhoe Iron Foundry, both established in the 1850s.

The iron foundry was initially owned by the brother of the Shildon railway engineer Timothy Hackworth, along with a partner called Fossick. It was owned by G. Blair

and Co., of Stockton, before it was closed in the 1870s. Foundry Row, a nearby street, has long since gone.

The establishment of Bowburn Colliery by Bell Brothers at Bowburn in 1908 provided new opportunities for Coxhoe miners, and this new colliery was much larger than the earlier Bowburn Colliery that was really located at Coxhoe.

Limestone quarrying has a long history at Coxhoe and the activity survived in Coxhoe after the collieries ceased to operate.

A major quarry opened in the Raisby-Garmondsway area about 1845, where lime was produced for roads and agriculture. Another major quarry existed on the hillside east of the main street before the 1850s. In 1906 this was bought by a company called Steetley, which built cupolas or furnaces for processing the lime. The cupolas were erected on the site of the earlier coke works and, along with a similar operation at Raisby, were known as the Basic Works. Basic refers to substances produced in a furnace and explains the name of Coxhoe's Basic Cottages, where workers once resided.

The former quarry at Coxhoe is now a refuse tip (NE)

The greater part of the Steetley Works shut down in 1966 and were completely demolished in 1981. A large part of the neighbouring quarry is now a refuse tip. Part of the Clarence Railway that brought about the birth and growth of Coxhoe in the 1830s had been used by Steetley as a mineral line but was completely removed in 1984.

It marked the final chapter in Coxhoe's industrial history. Nevertheless, Coxhoe still lives on as a very large and very proud village with new housing estates and lots of local shops clustered in and around a busy main street. It is a street that takes Coxhoe's history back to Roman times.

Bowburn and Park Hill

Compared to many of the other mining villages that lie in and around Durham City, Bowburn was a rather late arrival. Most mining settlements around the city were established in the early or mid-nineteenth century, but Bowburn only came into being during the first decade of the twentieth century.

A Bowburn Colliery opened about 1840, but it was a relatively small enterprise. Its owners were John Robson and Ralph Ward Jackson, who was the founder of the port and town of West Hartlepool. The colliery itself was located in what is now scrubland north of Coxhoe, just east of what is now the Park Hill housing estate.

Park Hill was named after a prominent farmhouse of the same name, most of which was demolished to make way for the A1(M) motorway interchange in the 1960s. The housing estate south of the house consists of homes built for miners before and after the war. It is now separated from Bowburn by the motorway and is often mistakenly thought to be a part of Coxhoe, but Durham County Council recently set the record straight by erecting road signs clearly showing that Park Hill is a distinct community.

The first Bowburn colliery was one of several nineteenth century pits near Coxhoe, and Coxhoe was one of several pit villages that had developed in the area. All the neighbouring pit villages like Quarrington Hill, New Cassop and Kelloe (East Hetton) were established long before Bowburn village came into being.

It was the Clarence Railway established in 1828 and named after the Duke of Clarence (later King William IV) that linked collieries in this area to ports at Stockton and Hartlepool and it was this railway that ran north to the first Bowburn colliery.

The Duke of Clarence connection is remembered in Bowburn's Clarence Street and in Park Hill's Clarence Villas. Clarence Villas stands close to Four Mile Bridge on the border of Park Hill and Coxhoe, where a beck runs beneath the road. Here stands the Kicking Cuddy pub, formerly a private house called Clarence Villa. It became the Clarence Villa Hotel around 1870.

Historic view of the Pit Laddie pub at Bowburn (MR)

By the 1850s, Coxhoe was a substantial mining settlement straddling the Durham to Stockton road but Bowburn was by comparison a tiny hamlet. In the late

nineteenth century, records show that there were only 11 stone cottages, a smithy and three pubs at Bowburn.

The smithy was on the eastern side of the main road opposite the Pit Laddie pub but today, the massive Bowburn motorway interchange occupies the whole site. Early Bowburn was located just north of here on the eastern side of the road. Here a small collection of farm buildings was situated on Crow Trees Lane just behind what is now The Cooperage pub.

Crow Trees Lane led to the village of Old Quarrington and a toll gate stood at the lane's junction with the main road. In Victorian times, the Cooperage was called the Wheatsheaf, and went by that name until renamed in 1993.

Just north, and on the same side of the road was a collection of houses forming the hamlet of Bowburn. In the nineteenth century, it consisted of no more than four or five houses, one of which is now the Post Office – probably Bowburn's oldest house.

Further north and slightly separated from the hamlet was the Hare and Hounds, which was the only pub noted on the 1860s map. In 1909, when Bowburn was undergoing transformation from hamlet to mining village, the pub was removed, rebuilt and renamed the Hare and Greyhound. It still bears this name today.

Before the twentieth century, Bowburn hamlet was hardly large enough to support a pub, so earlier patrons must have been local farmers or travellers passing through on the main road. The road in question now designated the A177 is arguably Bowburn's oldest feature. Its course is Roman in origin and is sometimes referred to as Cade's Road after a nineteenth century historian who first drew attention to its presence.

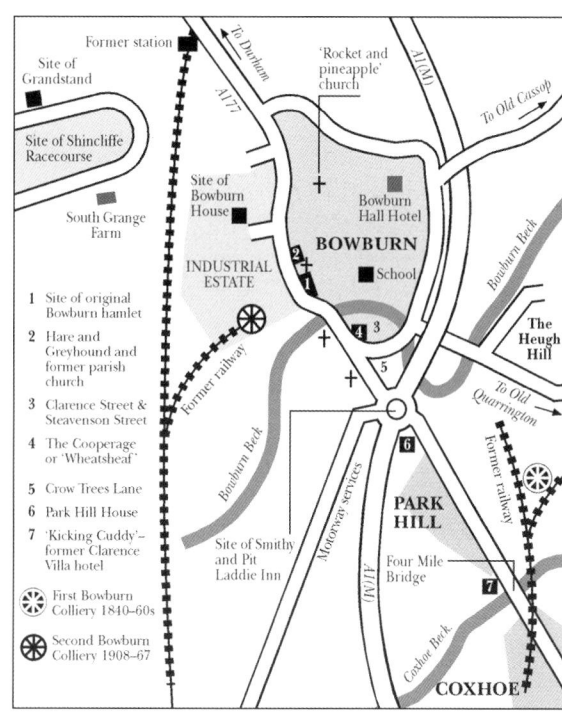

Map showing history of Bowburn (NE)

In the southern part of County Durham the Roman road crosses the Tees near Middleton St. George and continues north towards Sedgefield, before running through Coxhoe, Bowburn and Shincliffe. North of Shincliffe, its course is uncertain, but it reappears as Chester-le-Street's main street and continues on through Gateshead, eventually crossing the Tyne where the Swing Bridge stands today. Here it finally entered the Roman fort on Hadrian's Wall called Pons Aelius – better known to us today as Newcastle upon Tyne.

It has been suggested that there was a Roman settlement of some kind at Bowburn and that this might just explain the peculiar kink in the road here, but, unfortunately, there is no real evidence to support the theory. The kink may have simply avoided the meandering Bowburn Beck, a stream that gives Bowburn its name. Bowburn Beck was called Wedop Burn in medieval times, but it seems likely that it was also called Bow Burn at one time as it flows in an S-bend in two bow shaped meanders across the area. It passes under the old Roman road near the village library at Bowburn Bridge.

On the eastern (library side) of the road the beck runs through a culvert before emerging on the other side of the road alongside a former Methodist church. The name Bow Burn was not recorded before the nineteenth century, and while it is only a small watercourse, it is arguably the very heart of Bowburn village.

When Bowburn's first colliery of 1840 was abandoned in the 1860s, the old colliery site became a brick works. It was a local man called Tom Barker who invested his winnings from a handball championship to establish this enterprise. The championship was held in a handball court behind Coxhoe's Railway Hotel and around 7,000 people attended to see Barker defeat Dan Kelly of Tow Law who was the reigning world champion of the time. Barker's Bowburn Brick works operated into the early decades of the twentieth century and the old clay pits associated with his works can still be seen.

When the first Bowburn colliery closed, Bowburn village was little more than a hamlet and it was the second Bowburn Colliery that really brought about Bowburn's growth and development. The new colliery owners were Bell Brothers, an iron making firm of Middlesbrough who commenced mining near the Bowburn hamlet in 1908.

Bell Brothers were already owners of Tursdale Colliery, established a little further south, back in 1854. It was initially intended to call Bowburn Colliery New Tursdale

and it is possible that the new mining village may have also acquired this name. In the end both colliery and village took the name Bowburn.

From around 1900 Bell Brothers bought farms and farmland in the area for developing the colliery and the village. Amongst the farmhouses purchased was a property called Bowburn House. The colliery opened on land immediately to its south. Neither the house nor colliery can be seen today as the North and South Industrial Estates now respectively occupy their sites.

The old grandstand at Shincliffe (MR)

Bell Brothers played a big part in the development of the pit village, providing land and finance for the development of housing and a school. Early colliery streets in Bowburn included Clarence Street, Steavenson Street and housing developments along Durham Road. Steavenson Street is named from a Bell Brothers' colliery agent and engineer. A County School, now the junior school opened in 1909 in Wylam Street on land donated by Bell Brothers. The designer was H. T. Gradon, who built the Durham Miners' Hall at Redhills. In the previous year a Primitive Methodist Chapel built of iron was opened on Durham Road West and was followed in

the same road by the Wesleyan chapel near Bowburn Beck that was opened by Lady Bell in 1910.

By this time Bowburn was the home to approximately 1,200 people. For many Bowburn miners one particular attraction of the locality was the racecourse at neighbouring Shincliffe. This opened in 1895 and stood in fields near Shincliffe Bank Top railway station (until recently a restaurant) just north of Bowburn. Sadly the race meetings ceased in 1914 at the outbreak of the First World War and were never revived. The concrete grandstand was still standing until it was demolished in 1999.

On 20 March, 1912, during a minimum wages strike the race meeting at Shincliffe was called off because of cancelled trains. It was a great disappointment to many Durham miners but the Bowburn inhabitants hit upon the idea of racing pit ponies on a field behind the colliery. Money raised through this event went towards impoverished miners. Another industrial dispute arose in 1921 as a result of post war wage cuts and similar fund raising races were held in June of that year. Fortunately the strike was over by July.

By 1941 Bowburn residents had found a new form of entertainment in the form of the Crown Cinema on Durham Road which opened in that year. In its later days it served as a bingo hall and eventually closed in 1996. The building was demolished in 2002.

Bell Brothers concerns at Bowburn Colliery were taken over in 1923 by the Middlesbrough steel firm of Dorman Long who were later famed for building the Sydney Harbour Bridge. Following Nationalisation in 1947 the colliery was taken over by the National Coal Board. The NCB also acquired Bowburn Grange, a former colliery agent's house dating from the 1920s just to the east of Bowburn. The house was acquired by Ramside estates in the 1960s and is now better known as Bowburn Hall Hotel.

Bowburn Grange, is now a hotel (NE)

historian Nikolaus Pevsner. A free standing, cross-shaped spire stands alongside which the same critic called gimmicky. The local nickname 'Rocket and Pineapple' is perhaps a more accurate description of the church. It is probably more widely used than the official name of 'Christ the King' assigned to the church on its eventual completion in 1978. Unfortunately it was announced in 1994 that the building, which had suffered structural problems and roof leaks, was to be closed without replacement. It seemed that Bowburn residents would have to seek services elsewhere. However plans were approved for a new church in 2003 and at the time of writing the rocket and pineapple still await their fate.

The 'Rocket and Pineapple' church, Bowburn (NE)

East of the hall across the motorway out towards Quarrington lies the prominent magnesian limestone hill called the Heugh. This marks the very edge of the limestone region that dominates the eastern part of County Durham.

Quarrying continues in this area today but coal mining ceased with the closure of Bowburn colliery in July 1967. The suffering was partly eased by the opening of an industrial estate on the Bowburn colliery site. The proximity of Bowburn motorway interchange has also helped to attract development to the Bowburn area.

Finally, no visit to Bowburn would be complete without mentioning its peculiar parish church. The first Anglican church had been built in the village on the main street in 1926 but was too small for the village needs by the 1950s. In 1961 a new church was commenced on Bowburn council estate, where most of the village population now resided. The old church was converted into a bungalow in 1967.

The new church, designed by Harold Wharfe of Newcastle University has a glass-fibre, domed roof described as resembling 'a playground inflatable' by the architectural

Limestone escarpment at the Heugh near Bowburn (DS)

Chapter Five

Tursdale, Croxdale and Hett

The area between Bowburn in the east and the River Wear to the west is a relatively undeveloped district and there are no major colliery villages hereabouts. The largest settlements are Croxdale and Tursdale which are former pit villages but rather small ones. The main features of the area are a cap shaped hill on top of which stands the quaint little village of Hett, a wooded valley formed by the Croxdale and Tursdale Becks and the heavily wooded banks of the Wear where the river has changed its course from time to time.

Tursdale lies on the southern fringe of the area in question and is a former mining village. It is just to the south east of Bowburn and west of the A1(M) at Coxhoe. A colliery was established here by Bell Brothers of Middlesbrough in 1854 and a village was built nearby. Tursdale's colliery village never consisted of anything more than two or three terraces, a Methodist Chapel and a school. Two streets remain, but the colliery itself closed in 1960. The buildings of an extensive engineering works that supplied the coal industry from 1954 can still be seen but these were closed in 1999.

Several streams join together at Tursdale including the Coxhoe Beck and the Tursdale Beck, the second of which becomes Croxdale Beck before it joins the River Wear to the north. Close to Tursdale are old farms called Brandon Hill and Hoggers Gate and until the 1970s a farm called Standalone could be seen to the north east. A field belonging to this farm called Castle Field is thought to have marked the site of a medieval moated house or castle. It was the manor house for the ancient district of Quarringtonshire and may have belonged to the Baliol family. In truth little is known about the site.

On the eastern side of Tursdale towards the motorway can be seen several large ponds. These are not the moat of an ancient castle but were formed by the clay pits left over from a succession of brick works, the first of which was established by a Mr Goodyear back in 1864.

On the western side of Tursdale is a railway junction where the Leamside railway joins the east coast main line from London to Edinburgh. The Leamside line was built in 1844 and was once the main route north from London. It heads north around the eastern side of Durham City but the present main line departs from this course at Tursdale and heads around the western side of the city, which it has done since the 1870s.

A mile north of Tursdale the railway passes Hett Mill near the site of a much earlier village that was also known as Tursdale. This shrunken medieval village of Tursdale has virtually disappeared. The site is now occupied by an old farmhouse called Tursdale House that is located about 100 metres across the beck from Hett Mill. It stands at the southern end of a pathway from Shincliffe called Strawberry Lane.

Old Tursdale was originally Trollesden, a name first recorded in 1274, but dating back to Viking times. It was named from a Norseman called Thrall. The village name means Thrall's Dene, in other words the valley belonging to Thrall, but I suppose there is a feint possibility that it was once occupied by trolls! The main line railway runs close to Hett Mill at a level crossing and here the mill itself is located on the Tursdale Beck. The stream changes name hereabouts and becomes Croxdale Beck, eventually joining the River Wear just to the north at Croxdale.

The deep wooded valley or 'dene' of the Croxdale and Tursdale Beck is at the southern terminus of woodland that twists and turns its way as far north as Shincliffe. According to Whellan's 1894 Directory of Durham, part of the little valley alongside a wooded bank was associated with fairies and goblins.

Between Hett Mill and the village of Sunderland Bridge the wooded valley cuts off the land around Hett to the south, from the parkland of Croxdale Hall to the north. On the south side, the railway runs parallel to the dene and occasional glimpses of the beck in the little wooded valley can be seen from passing trains.

Hett Village and the Croxdale Beck

The village of Hett sits on the top of a hill about a mile south west of Hett Mill. Anglo-Saxons thought the hill resembled a hat and the village name simply means 'hat'. Despite some recent housing, Hett is still a charming rural oasis, slightly off the beaten track and gives an impression of how many Durham villages may have appeared many centuries ago.

Hett is best known for its duck pond, its large village green and as being the place where the fashion designer Bruce Oldfield lived as a boy. He was taught to sew here by his seamstress foster mother, Violet Masters.

The village pond at Hett (DS)

In the 1890s, Hett's population was over 350 and the village was described as 'pleasantly situated, possessing a green of some acres in extent, round which the houses form a square.' The village has changed very little since that time. The huge, if rather rugged looking village green, with its duck pond, looks rather like a farmer's grazing field so it is not surprising that a number of houses surrounding the green were originally farms. The oldest of these is Slashpool House near the south east corner of the green. A plaque shows the date 1708, but parts of the farm may be older. The roof is internally constructed from a 'cruck truss' wooden frame.

Like many villages, Hett began as an agricultural settlement but mining and quarrying were also of importance. To the west of the village, sand and stone quarrying took place in the nineteenth century but Hett was also very much a part of Durham's early coal mining history. Hett was never the site of a major colliery and cannot be called a colliery village in the modern sense of the word but mining was certainly carried out here in medieval times.

In the thirteenth and fourteenth century 'sea coal' was mined at Hett under the jurisdiction of the Priors of Durham Cathedral. In fact, Hett is one of a small number of places in County Durham that have documentary evidence for medieval mining. In 1407, it is known that the Prior of Durham made an agreement with Sir William Blakiston for the construction of a trench 'for carrying off water and winning of coal in the lands of Hette'.

Sir William Blakiston was related by marriage to the family called Hette (or Hett), who owned the manor in medieval times and took their name from the village. The site of the medieval mine at Hett is not known but shafts marked on old maps may be associated with the period. These were located immediately north of the village but could in fact be associated with later coal workings of the eighteenth century. Sadly, opencast mining destroyed the evidence in 1966.

Slashpool Farm at Hett village (DS)

Hett's village pub, the Hett Arms stands on the western side of the village green. It was one of two pubs located in the village in the nineteenth century. Nearby is the village hall, a striking and slightly incongruous feature. It opened in 1962 at a cost of £1,700 and is a salvaged Nissen hut, a barn-like building with a semicircular corrugated roof. Once a common sight during the war years, Nissen huts were named after their inventor Lieutenant Colonel Peter Norman Nissen. Hett village has no church of its own and in early times the locals had to attend services at Kirk Merrington church on a hill top about four miles to the south.

Former church at Hett village (DS)

In 1843 Hett village was transferred from Kirk Merrington parish to the parish of Croxdale where the church was much nearer. This added about 230 new people to Croxdale parish and in 1845 a new church was built for Croxdale in the village of Sunderland Bridge a mile to the north west. The new church was built by the Salvin family and dedicated to St. Bartholomew but in 1881, a chapel of ease dedicated to St. Michael was built on the north east corner of Hett's village green. It gave the Hett parishioners a degree of independence from Croxdale but it closed less than a hundred years later in 1978 and is now a private house.

Hett is a slightly isolated village and cannot be reached from Tursdale's old Colliery village, except on foot. In a car it can be reached via Hett Lane which is the back road from the village of Sunderland Bridge to the north. It can also be reached from the A167 or Great North Road at Low Butcher Race.

Low Butcher Race is situated to the north of the Thinford roundabout near Spennymoor and is home to the Coach and Horses Inn. The place is reputedly named because a party of foraging Scots were ambushed and butchered here shortly before the Battle of Neville's Cross in 1346.

The farmland surrounding Hett village is separated from the parkland of Croxdale Hall to the north by the wooded dene of the Croxdale and Tursdale Beck. There were at one time four mills along this little stretch of valley and three of the mills were involved in the making of paper. Hett Mill which we have already mentioned in connection with Tursdale stands at the eastern end of this stretch where the woodland reaches its terminus.

There are records of a Hett mill as early as 1451 but the present buildings are from a later period. The mill was worked by a family called Cooke around the 1820s and a Robert Cook (sic) is listed as miller here in the 1850s.

By the late nineteenth century one member of the family called James Cooke had become a rag merchant in Darlington. This was a related trade because paper was manufactured from the fibres of old rags. An Isaac Cooke was still resident at Hett Mill in 1881 but he worked as a railway signalman on the nearby railway line rather than as a paper worker.

Other residents at Hett Mill during this time seem to have been employed as railway plate layers including a member of the Ayre family. The Ayres worked as millers in the area during the nineteenth century. Hett Mill produced corn in early times and was probably converted to paper making in the 1700s. The mill site, now called Hett Mill Cottage is wedged between the level crossing on its south side and the Tursdale Beck on the north. A little to the west, but on the north side of the beck was Butterby Mill but its site lies within the grounds of Croxdale Hall. Despite its name this mill was a good mile south of Butterby.

Butterby mill was first recorded in 1795 when it was worked by William Lumley. On 29 December, 1816 the mill was destroyed by a freak wind that flattened the building. It was up and running again by the 1820s and operated by Joseph Teasdale before passing to the Martin family in the 1830s. In the 1850s the historian Fordyce mentions that the miller at Butterby was called James Cook but the mill itself was owned by Gerard Salvin.

Croxdale Mill (DS)

Butterby Mill was still operating as a paper mill at the time of the 1860s Ordnance Survey map but seems to have been converted for other work later in the century. By 1894 it was owned by worsted millers and yarn manufacturers called Matthew Dean and Sons and was managed by a Mr John Harding. The mill had fallen out of use by the mid-twentieth century and the buildings disappeared in the 1970s. Traces of the mill race and a sluice can still be seen.

At the western end of the little valley close to Croxdale Hall and the village of Sunderland Bridge were two mills that both seem to have been known as Croxdale Mill. One was Croxdale Corn Mill. Its mill house dating from the eighteenth century can still be seen between Croxdale

Hall and Sunderland Bridge. The mill was disused by the end of the nineteenth century.

A little south of here is the intriguingly named Crime Wood and the apex of a prominent meander called the Heugh formed by the beck. Here was Croxdale paper mill, first mentioned around 1678 when John Benson was the miller. From around 1738 until the early part of the nineteenth century the mill tenants were the Ayre family, but its owners were the Salvins of Croxdale Hall.

By the time of the 1860s Ordnance Survey map Croxdale paper mill was already a mass of rubble and has long since gone. In the late nineteenth century its remnants resembled the romantic ruins of an ancient chapel.

Old Croxdale

Croxdale lies on the southern boundary of the Durham City council area as boundaries stand in 2006 and forms an area that is particularly rich in history. It is however important to distinguish the old from the new where Croxdale is concerned.

Croxdale Hall (DS)

Most people are familiar with the striking stone terraces alongside the busy A167 just south of Durham and identify this place as Croxdale. In truth this is the former colliery settlement that sprung up in the second half of the nineteenth century and was until recent times known as Croxdale Colliery. The older and original Croxdale is a much smaller settlement being a hamlet of farm buildings clustered around Croxdale Hall half a mile to the north east.

The busy A167 makes the journey between old and new Croxdale rather precarious whether on foot or by car. Crossing the road can be dangerous and cars can easily miss the turn-off towards the village of Sunderland Bridge. The pretty village of Sunderland Bridge lies right in between the two Croxdales making Sunderland Bridge's history virtually inseparable from the other two places.

Old Croxdale, with Croxdale Hall at its centre, lies in beautiful wooded parkland east of the River Wear. It can be reached from the village of Sunderland Bridge by a footbridge that crosses over the beck. The village can also be reached by footpaths from Shincliffe, Butterby and Bowburn.

Woodland stretching from Shincliffe in the north to old Tursdale in the south has dominated this area since ancient times. The name of Croxdale has aroused much curiosity and place-name academics believe it is named after a man with the Viking name Krokr. His name could mean 'crooked back', but the name could refer to the crooked nature of the River Wear near here.

Croxdale could be a 'tail of land' as early spellings of Croxdale point to the explanation Croc's Tail rather than dale. The name could be due to Croxdale's location between two streams or because of its proximity to several tail-like loops of the River Wear. Some people may believe the age-old superstition that a cross or 'crux' was erected here in the deep and dark woods in ancient times to ward off evil spirits and demons.

The earliest recorded owner of Croxdale was Roger De Routhberi in 1291, whose family were presumably connected with the Northumbrian town of Rothbury. Roger was also owner of neighbouring Shincliffe, but his son renounced claims to that particular village and Shincliffe passed to the Priors of Durham.

By 1350, Croxdale belonged to Robert De Whalton, Treasurer of Brittany. It was his granddaughter, Agnes who married Gerard Salvin in 1409 and the Salvins would come to dominate the history of Croxdale right up to the present day.

The Salvins came to England at the time of the Norman Conquest and their patriarch was Joceus Le Flamengh, who received land in Sherwood Forest in Nottinghamshire. By virtue of his wooded habitation he took the name Silvan, a variation of Sylvan. Sylvan was an old French word that simply meant woodland. The Silvan surname was later corrupted to Salvin and it was Gerard Salvin and his heirs that inherited Croxdale upon the marriage to Agnes.

From that point the next ten owners of Croxdale were all rather confusingly called Gerard Salvin. The only break in this particular Salvin line came in the Civil War when Gerard, son of the ninth Gerard Salvin, supported the Royalists and was slain at Marston Moor.

The chapel at Croxdale Hall (DS)

Fortunately this Gerard's father, the ninth heir, was not engaged in active Royal service, so his estate was not confiscated. It passed directly to his grandson, who became the 10th Gerard Salvin to own Croxdale, though he should have been the 11th.

It is worth noting that part of the nearby Nickynack Beck, a stream that currently marks the southern boundary of the Durham City council area is known in part as Gerard's Gill. Which Gerard it actually refers to is anyone's guess.

The Salvins were principally known in Durham as staunch Roman Catholics, even after the Reformation when members of the Catholic faith were persecuted. For centuries they actively encouraged Roman Catholicism in the locality at places like Tudhoe and in the twentieth century they donated their mansion at Burn Hall alongside the A167 to a Roman Catholic mission.

However, the Salvins are more closely associated with another hall called Croxdale Hall that is situated in the old part of Croxdale. It is an especially beautiful part of Durham and the hall's parkland includes lakes, an avenue of trees and an eighteenth century orangery. It is only open to the public by appointment on limited occasions as detailed on the gate, but paths run through the grounds outside the hall and offer an opportunity to admire some beautiful surroundings and rather interesting buildings.

The hall itself dates mostly from the mid-1700s, but may include fabric from earlier times. It is thought to have been built on the site of a Tudor house. It incorporates a Roman Catholic chapel dedicated to St. Herbert that was built in Gothic style in 1807.

Outside the hall, enclosed by a wall stands a small, enigmatic medieval chapel with a Norman door. This was

Croxdale's original church and was designated by Hugh Pudsey, the twelfth century Bishop of Durham as a dependent chapel belonging to the parish of St. Oswald in Elvet.

This little church served the tiny Croxdale community, including Butterby and Sunderland Bridge until 1845. In that year, the Salvins built a new church for the locality. The new church was dedicated to St. Bartholomew and erected in the village of Sunderland Bridge. The Salvins retained the old Norman church for private burials.

The old barn near Croxdale Hall (DS)

Many centuries ago an ancient cross was found at the old church and can still be seen. Perhaps it was the very cross or 'crux' of Croxdale that is said to have warned off evil spirits in ancient times. Close to the hall and chapel stands Croxdale Home Farm which dates from the eighteenth century. The buildings include a huge and very remarkable hay barn that dates from the late eighteenth or early nineteenth century.

In the late nineteenth century the Salvins seem to have moved out of Croxdale Hall for a time but remained owners of the property when it was leased to John

Rogerson JP, a coal and iron merchant who was a Director of the Weardale Iron Company. This company owned several collieries in County Durham including Croxdale. The company's founder was Rogerson's uncle, Charles Attwood, who established the Tudhoe Iron Works in the 1850s. This enterprise brought about the birth and rapid growth of the town of Spennymoor. Properties in the neighbouring settlement of Tudhoe Grange were developed by the Salvin family to serve the iron works and collieries of the area.

Rogerson was clearly a man of great wealth and in the 1881 census he was the head of a substantial household at Croxdale Hall. The Rogersons were later owners of the grand house called Mount Oswald near Durham City.

Croxdale Hall continued to be the property of the Salvins throughout the twentieth century but around the time of the Second World War the hall served as a military hospital and maternity home. Many people throughout County Durham and beyond can proudly give their birthplace as Croxdale Hall even though they may have no family connection with the property.

Butterby

A woodland path leads a mile north from Croxdale Hall through the unspoilt scenery of the Salvin estate before we reach Low Butterby on the south bank of the River Wear. This farm is actually on the same side of the river as Shincliffe, but the river twists and turns here and if the crow were to fly the one and a half miles between the two places it would have to cross the river twice.

Low Butterby Farm sits in a river meadow rather defensively tucked away inside a meander with further protection offered by dense woodland and the marshy wetland around an oxbow lake. The swamp was formed by the old course of a long redundant loop of the River

Wear that was abandoned by nature many centuries ago. As if all these natural defences were not enough, Low Butterby Farm also has the remnants of a deep man made moat. The chain mail of a long forgotten knight was recovered from this moat during the nineteenth century.

The first inhabitants of Butterby were clearly security conscious and at a guess you might expect them to have been Vikings of the Danish variety. The reasoning is simple. Place names ending in the letters 'by' are usually Danish in origin. This would make Butterby, Croxdale and Tursdale some of the most northerly Viking place names in County Durham. However, we may be mistaken as the first settlers at Butterby were seemingly a Norman family called D'Audre and they gave the site the French name 'Beautrove' meaning 'beautiful find'. It seems that the locals corrupted the name to 'Butterby'.

In around 1240 the D' Audres were succeeded by the Lumleys and then by Christopher Chaytor in 1556. Butterby then passed to the Doubledays and subsequently to the Wards of Sedgefield. The salt springs and any possible salt mines that might be excavated on the site were retained by the Doubledays.

In the early 1600s the riverside at Butterby was noted for mineral and salt springs that were first mentioned in 1607 by Camden. Reddish salt water and a sulphurous spring attracted much interest at this time.

Today Low Butterby belongs to the Gerard Salvin, but sadly only the moat and walls of the old manor house remain. The present building dates from the seventeenth or eighteenth century.

Just across the river north of Butterby is High Houghall Farm which lies at the southern end of the extensive area of land known as Houghall. In order to reach Houghall from Butterby you would have to head for the nearest bridges which are at Shincliffe in the north or Croxdale to the

south. In times gone by the river seems to have been crossed by a ford here that lead north onto Butterby Lane, but a ferry is also known to have operated here. Butterby Lane, now called Hollinside Lane was an old route into Durham City and is now best known as the site of Hollingside House and Durham University's Grey College.

High Houghall Farm should not be confused with High Butterby Farm which lies to the east of Low Butterby on the path leading towards High Shincliffe. Although this lies on the same side of the river as Low Butterby, High Butterby is separated from its more historic namesake by a loop of the river and by the thick woodland of Croxdale and Butterby Woods. During the time of the 1881 census High Butterby was farmed by Roger Naisbit and Low Butterby by Charles Wearmouth.

In between the two farms is Croxdale Wood House, a mid-eighteenth century building with an 1860s wing. By the end of the nineteenth century this house was occupied by the Salvins when Croxdale Hall became the home of the Rogersons. In the 1881 census it was home to Henry Thomas Thornton Salvin and his family, as well as a coachman and a gardener.

Low Butterby and High Butterby never grew into anything more than farms and there was certainly never a church here. There was at one time a well known local saying to 'go to Butterby Church'. To go to Butterby church meant to skip church altogether.

Sunderland Bridge and Croxdale Colliery

The pretty little village of Sunderland Bridge lies wedged between the A167 and Croxdale Hall. Like its more famous Wearside namesake the village is named from being 'sundered' or 'separated' land. It was an isolated or sundered portion of the parish of St. Oswald in Elvet

from which it was separated by the River Wear. The word 'Bridge' was added to the name to distinguish it from the other Sunderland.

The village of Sunderland Bridge (DS)

In historic times Sunderland Bridge was also called 'Sunderland juxta Croxdale' or 'Sunderland-by-the Bridge' and the bridge in question crosses the River Wear. It is still there and incorporates some thirteenth century stonework.

The bridge once carried the Great North Road (now the A167) over the River Wear but was superseded by a new road bridge in the mid-twentieth century.

Sunderland Bridge village is a collection of cottages in two rows at right angles to the A167. Near the A167 at the western end of the village is the Victorian church of St. Bartholomew built by the Salvin family in 1845 as the successor to the earlier chapel at Croxdale Hall.

Croxdale Hall itself is reached from the extreme eastern end of Sunderland Bridge village by a footpath over a bridge. Here at the east end the main street through the village takes a sharp bend as it heads south towards Hett. On the corner of this road is a house called The Hermitage that dates partly to the 1600s. It has an unusual embattled summerhouse in the garden and is one of the last houses in Sunderland Bridge.

Sunderland Bridge belonged to William De Kilkenny in 1321 but by the 1400s belonged to the Neville family. The Salvins of Croxdale Hall were mentioned amongst Sunderland Bridge landowners in the 1600s and it was the Sunderland Bridge branch of the family that were ancestors of the famous London architect Anthony Salvin (1799-1881). Salvin was married to the daughter of a Rector of Brancepeth and his work can be seen across the length and breadth of Britain. He was responsible for the restoration of castles at Alnwick, Brancepeth, Windsor and Durham.

Historic view of bridges at Sunderland Bridge (NE)

Until the 1870s when the railway line was constructed through the area there was no coal mining at Sunderland Bridge or Croxdale. A mine called Croxdale Colliery had opened back in 1845, but was closed by 1870. The little colliery was located near Low Burn Hall Farm, beyond the River Wear, about a mile north of Sunderland Bridge and was served by a wagonway from Houghall and Shincliffe.

The wagonway passed through a tunnel beneath Hollinside Wood and joined the railway line from Sunderland at Shincliffe. A stationary engine was located on the fields that now lie between Low Burn Hall Farm and the site of the Cock o' the North pub. It hauled coal wagons along an incline formed by the wagonway.

In the 1870s part of the main line from London to Edinburgh via Tursdale was completed near Sunderland Bridge. Here it still passes underneath the A167 near the village and then over a viaduct that crosses the River Wear. Railway houses including a station house were built alongside the A167 and can still be seen.

Railways provided a means of coal transportation, so in 1875 the Weardale Iron and Coal Company, who already owned the colliery at Tudhoe, opened a colliery at Sunderland Bridge. Like its more northerly predecessor at Low Burn Hall, this colliery was called Croxdale Colliery but was a much larger concern. Also known as Sunderland Bridge Colliery or Thornton Pit, it was situated south of Sunderland Bridge on the western side of the Tudhoe road.

Railway sidings linked the colliery with the main line and a station was opened nearby. Croxdale colliery village, now simply called Croxdale, developed in the previously empty fields alongside the main road next to the colliery. Houses were built in long stone terraces called Rogerson Terrace, Wood View and Salvin Street and the population of the district quickly grew. The church of St. Bartholomew at Sunderland Bridge was extended to accommodate the expanding population, but two Methodist churches and a school were also built in Croxdale Colliery village.

St. Batholemew's church Sunderland Bridge (DS)

The Primitive Methodist Chapel opened in 1877 and the Wesleyan Methodists in 1897. Both buildings can still be seen as can the old school of 1878 that now serves as Croxdale Community Centre.

Like many collieries around Durham, Croxdale Colliery specialised in coking coal and employed around 470 people at its peak. It could output up to 600 tons of coal per day in the late nineteenth century and continued to operate until closure in 1934. Older residents may remember the colliery chimney incorporating some white bricks that were shaped to show the year of its foundation in 1875.

The old pit houses in the village have had to undergo some refurbishment in recent decades to bring them up to acceptable modern standards but they now form an attractive collection of houses some of which have excellent views across the countryside towards the estate of Burn Hall.

Burn Hall

Burn Hall is a magnificent nineteenth century mansion in a wooded setting on the western side of the A167 three quarters of a mile north of Sunderland Bridge. It can be seen from the car, fleetingly glimpsed in the distance when heading north through Croxdale.

A better view of the hall and its estate can be obtained from passing trains on the London to Edinburgh line. This is a very impressive house in a beautiful valley setting, almost encircled by the River Browney, that flows into the River Wear near this point.

Nineteenth century illustration of Burn Hall

The River Browney passes underneath Browney Bridge on the A167 close to here, just north of Croxdale's former Bridge Hotel. This hotel reopened as the Honest Lawyer in 2004.

After passing under the road the little river Browney joins the River Wear about a quarter of a mile to the east. We will explore the valley of the Browney in later chapters of this book.

The present mansion at Burn Hall was started in 1821, but there was an earlier manor house of some kind called Great Burn. The earliest known owners of Great Burn

were the Brackenbury family who were mentioned in 1307. They leased the land from the powerful Nevilles but in the 1380s Great Burn passed through marriage to Sir John Claxton.

In 1569, a successor called Robert Claxton supported the Nevilles in a rising against Elizabeth I and was fortunate not to lose the property not to mention his life.

In the 1600s, the manor was sold to the Lawsons of Usworth and exchanged hands on a number of occasions during this period. Some owners may have been frustrated by the special tax at Burn Hall that was used for the upkeep of the neighbouring highway – the Great North Road – which divided the estate in two. There was also a constant threat of horse and carriage theft on estates situated close to major roads like this.

Sometime around 1800 Burn Hall was sold to Brian John Salvin of Croxdale, who employed the great Durham architect Ignatius Bonomi to design a great mansion house. The house was completed to Bonomi's designs between 1821 and 1834 with work undertaken by a builder called Moody of Ushaw.

So impressive was the finished result that Queen Victoria is said to have described it as 'the finest looking estate between the Humber and the Tweed'.

The hall remained in the hands of the Salvin family until 1926 when it was sold to a Roman Catholic mission for the training of young boys destined to become missionary priests in foreign lands.

However, by 1995 the cost of maintaining such a huge building, with its 69 acre estate had grown too high and the mission sold the Grade II listed hall to a developer for a tasteful conversion into apartments.

Access into the grounds of the hall is now only to residents through a gateway. It is a sought after spot because not only is it very beautiful and conveniently located for the main road heading to Newcastle or the south, but it also lies a stone's throw from the City of Durham.

The Cock o' the North roundabout at Farewell Hall Farm on the outskirts of the city lies just to the north of the hall. Farewell Hall was yet another Salvin property but here we have strayed into the realms of the accompanying book that features Durham City.

Trainee missionaries at Burn Hall in the 1960s (NES)

Chapter Six

Langley Moor, Brandon and Brancepeth

The River Wear and its tributary the River Browney separate the Croxdale area in the east from the Brandon and Brancepeth area to the west but it was the Browney which loops its way around Burn Hall on the eastern side that formed the historic boundary between these two areas. This little river flows along the eastern edge of Durham City Golf Club before skirting the industrial estates of Littleburn and Meadowfield near Langley Moor.

A house called Littleburn Farm lies hidden amongst the bunkers and greens of the golf course and has an unexpected connection with Burn Hall on the opposite bank of the river. The farm dates in part from the early 1600s and includes the remains of a moat.

Littleburn was the seat of the Calverley family in distant times and was later the seat of the Doubledays and Reeds. In the nineteenth century it was home to the Cunninghams and then held later by the Russells.

During the medieval period the settlement of Littleburn, which is now nothing but a farm, was called Burn Parva, meaning Little Burn to distinguish it from Burn Magna or the manor of Great Burn across the river to the south.

Great Burn was the early name for Burn Hall, probably because its lands covered a greater extent than those of Littleburn. Another possibility is that Great Burn refers to the Browney and Little Burn to the Deerness which joins the Browney just north of Littleburn at Langley Moor. The two places belonged to different parishes since the River Browney divided the parish of Brancepeth in the west from that of St. Oswald in Elvet to the east.

Historic view of Browney Colliery village (JK)

The main London to Edinburgh railway now runs through the industrial estates at Littleburn but in the nineteenth century this railway gave rise to the development of two collieries hereabouts. One was Browney Colliery of 1871 that was opened in sidings just off the main line by Bell Brothers of Middlesbrough. This company was involved in iron and steel production and converted coal to coke at the colliery before transporting it by rail to Teesside for use in the iron and steel works there. Bell Brothers' concerns, including Browney Colliery, were eventually taken over in 1924 by another Middlesbrough steel company called Dorman Long. This company was later famed for building the Tyne Bridge and the Sydney Harbour Bridge in Australia. Browney Colliery closed in July 1938 after serious flooding in the pit.

Most of the early colliery houses in Browney colliery village have now been demolished, along with a Primitive Methodist chapel, a Wesleyan Methodist Chapel and a mission church that stood nearby. The Wesleyan Chapel here was purpose built in 1887 but the Primitives worshipped in a nearby shed that was originally used for colliery stores. Both of the chapels and the mission church stood in fields on the north side of the village overlooked by Office Street. My grandmother grew up in this street and her father was the colliery electrician.

Apart from Office Street, the only other streets in the village were Middle Street and Front Street on the road between Croxdale and Meadowfield. Browney British School, now called Browney Primary School still stands in 2006. It was built by Bell Brothers in 1881. The village stood south of the school with the colliery located further south towards the main line. The colliery streets were demolished after the war and Browney village was rebuilt on the north west side of the school where it has more or less become part of Meadowfield.

To the north east of Browney village, alongside the main railway line stood Littleburn Colliery. This was opened in the late nineteenth century by the North Brancepeth Coal Company and operated until closure in December 1950. It was situated north of Littleburn Farm, in the area now occupied by Meadowfield Industrial Estate.

Littleburn pit village consisted of Railway Street, Princes Street, Office Street and a pub called the Colliery Inn. All have since been demolished and the colliery village site is now occupied by new streets that are tucked away on the south side of Langley Moor.

Langley Moor and Meadowfield

Langley Moor and Meadowfield were a focal point for neighbouring colliery villages on either side of the main road including Brandon and have now practically merged together along the A690. In the 1890s Langley Moor was described as 'a long straggling village where most of the shops are' Meadowfield was a much smaller village consisting of terraces called John Street and Frederick Street alongside the main road. Although many of the houses in the two villages were occupied by miners neither had a colliery to call their own.

Aerial view of Meadowfield (NE)

Both places had grown as a result of the surrounding collieries and at the time of the 1860s map Meadowfield consisted of nothing more than a farm called Low Barns on the north side and another farm called Humble Sledge on the corner of the road to Croxdale.

Meadowfield became the home to some of Durham City's council offices but was previously the headquarters for the intriguingly named Brandon and Byshottles Council that was created in 1877 from part of the parish of Brancepeth. Brandon and Byshottles became an Urban District in 1894 and included Brandon, Browney village, Meadowfield and Langley Moor as well as Deerness Valley mining villages like New Brancepeth, Ushaw Moor, Esh Winning and Waterhouses. The

Urban District Council was abolished in 1974 and was incorporated into Durham City.

Langley Moor, to the north of Meadowfield could be described as the village at the junctions. Not only does it lie near the junction of the two little rivers called the Browney and Deerness that dominate the scenery and history to the west of Durham city, but it also lies close to what was once a major railway junction at Relly. It was the railways that shaped the colliery history of Langley Moor and neighbouring settlements like Browney, Littleburn and Broompark.

In the first half of the nineteenth century most of the area around Langley Moor consisted of open fields and although there was small-scale mining in the area, most people were employed on farms. On the main road where Langley Moor stands today there was nothing more than a solitary farmhouse simply called Langley Moor.

There was however a small hamlet of farmhouses just to the north. This was the old farming hamlet of Langley and can still be seen today near Langley Moor. To reach it we have to pass through the remnants of yet another colliery village.

Today the main road through Langley Moor is the A690 and this forms Langley Moor High Street. To reach the hamlet of Old Langley we have to turn off from the High Street at the Lord Boyne pub to join the road to New Brancepeth and Alum Waters.

At this point we enter the Front Street of what was once a quite separate village called 'Boyne' or North Brancepeth. Boyne Front Street should not be confused with Langley Moor High Street (the A690) which it joins at right angles. The colliery village of Boyne or North Brancepeth was named from Viscount Boyne who owned the

Brancepeth Castle estate upon which Boyne, Brandon, Meadowfield and Langley Moor were all built.

Historic photograph of the Lord Boyne pub at Langley Moor near the site of Boyne Village (JK)

If we continue along Boyne's Front Street out into the open countryside we cross the Brandon-Bishop Auckland long distance footpath. This footpath follows the course of what was once the North Eastern Railway's Bishop Auckland to Durham line. It was this railway that brought about the opening of Boyne and Brandon Colliery as well as providing a local passenger service.

Boyne (or North Brancepeth) Colliery came into being in the late nineteenth century and is shown on Ordnance survey maps of the time. Unfortunately the dates for its opening and closure are not certain. We only know that it was short-lived, and that it lay alongside the Bishop Auckland to Durham line near the farming hamlet of Old Langley. We also know that it was owned by the North Brancepeth Colliery Company and is marked on an 1897 map as disused.

Old Langley, which stands just to the north of the colliery site consists of stone built farm houses like Field Hall, Langley Old Hall and Langley Hall Farm. There are pleasant walks here that take us north across the River

Deerness to Relly Farm and to a picnic area near Broompark on the outskirts of Ushaw Moor.

Relly is known to have belonged to Richard, a clerk of Barnard Castle in the fourteenth century but from the mid nineteenth century it was an important railway junction where the Bishop Auckland-Durham Railway was joined by the Dearness (sic) Railway and the Lanchester branch of the North Eastern Railway.

Historic photograph of Relly Mill junction

The Dearness Railway opened in the 1850s and crossed the Deerness by a wooden viaduct at Relly. It then followed the course of the Deerness river valley through Ushaw Moor, New Brancepeth, Esh Winning and Waterhouses. In fact the railway gave rise to all of these colliery villages. Today the line has gone and it is now the Deerness Valley walk.

The Lanchester branch of the North Eastern Railway also joined the main line at Relly and opened in 1862. It followed the course of the River Browney valley northwards. This railway gave rise to the mining villages of Broompark, Bearpark and Langley Park but departs from the Browney valley at Lanchester. The railway's ultimate destination was the iron works at Consett. The

railway has now gone and the whole Lanchester branch railway now forms another long distance footpath called the Lanchester Valley Walk.

It was in the 1870s that Relly junction was joined by the main line north from London and this is now the only surviving railway at Langley Moor. This line crosses over Langley Moor's High Street near the Lord Boyne pub very close to the junction of the two little rivers that lie to its east.

Here the River Deerness joins its larger brother the River Browney in Langley Moor's Holliday Park. The park is named from a former manager of the North Brancepeth Colliery Company and was in earlier times the site of a paper mill. Martin Holliday, a colliery manager resided in a house here called Langley Grove. In historic times the land formed by the junction of the two rivers was called Brunespittle and was part of the district called Relly.

The River Deerness has an ancient Celtic name meaning 'roaring river' and is one of the oldest, if not the oldest, name on the map of County Durham. Browney is a much later name of Anglo-Saxon origin and means 'brown river'. In times gone by it was called the 'Brune' or 'Brun Ea'.

The Browney valley around Stonebridge and Langley Moor was noted for its paper mills, but most of the workers lived in Crossgate Moor or Neville's Cross. There was however a street called Paper Row between Langley Moor and Stonebridge that housed some of the workers for a time. The history of these paper mills is featured in the accompanying book on Durham City.

Paper was made using old rags that were brought into Brandon railway station throughout the nineteenth century but the four paper mills along the Browney at Stonebridge, Langley Moor, Relly and Moorsley Banks near Bearpark were established in the late 1700s.

Old mill house at site of Relly paper mill (DS)

The remnants of Relly paper mill can still be seen alongside the Browney and it was still operating during the first decade of the twentieth century. Langley paper mill has gone as has Langley Grove the former home of Martin Holliday. His house had previously belonged to a paper manufacturer. Langley paper mill dated back to 1777 but ceased trading in the late 1870s in favour of Relly. It should not be confused with Langley corn mill which was a little further to the south near Littleburn. The paper mill at Stonebridge had also become a corn mill by 1834.

Although paper making had been important around Langley Moor the village really grew as a result of the burgeoning mining settlements in the area during the late nineteenth century and because of the important location on the main road from Durham to Willington.

Chapels were built alongside the road in the village by the Primitive Methodists in 1874, by the Wesleyans in 1876 and by the New Connexion Methodists. The last of these was built by Mrs Love, wife of a local coal owner and was converted from a short-lived music hall, but along with the other chapels it has now gone. A small Baptist church donated by Mr George Angus of Newcastle also stood at the north end of the village.

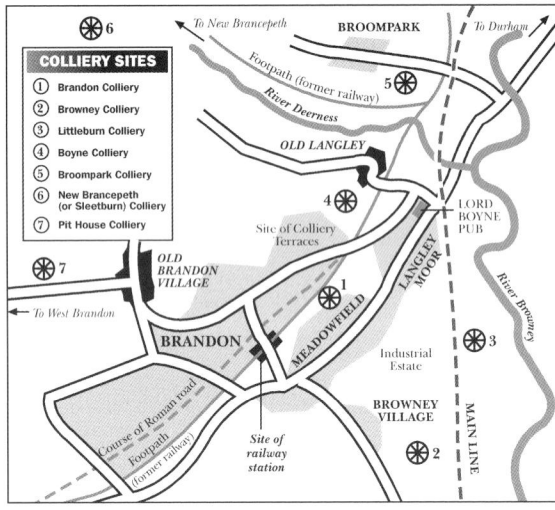

Map showing history of Brandon area (NE)

The Anglican parish church of St. John (1875) on the northern edge of Meadowfield and the Roman Catholic church of St. Patrick (1878) on the southern edge of Langley Moor were built in what was once open land between the two villages. Langley Moor also had a Catholic school built of corrugated iron. The Anglican and Catholic church are still in use today.

Langley Moor School was originally called North Brancepeth School and is still situated at Boyne village. It was opened by the North Brancepeth Colliery Manager Martin Holliday in 1883.

Pubs established in Langley Moor in the nineteenth century included the Shafto Arms and Littleburn Hotel as well as the Lord Boyne. In the early twentieth century the village became the home of a cinema with the opening of the Langley Moor Empire in 1915. It closed in 1961 in the same year as the Central Palace picture house or Kinema of 1913 closed at Meadowfield. This cinema occupied an upper storey of a large Co-operative store dating from 1882

Brandon

Brandon lies south west of Durham City and is one of the largest former mining settlements in the area. Surprisingly the village has a history that predates the intensive mining activity of the nineteenth century as in the far north west corner of Brandon we can still find the old farming village known locally as old Brandon or Brandon village.

The old village was the largest of four farming settlements in the area that were all called Brandon, but the others were little more than farmhouses called West Brandon, East Brandon and South Brandon. These farms stood in what is still mostly open moorland to the west of Brandon and were spread out towards Esh Winning.

Historic view of old Brandon village (JK)

East Brandon farm has now gone, but West Brandon Farm is still there. It achieved fame under the new name of Brancepeth Manor, as the home of the Grand National winning horse, Red Marauder in 2001.

Archaeological dig at East Brandon in 1904 (JK)

Ancient man knew the Brandons well. Two Iron Age settlements were excavated at West Brandon in the early 1960s showing evidence of circular huts, ditches and fenced enclosures. A smelting furnace with recesses for bellows was also found. Used in the extraction of ore, it was an extremely rare find and aroused great interest. Consisting of a bowl cut into the rock, it was worked by skilled operators who were experts in keeping the furnace at the correct temperature for several days at a time.

Evidence of pre-historic enclosures have also been found near old Brandon village and in 1904 a crouched Bronze Age skeleton was found not far away in a coffin beneath an imposing mound at East Brandon Wood. Unfortunately, open cast mining destroyed this site in 1979.

A local farmer tells me that the East Brandon area is reputedly haunted by the strange figure of a woman on horseback. The farmer has never seen her but recalls that a neighbouring farmer once did see something strange and frightening run in front of his car on the road between South and West Brandon. Perhaps it was an apparition from ancient times.

The Romans were no strangers to the Brandon area. They built not one, but two roads in the district. One was Dere Street, the great Roman road between York and the Scottish Borders. It can be traced through the fields at West Brandon. The other road, a north eastern offshoot of Dere Street near Willington, has no name, but goes through neighbouring Brancepeth village and is apparently destined for Durham. Unfortunately its course then disappears amongst the houses on the southern edge of Brandon. In Brandon it runs parallel and slightly to the north of the former railway that is now the Brandon-Bishop Auckland walk. The course of the actual Roman road between Brandon and Durham City is a mystery.

It was the Anglo-Saxons who succeeded the Romans in the area and gave Brandon its name. Early spellings suggest it meant 'Broom-Don' – 'the hill where prickly bushes grew'. The hill in question is Brandon Hill which forms a substantial moorland area with magnificent views to the west of Brandon village.

Popular belief favours another theory realting to Brandon's name and it is said that a wild boar or 'brawn' roamed the path between here and Brancepeth. Brandon was reputedly the brawn's lair and this legend has given rise to the name of an old farm called Brawn's Den near South Brandon. Brawn's Den is also the name of a Brandon pub but it was only named in 1982 as the result of a competition.

For centuries Brandon was part of the vast country estate of Brancepeth Castle and belonged in medieval times to the powerful Neville family. In 1569, the Nevilles rebelled against Queen Elizabeth I in the Rising of the North and their lands including Brandon were confiscated by the crown and broken up.

In 1630 Brandon was sold to a London silk merchant called Edward Copley but his family sold it to the Earl of Shaftesbury in 1711. It was a succeeding Earl of Shaftesbury who sold Brandon to William Russell, one of the most powerful coal owners of the time.

Russell had purchased Brancepeth Castle in 1796 and set about restoring lands to the Brancepeth estate. William's granddaughter, Emma, who inherited the estate married the seventh Viscount Boyne and their family owned Brandon right up into the early part of the twentieth century. The Boynes would see the Brandon area change from being a largely agricultural community of only a few hundred or so people into a populous mining community of thousands that was dominated by six large collieries all within a one-mile radius of old Brandon village.

Brandon Colliery (JK)

Some coal mining had been carried out near the old farming village of Brandon in the 1830s when records describe a man raising coal from a mine using a whim-gin operated by a bull. However the area was largely agricultural and there was no major colliery.

Things changed in the 1850s with the arrival of Brandon's first railway and an increasing nationwide demand for coal provided stimulus for growth. Brandon Colliery was opened in 1856 by the coal owning company called Strakers and Love just as the Durham to Bishop Auckland Railway was being completed nearby. It was no coincidence. Railways were essential for transporting coal.

The railway skirted the fields half a mile south of old Brandon village and continued east where the colliery was built close to where Meadowfield Sports Centre now stands. Strakers and Love had leased a third of Viscount Boyne's huge Brancepeth Castle estate for the purpose of mining and the land included Brandon.

Mines need manpower and the company built the new colliery village to house the workers. It was located north east of the colliery and called Brandon Colliery village. It was three-quarters of a mile across the fields to the east of old Brandon village.

It was a substantial colliery village and consisted of rows of terraces like Cobden Terrace, Russell Street, North Street, West Street, Durham Street, Sunderland Street, High Street and several more. All have now gone and modern streets like Hemmel Court and the Riggs now stand in their place.

A second railway came to the area in the 1870s and brought further industrial growth. This railway was the main line from London and the nearby collieries of Littleburn and Browney opened up in the adjoining sidings.

There were 260 houses at Brandon Colliery by 1871 and the sudden growth must have been quite a shock to the people of old Brandon village where there were only twenty-five houses. The old Brandon villagers must have wondered where all the new people came from.

In fact by the end of the nineteenth century many men had migrated to the area from other parts of County Durham, but were joined by substantial numbers from Yorkshire, Northumberland, the Lake District, Lancashire, Derbyshire and Ireland. Many were agricultural labourers from farming areas attracted by the better wages of industry. The population influx and geographical origin of the workers was typical of that of many burgeoning nineteenth century pit villages in County Durham.

Shops, schools, and churches opened up to serve the growing communities and there was no shortage of pubs. By the 1890s Brandon colliery miners could visit any one of at least seven pubs in the Langley Moor and Meadowfield areas or could take a short walk west across the fields to old Brandon village where there were three.

The less adventurous could stay in Brandon Colliery itself and visit the Brandon Inn near the colliery's 'A' Pit. Alternatively they could head east to Brandon Colliery's other pub, the Red Lion, an isolated establishment in the fields near the fiery colliery waste heaps. Known locally as 'the Bleazer' this particular pub was demolished in the 1960s.

Old Brandon village had no church to call its own and the parishioners in the old farming village had always attended the ancient parish church of St. Brandon in the neighbouring village of Brancepeth. Despite its appropriate name, St. Brandon's Church was too small for Brandon's expanding population and a new church dedicated to St. John was built on land donated by Viscount Boyne at Meadowfield. It became Brandon's parish church in 1877. A vicarage was built for the church on Sawmills Lane.

Sawmills Lane is the road linking old Brandon village to Meadowfield but the vicarage is now a private residence. Sawmills Lane was named after a sawmill that stood on the north side of the railway (now the footpath) to the north of the road. The mill appears on the 1890s Ordnance Survey map along with some nearby houses called Sawmill Cottages. The mill must have been relatively new at that time, as it did not exist at the time of the 1860s map a few decades earlier.

As Brandon grew St. John's Church at Meadowfield proved insufficient for the village needs so in 1893 a new church dedicated to St. Agatha was opened on the northern fringe of the colliery village. Now demolished, St. Agatha's is only remembered in the name of a modern street called St. Agatha's Close.

Of course not all of the late nineteenth century population in Brandon was Church of England. Several Non-conformist chapels were built, whilst Roman Catholics, many of Irish origin, attended St. Patrick's Roman Catholic Church in Langley Moor.

Chapels in Brandon Colliery village included a Victorian Wesleyan chapel of uncertain date in the now demolished High Street. This chapel stood approximately midway along what is now St. Agatha's Close. A second Wesleyan Chapel was built in 1905 close to the railway station in Station Avenue.

A Primitive Methodist Chapel of 1871 called Mount Calgary was located on the south side of Commercial Street in the colliery village and was demolished quite recently. It once included a Sunday School. Finally, the New Connexion chapel of 1863 stood close to a small square and was originally built as a school. The square and the chapel are now gone. The square, was little more than a road junction with a reservoir at its centre and stood approximately where the present road junction between Commercial Street, Brandon Lane and St. Agatha's Close stand today.

All of the Methodist chapels in Brandon were superseded by the present chapel dedicated to St. Andrew in Carr Avenue. This only opened in 1983 and stands close to the library and post office. Just along Carr Avenue to the south is the handsome Brandon Primary and Infant School. There were two schools at Brandon by the 1890s. These were the National School, in old Brandon Village with 40 pupils and the British School, just north of the colliery village. The British School which housed around 150 pupils was built by Strakers and Love near St. Agatha's Church in 1874. Both the school and church have now gone but the old school wall can still be seen running along the northern edge of the estate near St. Agatha's Close.

From 1878 Brandon's growing nineteenth century population was served by a railway station. This was located, like the colliery on the line that is now the Brandon to Bishop Auckland Walk. The station closed in 1964 and was subsequently demolished but Station Road and Station Avenue still point to the site.

During the twentieth century Brandon continued to prosper as a colliery village particularly following the opening of Brandon Pit House Colliery in 1924. This stood out in the moorland to the west of old Brandon village on the road to New Brancepeth and was operating until closure in 1968. It outlived the original Brandon Colliery which closed in 1960 as well as those at Browney village and Littleburn which closed respectively in 1938 and 1950.

Housing development has been a constant feature of Brandon history since the 1950s and although the former farming community of old Brandon village still remains, there is little trace of the huge colliery village that stood nearby.

New houses have replaced the basic but characterful colliery terraces of times gone by and large parts of Brandon are now a collection of housing estates on the top of a hill.

Pit House Colliery, Brandon (JK)

The atmosphere of Brandon colliery village as it was in earlier times is well captured in the wonderful children's novel called The Bonnie Pit Laddie. This is set in a fictional village called Branton but very clearly uses Brandon as its model. Set in the early twentieth century, the novel was actually written in the 1960s.

The novel was the work of the Brandon writer Frederick Grice and rather movingly observes the lives of a young pit boy and his brother growing up in Brandon at the beginning of the twentieth century.

Durham City is featured in the novel which also alludes to a number of local pit villages. The discovery of an ancient burial chamber also features in the story and we have already noted that a discovery of this kind did actually take place in Brandon.

By the 1960s the demolition of the terraced houses and relocation of people to new houses in Brandon Colliery

village caused the old farming village of Brandon and the colliery village to virtually merge across the fields into one place.

Many of the old terraces in and around Brandon have been removed and replaced with industry or new housing developments. At nearby Littleburn the terraces made way for much-needed jobs on the developing industrial estate. The last of Brandon's colliery terraces were themselves demolished in the 1970s for new housing. Neighbouring pit heaps have also been flattened to the ground. For many years the heaps had been known as the 'fiery heaps' because of their tendency to ignite without warning. No trace of them remains today and although Brandon is still occasionally described as a mining village the collieries are no more.

Brancepeth Village and Castle

Few places of Brancepeth's size possess as much history as this little village four miles south east of Durham. Despite recent, small-scale housing development Brancepeth is still a tiny village by Durham standards and its old-world charm is partly due to the fact that Brancepeth was never a colliery village. It will therefore come as a great surprise to learn that there were actually four Brancepeth Collieries.

Firstly there was Brancepeth Colliery but this was located two miles south east of Brancepeth at Willington. It was at Willington that the Brancepeth miners actually resided. Strakers and Love, who also owned Brandon Colliery, opened Brancepeth Colliery in 1840 and the mine operated until closure in 1967. However, Willington lies outside the scope of this book.

Another Brancepeth Colliery that lies outside the area covered by this book was South Brancepeth Colliery, owned by Bell Brothers and later by Dorman Long. It operated from 1855 to 1931 and was otherwise known

as Page Bank Colliery. In truth Page Bank was a more accurate description of this colliery's location about two miles south of Brancepeth.

The other two collieries called Brancepeth were New Brancepeth Colliery, in the Deerness Valley two and half miles north of Brancepeth and North Brancepeth Colliery better known as Boyne which operated at Langley Moor for an uncertain period in the late nineteenth century.

The use of Brancepeth in these names is not altogether unjustified as all were built on land that formed part of the vast estate of Brancepeth Castle. Coal owners leased land from the castle's illustrious owners and the castle's occupants ultimately profited from the extensive coal mining of the district. However Brancepeth was of great importance long before the coal-mining era.

Aerial view of Brancepeth Castle (NE)

Early spellings of the name suggest that in pre-Norman times Brancepeth belonged to someone called Brand who perhaps owned the 'peth', which is in this case the climbing Roman road linking Brancepeth with Brandon. Other theories suggest Brancepeth means 'road to Brandon' or the 'path frequented by the brawn', a ferocious wild boar of medieval times. According to legend, a man from Ferryhill called Hodge eventually captured this beast by luring it into a pit. However, it is thought that Robert Surtees, the nineteenth century Durham historian, may have invented the legend.

If Brand was Brancepeth's earliest owner, nothing is known of him. By the 1100s the place belonged to a prominent local family of reputed Anglo-Saxon origin called Bulmer.

The Bulmers somehow managed to hold onto Brancepeth after the Norman Conquest along with land held at Sheriff Hutton near York where they were the Sheriffs of the name.

A church already existed at Brancepeth in Anglo-Saxon times and the first known rector was a Durham monk called Haeming, mentioned in 1085. The dedication of the church to St. Brandon is an unusual and interesting choice, being one of only two dedicated to this saint in the country. The other is in the village of Brendon in Devon. Also known as St. Brendan the Voyager, this Irish saint made some visits to the British mainland and it is tempting to think he may have come to Brancepeth.

It is likely that there was a prominent manor house, possibly fortified, belonging to the Bulmer family at Brancepeth in early times. In 1166, Bertram, the last male heir of the Brancepeth Bulmers, died and his property passed to his daughter Emma. It was through her marriage to Geoffrey Neville that Brancepeth began its four centuries of association with the Neville family.

Geoffrey Neville was from a family of Norman origin, being the grandson of William the Conqueror's Admiral of the

Fleet. The Bulmers must have been considered a family of some importance because sometime after Geoffrey's marriage, the Nevilles adopted the bull's head as their family emblem in recognition of their Bulmer blood.

The Brancepeth Nevilles later acquired Raby, in south Durham through a subsequent intermarriage with the Fitzmaldred family, but Brancepeth was still of primary importance. From 1397, the leading Nevilles were titled the Earls of Westmorland although their land was

concentrated in Durham and Yorkshire. The first earl was largely responsible for building Brancepeth Castle, although only a little of his work remains today.

Brancepeth was a great military stronghold, swarming with soldiers and always stronger, defensively, than Raby Castle. Its solid walls reflect the major role the Nevilles played in the North. Famously, the Nevilles helped to fight and defeat the Scots at Neville's Cross, near Durham, in 1346, and they were one of the most

Brancepeth Castle (NE)

powerful families in England during the Middle Ages. Always well prepared for battle in Scotland, England or France, the Neville retinue at Agincourt in 1415 included 30 horses and 80 archers from Brancepeth. Only the Percys of Alnwick in Northumberland could match the Nevilles in the North. Ironically, it was an allegiance of the two families that brought about their downfall.

In 1569, the Percys and Nevilles colluded in a northern Catholic rising. This was the Rising of the North, an attempt to restore Catholicism and release the imprisoned Mary Queen of Scots in defiance of Queen Elizabeth I. A great military assemblage gathered at Brancepeth prior to the rising. The atmosphere of this event was captured, 200 years later by William Wordsworth, the famous Cumberland poet in part of his lengthy poem called The White Doe of Rylstone:

> From every side came noisy swarms
> Of peasants in their homely gear;
> And mixed with these to Brancepeth came
> Grave gentry of estate and name
> And captains known for worth in arms
> And prayed the earls in self defence
> To rise and prove their innocence.

The leaders amassed 4,000 soldiers and 600 horses but were still disappointed by this level of support. Walter Devereux, the Earl of Essex, had raised a much larger force against the rebels at York. The rebels were quickly disheartened and fled north to Scotland without battle. As far as rebellions go it seems to have been a bit of a flop.

The Earl of Westmorland escaped to Flanders to avoid punishment and lived there until his death. It was safer to be abroad. Rebels were executed in every town and village from Wetherby to Newcastle. Sixty-six were hanged at Durham City alone.

Brancepeth Castle, the home to the Nevilles for 400 years, was seized by the Crown and lost from the Nevilles forever. With the death of Queen Elizabeth in 1603, the lands of the Crown passed to the new monarch James I, who gave Brancepeth and other territories to his Scottish favourite, Robert Carr (or Ker), the Earl of Somerset. However, Carr and his wife were implicated in a poisoning scandal and Brancepeth was confiscated once again.

In 1633, the King's Commissioners sold Brancepeth to three buyers, who sold the property three years later to Ralph Cole of Newcastle.

Later, Ralph Cole's grandson, a Durham City MP, also called Ralph, sold the property to Sir Henry Belaysyse. Sir Henry, who also became Durham's MP, was succeeded at Brancepeth by his son, William. William's daughter and only heir was Bridget Belaysyse, who reputedly fell in love with the Durham MP Robert Shafto. He lived at Whitworth Hall, two miles south of Brancepeth between Spennymoor and Page Bank.

Unfortunately, Bridget's love for Mr Shafto was unrequited and it is said that she died of a broken heart. Her ever-hopeful love for Mr Shafto was supposedly immortalised in the famous North East folk ballad:

> Bobby Shafto's gone to Sea
> Silver buckles on his knee
> He'll come back and marry me
> Bonny Bobby Shafto

Bridget Bellaysyse succeeded to the Brancepeth estate in 1769, but in 1774 it was left to the Earl Fauconberg and subsequently sold to John Tempest. The Tempests then sold it to William Russell for £75,000 at the end of the eighteenth century.

William Russell, of Newbottle, was a Sunderland banker, coal owner and one of the richest and most powerful men in the North. Russell was one of 'the Grand Allies' – a cartel of coal barons who dominated the region's eighteenth century coal trade. His son, Matthew, the MP for Saltash, was reputedly the richest commoner in England and it was he who instigated the virtual rebuilding of Brancepeth Castle in about 1817.

Russell spent £80,000 a year for several years on the project, employing labourers from nearby Brandon working under the guidance of a Scottish architect called Patterson. The notable architect Anthony Salvin also undertook restoration of the castle in the 1860s and 1870s.

Matthew Russell was married to Elizabeth Tennyson, aunt of Lord Tennyson, the famous poet and it appears that Tennyson composed 'Come into the Garden Maud' during a Brancepeth visit. The poem begins:

> Come into the garden, Maud,
> For the black bat, night, has flown,
> Come into the garden, Maud,
> I am here at the gate alone;
> And the woodbine spices are wafted abroad,
> And the musk of the rose is blown.

Matthew Russell was succeeded at Brancepeth by his son William, yet another Durham MP. William left no heirs so the estate passed to his sister, Emma Maria, who, in 1828, married Gustavus Frederick John James Hamilton, the son and heir of Viscount Boyne.

The Viscount Boynes adopted the name Hamilton-Russell and continued to live at the castle until the 1920s, when heavy taxes and maintenance costs forced them to depart for Burwarton, in Shropshire.

During their long residence at Brancepeth, the Boynes had seen the birth of the railways and a boom period for collieries, many of which were built on land leased from their estate. Places like Hamilton Row near Waterhouses and the Lord Boyne pub at Langley Moor commemorate the family name in the surrounding area.

Brancepeth Castle (DS)

By the beginning of the twentieth century, the future of Brancepeth Castle was uncertain. During the First World War part of the castle was converted into a military hospital where 126 patients from Newcastle General Hospital could convalesce at any given time. By the end of the war it had cared for about 4,000 soldiers. Afterwards, it became the regimental headquarters for the Durham Light Infantry.

A huge military camp of more than 100 huts was built south of the village during the Second World War. It seemed as though Brancepeth's history had come full circle with the castle reverting to its original military role. However, the withdrawal of the Durham Light Infantry from the castle and its subsequent disbanding in the 1960s made the building's future uncertain once again.

Several ideas were forwarded for its use, including conversion into a private school, a nightclub, or country club, but nothing came of these plans. Interest was subdued and the agent in charge of selling the castle even considered advertising the property in Playboy magazine.

The locals of this quiet village, without even a pub on their doorstep, were highly concerned that life in their village was about to change. It was ironic that while properties in the village were expensive and highly sought after, nobody seemed to want the castle. After a brief tenancy by a London businessman, the castle eventually came to be occupied by a Sunderland glass firm as a research centre in 1966, but it was back on the market again in the early 1970s.

There were rumours that the castle would be purchased by an oil sheikh and in another rumour it was believed that the actor Telly Savalas, famous for his role as Kojak, was about to move in. It was reported that he would like to live in an English castle. Some witnesses said they had even seen his limousine parked near the castle gates, but the rumours were denied.

The eventual purchaser turned out to be Margaret Dobson, the head of a London publishing business, who moved to Brancepeth in 1978. The castle became Mrs Dobson's family home and a headquarters for the business started by her late husband. Other parts of the 260-room castle were rented out to small businesses or students and in 1981 the village post office was set up in the castle gatehouse and operated here for a time. Mrs Dobson and her family brought new life and purpose to the castle without destroying the quiet charm of the neighbouring village.

It is clear that the history of Brancepeth village is inextricably tied to the story of its castle, but the village and its surrounding farms also have a history of their own. We know that the Brancepeth estate covered a vast area of land and that much of the area came to be occupied by mining villages, but there are other, smaller farms and settlements in undeveloped land close to the castle that are worthy of note.

Holywell Hall, near the River Wear a mile and a half west of Brancepeth was a reputed place of rest for the coffin of St. Cuthbert in Anglo-Saxon times. It later belonged to the powerful Neville family and in medieval times was the residence of the Brancepeth Castle constable from 1402. The present house dates from the eighteenth century.

Other farmhouses and lodges scattered around the old castle lands were often associated with the castle's medieval parkland that was redeveloped in the nineteenth century.

East Park Cottage, just south east of the castle is a reminder of one of two medieval deer parks. The other was the West Park. East Park contained a rare herd of wild white cattle, like that still found at Chillingham in Northumberland. The cattle were locked into the park when it was enclosed in medieval times and still existed in the early 1600s. Unfortunately the herd died out, possibly due to mismanagement. Brancepeth Castle Golf Club which opened in 1924 now occupies a substantial portion of the former park.

Brancepeth village 1959 (NE)

Brancepeth army camp (NE)

The road from Page Bank runs along the western flank of the golf course before joining the A690 on the southern edge of Brancepeth village. In the field bordered and nearly enclosed by the two roads there once stood an almost separate village. This was Brancepeth army camp. Located here from the time of the Second World War it was conveniently close to the Durham Light Infantry headquarters at Brancepeth Castle.

Brancepeth camp consisted of over a hundred huts that served as accommodation and offices for soldiers. The camp even had its own gymnasium and cinema. The buildings were still standing at the beginning of the 1970s and in their later days housed a collection of historic artefacts that had been built up by a Mr Frank Atkinson. The collection would form the basis of what would become Beamish Open Air Museum near Stanley in the northern part of County Durham.

Nothing remains of Brancepeth Camp except for a field. All of the huts at the camp were dismantled and sold at auction in 1971. Successful bidders included local social clubs and amateur football teams who used the removed buildings as changing rooms.

The later history of the camp could have taken a very different course. There was great controversy in the

1960s when the Home Office seemed determined to re-utilise the 120 acre site as a prison. Intense opposition from villagers and local councils brought about the eventual abandonment of the plan in 1968 and the prison was eventually built at Frankland near Brasside on the northern outskirts of Durham City in the 1980s.

The village of Brancepeth was of course the estate village for Brancepeth castle in historic times and today consists of a number of pretty eighteenth century houses. They include the beautiful row on the south side of the road simply called 'the village' that leads to the gateway of the castle grounds.

Taller and slightly more elaborate nineteenth century 'Tudoresque' houses form gable ends to the street. There are other picturesque houses on the opposite side of the A690 including the pretty Magnolia Cottage that was once the village post office.

A more recent estate of executive type houses also occupies this northern part of the village near the Brandon to Bishop Auckland walk. This walk was the former railway line and provides a lovely stroll for visitors and locals alike. The former Brancepeth railway station, now a private house can still be seen alongside the walk. It operated from 1864 until closure in 1965.

Brancepeth once had its own school but it closed in 1933 when pupils were transferred to Brandon. There was once even a brewery in the village but there hasn't been a pub here since the nineteenth century. Some villagers prefer to keep it that way.

The spiritual heart of Brancepeth village is of course the medieval church of St. Brandon, located in the castle grounds. The most remarkable aspect of the church was its beautiful 'Gothick revival' woodwork instigated by John Cosin. He was Rector of Brancepeth from 1626 to 1640 and Bishop of Durham from 1660.

The architectural historian, Nikolaus Pevsner described Cosin's work at Brancepeth as one of Durham's 'most remarkable contributions to the history of architecture and decoration in England'. Sadly these comments only serve to emphasise the scale of the disaster that beset the church in 1998.

At 4.10am on the 16 September, 1998, while the residents of the village lay asleep, a routine police patrol travelling the road from Page Bank was drawn towards a distant glow. The church was on fire. It was too late to save the beautiful woodwork. Temperatures reached an estimated 1200 degrees during the inexplicable blaze and a crew of seven fire engines took one and a half hours to extinguish the flames.

The oak-beamed roof of the church was completely destroyed, exposing an earlier roofline that proved the church's Saxon origins. Interior masonry of the church was severely damaged and stone effigies of the Nevilles were coated with a yellow glaze of melted lead. It was so hot that a Frosterley marble font exploded.

St. Brandon's church, Brancepeth (NE)

Brancepeth village – the north side (NE)

The villagers of Brancepeth who had fought hard to preserve the unique appearance and appeal of their village throughout the years were grief stricken by the destruction of their church.

Over the next seven years the villagers set about refurbishing the interior of their church. Charitable events were held such as art exhibitions, fashion shows, dances and meals which raised hundreds of thousands of pounds. The work also attracted various grants and insurance paid £1.9 million towards the total cost of £3.2 million. The refurbishment resulted in a more roomy and brighter building inside. Once the work was complete it was officially blessed and rededicated by the Bishop of Durham, the Right Reverend Tom Wright on the 23rd October 2005.

New Brancepeth and Alum Waters

New Brancepeth lies on the south bank of the River Deerness two miles north of Brancepeth village and two miles west of Durham. Despite its name New Brancepeth has little in common with Brancepeth village itself.

Brancepeth isn't even New Brancepeth's nearest neighbour since Esh Winning, Brandon and Ushaw Moor are all much closer. However the village did come into being on land that once formed part of Brancepeth Castle's vast estate.

Until the second part of the nineteenth century, what is now New Brancepeth consisted of a few farms and open farmland on the south bank of the River Deerness. Despite the subsequent mining development some farms like Unthank, just east of New Brancepeth still survive. Unthank was first mentioned in 1314 and may refer to the occasionally thankless task of farming although it is sometimes said to refer to squatters who may have lived here in times past.

West of New Brancepeth is Hareholme Farm, where a chapel once stood close to the river. It was reputedly founded around 1170 by one of Thomas Becket's murderers called Redpath. The fugitive apparently fled here, but in truth the name Redpath does not appear amongst the list of Becket's murderers. The origin of the chapel, marked on Victorian maps, still remains a mystery.

Two streams, both tributaries of the Deerness, cut through the land east and west of New Brancepeth and the larger stream in the west is called the Red Burn. A house called Sleetburn stood nearby but was demolished in the nineteenth century to make way for Sleetburn Colliery.

The colliery owners adopted Sleetburn as the name for both the colliery and the village that was built to house the miners, but the name Sleetburn was dropped during the nineteenth century in favour of New Brancepeth, perhaps to avoid confusion with Sleekburn Colliery in Northumberland. Nevertheless many locals still use the name Sleetburn today.

A smaller stream on the eastern side of the village is not named on maps, but a Sleetburn corn mill once stood nearby. This stream could very well be the actual Sleet Burn and its proximity to the little nineteenth century hamlet called Alum Waters could be a clue.

A local farmer informs me that the stream occasionally turns white as a result of alum present in the water. Whiteness would certainly give the stream a sleety appearance. Alum is a metallic solution occurring in many forms and was traditionally used as a fixative in the dyeing process. A bleaching mill called Primroseside Mill existed quite close to here in the early nineteenth century near a farmhouse called Bleach Green.

Alum Waters was built for miners in the nineteenth century before New Brancepeth came into being. In 1856 an industrialist called Cochrane leased mining rights south of the Deerness from Viscount Boyne of Brancepeth Castle. The new Dearness Railway facilitated mining development and the Cochranes needed coal for their coke ovens and ironworks at North Ormesby near Middlesbrough.

Alum Waters (DS)

Colonel Samuel Cody at Brandon (JK)

At first a small mine called Witty Pit opened at Unthank and the miners resided at Alum Waters. However it was the sinking in 1872 of a shaft for the much bigger colliery at Sleetburn House that resulted in the birth of New Brancepeth village.

Cochrane took two unusual steps in establishing his mining village. Firstly, he decided to live nearby when most coal owners kept their mining villages at arm's length. Initially the Cochranes lived at Aldin Grange, between Bearpark and Neville's Cross but they relocated to a nine-acre woodland site, less than a mile to the west of the new colliery. Here a mansion called Eshwood Hall was specially built for the family.

Cochrane's second unusual step was building New Brancepeth as two separate villages. A northern village called 'Low Side' consisting of terraced streets like Plantation Row overlooked the Deerness and was solely for pitmen.

Further west, colliery officials and colliery craftsmen lived in a separate village of slightly better terraces like Eshwood Street. Assigning particular houses to certain types of employees was not unusual, but two villages separated by fields made a powerful social statement.

Henry Heath Cochrane, the colliery owner relished his almost feudal role. Villagers stood still and silent as he rode through their streets and women would receive reprimanding letters if they gossiped. The rule of fear seemed to work, as lawlessness was uncommon. Even unruly colliery officials could face relocation to Low Side.

Eshwood Hall was an esteemed residence, with impressive gardens and an ornamental lake. A railway was built through the grounds simply for delivering the landscaping materials.

View of Durham Cathedral from New Brancepeth (DS)

One unusual visitor to the hall was the pioneering American aviator Colonel Samuel Cody. At 8am on July 25, 1911 Cody made an emergency landing at Pit House near Brandon during a London to Newcastle air race. Cody had breakfast with a New Brancepeth family before staying at Eshwood Hall for two nights while his plane was repaired. The delay was enough to cost him victory.

As for Henry Cochrane, he died without issue in 1924 and the North Ormesby branch of his family showed no interest in Eshwood Hall. Subsequent owners retained the gardens, but a smaller modern hall replaced the original hall in 1935.

From 1933 Sleetburn colliery was managed by the Weardale Steel, Coal and Coke Company and from 1947 it was owned by the NCB. The colliery finally closed in 1953, but some miners found work at the nearby Brandon Pit House Colliery. An aerial ropeway for moving coal had once linked Brancepeth Pit House Colliery to Sleetburn Colliery. Netting protected the New Brancepeth streets from falling coal.

New Brancepeth had seen many changes by the 1950s. No further development took place at Low Side but the other village expanded eastward until the 1900s with new terraces like Harvey Street, Jubilee Street, Prospect Terrace and Rock Terrace. Some of these later terraces still exist.

Harvey Street, New Brancepeth 1963 (NE)

Schools were built in the fields between the two separate villages making New Brancepeth more like a single entity but the schools have now gone, as have the earlier terraces of the two original villages. Pringle and Braunsepeth Council estates were built during the twenties and thirties and most of the older terracing was gradually demolished.

A nineteenth century illustration of Brancepeth Castle

Chapter Seven

Ushaw Moor and Esh Wining

The River Deerness joins its larger brother the River Browney between Stonebridge and Langley Moor and although it is a rather small river it forms a significant valley to the west of Durham City. This valley was once the site of a railway that brought about the opening of several large colliery villages along its course. The valley includes the village of New Brancepeth on the south bank and on the north bank the villages of Broompark, Ushaw Moor, Esh Winning and Waterhouses. Further beyond are the villages of East Hedleyhope and the former iron town called Tow Law. It is at Tow Law that the Deerness begins its course as nothing more than a Pennine trickle but unfortunately Tow Law lies outside the scope of this book.

The former mining village of Ushaw Moor lies on the north side of the River Deerness half way between Durham and Esh Winning. Centrally located amongst the mining communities of the Deerness and Browney valleys, roads from neighbouring places converge upon the offset crossroads at the village centre.

The crossroads was there long before Ushaw Moor village came into being. There was no housing on the crossroads in the 1850s as the nearest structures were Cockhouse Farm, half a mile to the west and Broom Hall on a hill to the east.

Ushaw Moor's mining community was born in the second half of the nineteenth century on previously empty moorland. Some settlement of the area came in the early nineteenth century when Ushaw College was opened but this famous institution existed half a century before Ushaw Moor village came into being.

There had been an earlier farming settlement called Ushaw first mentioned in 1312. Now gone, it was located either on or just to the west of the site where Ushaw College Farm now stands. Early spellings suggest Anglo-Saxons called Ushaw 'Ulfs Shaw' meaning Wolf's Wood but it may be named after Ulf, a man who held land west of Durham in the 1100s.

Little is known of the early Ushaw, except that a bake-house belonging to the Batmanson family existed here in the seventeenth and eighteenth centuries, perhaps where the college now stands. It was a communal establishment used by the poor and needy for a small fee.

Ushaw's moorland, originally called Middlewood Moor lay mostly east of this early settlement. For centuries small-scale drift mining was undertaken at nearby places like Esh, but in 1755 attempts to reach coal on the moor ended in failure.

In 1858, success came when the Pease family of Darlington opened a railway through the Deerness Valley to serve their colliery at Waterhouses and this provided stimulus for further mining development. After the successful finding of coal, Ushaw Moor Colliery opened around 1870.

The colliery's first owners were probably the Holliday family who owned drift mines near old Esh and Hilltop. By 1873, it belonged to John Sharp but then passed to the aristocratic Henry Chaytor of Witton Castle in 1879.

Ushaw Moor's first colliery village developed on the north side of Cockhouse Lane (the B6302), three quarters of a mile west of the present village of Ushaw Moor.

The early colliery village included West Terrace, East Terrace and Double Row and is thought to have included a significant number of Irish inhabitants. The colliery itself lay on the opposite south side of the road overlooking the River Deerness. However the colliery and terraces of this early pit village were cleared in the 1950s and the colliery itself permanently closed in August 1960 before that too was cleared.

Deerness View, a lonely, isolated hamlet on the B6302 now stands close to the site. This hamlet consisting of a single terrace came later, in the mid-twentieth century, but the terraces of the first colliery village stood in the fields just to its east.

Ushaw Moor's early colliery village was the scene of a troublesome strike in the 1880s. It seems that Henry Chaytor was an uncompromising master and sanitary conditions in his terraces were appalling. Wooden huts housing additional miners in the village were described by one observer as 'the most wretched dwellings it was possible to conceive'.

Conditions in Chaytor's mine were no better and men complained of working in 18 inches of water. Chaytor hated unions and appointed Thomas Robinson, a ruthless colliery manager who assigned the best seams to his favourite employees and reduced the wages of others.

Ushaw Moor Colliery in 1969 (NE)

Robinson was especially hard on miners with union connections. Before 1881 two union representatives were removed from the colliery. Robinson threatened to expel a further 60 miners when the union complained.

In December 1881, a colliery overman instructed a miner called Thomas Westoe not to load tubs with poor quality coal from a geological fault. Robinson apparently overruled this and told Westoe it was acceptable.

However, when Westoe's coal arrived at the surface Robinson was unhappy with its quality and Westoe was sacked and his family evicted from their colliery-owned home. Westoe was the union representative.

Ushaw Moor's miners came out in support and handed in a fortnight's notice. If they thought Chaytor would crumble, they were wrong. A fortnight later Robinson arrived with helpers to evict the mining families from their homes. They systematically removed furniture and dumped it outside the houses. Police attended to prevent violence, but only intervened when Robinson personally attempted the removal of a seriously ill boy from his bed.

The miners regarded their protest as a strike and relied on support from workers at other mines. Help also came from

Father Philip Fortin, the Catholic priest of Newhouse in Esh Winning where there was a notable Irish community. He allowed evicted women and children to reside in a corrugated school he had built near Ushaw Moor Colliery in 1874. Ushaw College also helped, allowing strikers to pitch a large tent in the college grounds.

Robinson brought new workers to the colliery and this caused great resentment. Thomas Pyle, a platelayer of Crossgate Moor, who worked at the colliery was murdered. He was found dead in Durham's Redhills Lane with a severe blow to his throat. Westoe was amongst those suspected but was cleared. The murder was the worst of several violent incidents during the strike.

In 1882 several men hired by Robinson in Staffordshire arrived at Croxdale and walked to Ushaw Moor for work. They were unaware of the situation in the village and upon arrival were persuaded to leave by Durham union officials who provided their train fare home.

As they walked to Durham Station, Robinson rode up and told the men they were breaking a contract. Union officials argued otherwise so Robinson departed,

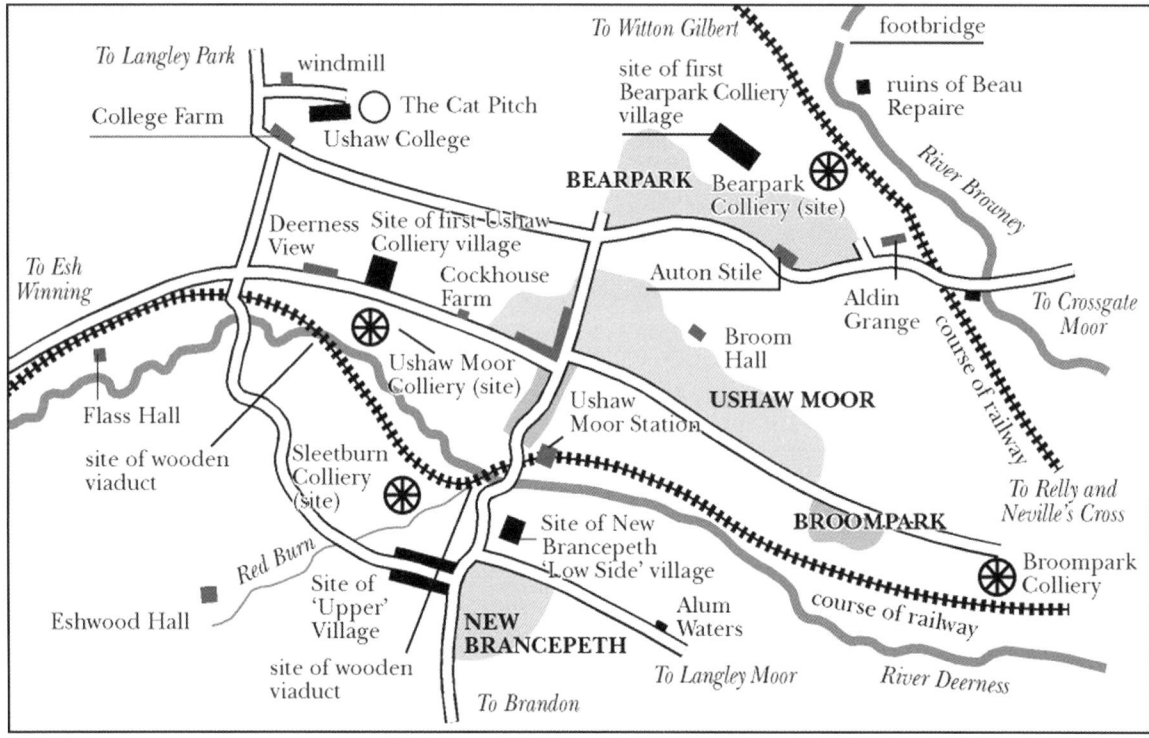

Map showing history of Ushaw Moor and surrounding area (NE)

threatening to return with police. The men avoided confrontation by diverting to Croxdale station before returning home.

Robinson was desperate to find colliery workers and resorted to faking documents to mislead recruits about the location of their work. He became increasingly frustrated and ended up in court on several occasions.

Ushaw Moor Station (JK)

During one appearance, a magistrate described Robinson's employer, Henry Chaytor as 'a very rich and very determined man who would never submit'. In truth Chaytor sat in the comfort of his castle while Robinson did the dirty work. In fact Robinson was almost out of control. He became involved in various trespassing disputes with the coal-owning Cochrane family of New Brancepeth and with Captain Leadbitter of nearby Flass Hall.

Father Fortin was also a focus for Robinson's wrath. Robinson said that if he had twenty pounds of dynamite he would blow up Fortin and his school. Robinson, attempting to have the overcrowded school closed, illegally entered the building to check its condition and assaulted a striking miner's wife.

Another incident occurred in September 1882 when Ushaw Moor's working miners arrived at Waterhouses station at Esh Winning on return from an excursion organised by Chaytor. Angry strikers gathered at Esh Winning's Stag's Head pub to greet the workers. Robinson opened fire on the crowd. He was using blanks, but a boy claimed that a bullet scathed his back. Robinson, now a liability for Chaytor, was replaced by a new manager later that year.

By 1883 it was all over. The protest petered out as strikers found work at other collieries. Chaytor, weary but victorious, was now in his 80s and sold the colliery to the Peases. In the meantime the corrugated Catholic school near the colliery had lost its licence during the strike. It was dismantled in 1898 and rebuilt as a Catholic club at Newhouse, Esh Winning. The Peases opened a new school in Ushaw Moor's centre the following year and a new Catholic school opened to the east in 1910.

In addition to the Ushaw Moor Colliery village there had been some development of buildings around the crossroads in what is now the centre of Ushaw Moor before the 1890s. Early buildings here included a pub called the Flass Inn, but most of the population was still concentrated in the terraces of the early mining village about three quarters of a mile to the west.

When Ushaw Moor railway station opened just south of the crossroads, Ushaw Moor's development was increasingly concentrated around the crossroads area. The station itself was located just down the bank from the crossroads near the River Deerness at the foot of Station Road. The station also served the village of New Brancepeth just across the river but it closed to passengers in 1951 and then to goods in 1964. The Station House can still be seen. Two impressive wooden viaducts transported the railway over the Deerness between New Brancepeth and Ushaw Moor but were demolished in 1966.

Wooden viaduct at Ushaw Moor in the 1960s (NE)

In the early twentieth century the crossroads and station area became the focal point for the village. It was seemingly a lively place to live as there were two cinemas in Station Road. The Empire Cinema of 1912 is now a billiard hall, while Club Hall Cinema was located in the Workingmen's Club.

Unfortunately hard times returned to Ushaw Moor during an economic depression in the 1920s and the colliery was temporarily closed between 1927 and 1929. Tragedy would also pay its visit. On 14 November, 1932, two young miners were killed in a gas explosion in the Victoria Seam. Of course, this was, rather sadly by no means an unusual event in the colliery villages around Durham City and I mention it here because of the rather striking *Northern Echo* picture showing the crowds gathered waiting for the news.

Miners await news of a gas explosion at Ushaw Moor on 14 November, 1932 (NE)

From the crossroads in the centre of Ushaw Moor, the B6302 or Cockhouse Lane leads east towards the Ushaw Moor colliery site. The B6302 is the main road leading to Esh Winning and Waterhouses but before the collieries developed in these two villages the lane terminated at Flass Hall, about a mile west of Ushaw Moor. This hall's name derives from an Old Danish word 'Flask' meaning swamp and has the same meaning as Flass Vale in Durham City.

Established in the 1570s, Flass Hall lies on the site of a medieval farm called Flass that is marked on Saxton's map of Durham in 1576. The hall's first occupant was William Brass who was succeeded by his son, Cuthbert in 1600. The last Brass at Flass still lived there in 1697 when it became the hall of the Halls.

By the nineteenth century Flass belonged to Jane Smythe of Esh Hall who married Sir Robert Peat, a friend of the Prince Regent. Robert had serious gambling debts and probably married Jane for her money. Later, they were estranged, partly because of Jane's kleptomaniac tendencies. She chose to live at Sunderland, renting Flass Hall to the Reverend Temple Chevalier of Esh village while her property at Cockhouse Farm was leased for a time to John Leadbitter of Gateshead.

Flass Hall became a property of the Peases in the 1920s before passing in the 1930s to a local farmer who kept pigs in the house. It was taken over by the NCB in 1947 and converted into a private residence in the late 1960s. Locally it is called 'the haunted house', but the identity of its spectral resident, if indeed there is one, remains a mystery.

Broompark

Broom Hall, now a farm is another notable hall associated with the area but is located at the eastern end of Ushaw Moor village. Once situated in empty fields, it was almost swallowed up by Ushaw Moor's housing developments in the 1960s. It belonged to the Batmanson family in the later half of the sixteenth century.

Broom Hall is really associated with the tiny former farming village of Broom that is just to the east. Old Broom is now called Broompark, but Broompark was really the name for a separate but adjoining colliery village that developed in the nineteenth century.

The original colliery village of Broompark has now gone and the site is now occupied by a housing development called Cooke's Wood. Older parts of the original Broom including several old farmhouses remain, but the whole village is now called Broompark.

Mining had taken place on a small scale in the Broom area since the 1300s when its coal was sold to the Prior of Bearpark. North Brancepeth Colliery Company who also operated Littleburn colliery at Meadowfield opened Broompark colliery here around 1870 near the site of a medieval moat. The neighbouring Boyne Colliery was also owned by the company.

A spur of land formed by the junction of the Browney and Deerness rivers in the Broom, Relly and Langley areas would have made this area attractive as a defended site and this may explain the presence of a moat hereabouts. The history of the moat here at what was once known as Brunespittle is however uncertain. As for Broompark colliery, it closed in 1904 after a major fire from which the miners very luckily escaped by means of an old drift. The Relly and Langley Moor areas were featured in an earlier chapter.

Broompark village (DS)

In recent decades housing growth at Ushaw Moor has meant that Broompark is now only separated from Ushaw Moor by a road and a recreation ground. One intriguing feature of Broompark is the Loves public house. Built in the nineteenth century it was originally called Love's Hotel after Joseph Love, a Durham coal owner who owned a brick foundry. The pub was built with Love's bricks, each rather romantically inscribed with the word Love.

Love Brick from The Loves at Broompark (NE)

Ushaw College

Where in the North East might we find a 400-year-old college with magnificent buildings, beautiful grounds, a cathedral-like chapel and a library modelled on Oxford and Cambridge? Near Durham City is the answer, but if you thought we were talking about Durham University you would be wrong, since this college came to Durham more than 30 years before Durham University was even established.

We are of course talking about Ushaw College, or the College of St. Cuthbert to use its full name. Located on a hilltop, a mile west of Bearpark, Ushaw College is a Roman Catholic seminary steeped in history and tradition. It even has a unique ball game all of its own.

Situated close to mining villages like Bearpark, Ushaw Moor, Langley Park and Esh Winning, it seems an incongruous feature of the landscape, but none of these mining villages even existed when the college was built on the site in 1808. However 1808 was by no means the beginning for Ushaw College. In fact the story of the college may be traced right back to Elizabethan times.

When Elizabeth I became Queen in 1558 she enforced the suppression of Catholicism which had once been the official religion of England. The religion was abolished by her father, Henry VIII but despite the suppression, many continued to secretly practise Catholicism, particularly in the North. Of course this was only possible with properly trained priests but they were now banned from working in England. Many priests fled to France or the Low Countries to escape persecution.

It was in the ancient French University town of Douai, 20 miles south of Lille, that a Lancashire born, Oxford educated priest called William Allen (later Cardinal Allen) established a college for training English priests in 1568. Allen hoped the college would provide priests ready for a time when Catholicism returned to England. However, the restoration of Catholicism became increasingly unlikely so the college secretly sent priests to England. Approximately 270 trained priests arrived in England from Douai in the period 1574 to 1585 and many were captured and executed.

Even when executions ceased, Douai's work continued but in the 1600s and early 1700s the lives of English Catholics were still severely restricted. Catholic priests or Catholic teachers faced life imprisonment but as the years passed Catholics gained greater freedom. In 1791 Catholic mass was legalised but the foundation of Catholic academies or colleges remained illegal.

In 1790 William Gibson of Stonecroft near Hexham had completed his term as President of Douai College and was succeeded by Edward Kitchin, Chaplain of Lartington Hall near Barnard Castle. Kitchin took control of Douai

in a troublesome period, when revolution was taking hold in France.

Douai would not escape the rioting that swept the French nation and on two occasions mobs of drunken soldiers and townsmen invaded the college. On one particularly dangerous raid, three quick-thinking Douai students from northern England shouted 'vive la nation' to get the crowd on their side. They were greeted with cheers and carried shoulder high through the streets of Douai.

Ill health forced Kitchin to return to England as the French instability increased. In 1793 the French king was executed and England declared war on France. The English were ordered to leave Douai and French Republicans occupied the college. Many students fled but 47 students and teachers remained and were imprisoned. Eleven escaped the following year and others were released later. Douai College's history had finally come to an end.

English Catholics sought to establish the institution elsewhere, but Catholic colleges were illegal in England. Fortunately some of the more influential Catholics persuaded William Pitt, first Lord of the Treasury that an English-based college would keep money in the country.

Douai College near Lille pictured in the eighteenth century

Ushaw College (DS)

A college location had to be decided upon and William Gibson, now the most senior Catholic in Northern England wanted it to be in the North. In the meantime while a new location was sought, former Douai pupils were educated at Old Hall near Ware in Hertfordshire and in a school at Tudhoe, County Durham.

Gibson eventually acquired Crook Hall near Leadgate (not to be confused with Crook Hall in Durham City) for his school. The pupils were housed at nearby Pontop Hall while the building was prepared.

It was initially agreed that Durham's college would serve all England, but southern factions favoured the Hertfordshire site. So it was decided that separate colleges should serve northern and southern England and Hertfordshire's Old Hall became St. Edmund's College.

The northern college received a boost as the result of a peculiar argument between two teachers (a northerner and a southerner) that took place at the Hertfordshire site. The argument concerned the relative strength of a cat and was to be settled by a bizarre tug of war contest.

A terrified cat was tied to a rope on one side of a pond, while a teacher – the southerner – was tied to the other end of the rope. When college students insisted he turned his back to give the cat a chance, they pulled the teacher towards the pond. He angrily responded, calling the culprits 'vulgar fellows and Lancashire blackguards'. This offended Hertfordshire's contingent of northern students and several departed to join Gibson in Durham. Some are said to have walked all the way to County Durham carrying luggage in a wheelbarrow.

Other students later joined Gibson straight from Douai and all moved into Crook Hall in October 1794.

Crook Hall was quite small and it became increasingly apparent that a larger, grander establishment was needed. Many sites were considered including Gainford on Tees and Flass Hall in the Deerness Valley. Flass Hall then belonged to a Catholic family called Smythe and it was Smythe farmland at nearby Ushaw Row that was eventually purchased in 1798 for the site of the college.

The construction of Ushaw College commenced in 1804 on the newly acquired land. The Smythe family who were principally associated with Esh village had owned much land in this neighbourhood since the reign of Henry VIII and had taken part in the Catholic rebellion called the Rising of the North in 1569. The rising failed, but fortunately, although the Smythe land was confiscated as a result of the rebellion, it was restored in 1609.

Sir Edward Smythe was no doubt happy to sell 200 acres of his land for the establishment of an important Catholic seminary. In fact Smythe property at Acton Burnell in Shropshire was once used as a place of refuge for schoolmasters from Ushaw College's forerunner at Douai.

When the revolution in France forced the college to relocate to England in the 1790s around 40 students and

teachers came north and eventually moved into the completed Ushaw College in 1808. James Taylor, an architect from Islington, constructed the early parts of the college around a quadrangle in Georgian style but this was only the beginning.

As the century passed, the college and its land continued to expand. In 1817 John Gillow, the college president built a 70ft windmill to provide 'unadulterated' flour for college consumption. It remained in use until the morning of New Years Day 1853 when a gale force wind decapitated the mill and sent its sails crashing to the ground.

The remains of the windmill can still be seen today in a little nameless row of houses just north west of the college. It was intended that the college should be agriculturally self-sufficient and in 1852, a year before the unfortunate gale, a model Home Farm was built for the college 200 metres down hill from the mill. This enormous and rather unusual farm, built in Gothic style encompassed everything needed in the way of farm buildings all under one roof.

Gothic farm near Ushaw College (DS)

Brandon Hill looking towards Durham City (DS)

Brancepeth village – the north side (DS)

Brancepeth Castle (DS)

Brancepeth village – the south side (DS)

The Deerness valley viewed from Brandon Hill (DS)

Flass Hall near Ushaw Moor (DS)

Ushaw College farm overlooks the Deerness Valley (DS)

Ushaw College (DS)

Esh Hall, Esh village (DS)

Esh Cross, Esh village (DS)

The beautiful Esh Laude (DS)

The Heugh at Quarrington Hill looking towards Bowburn (DS)

St. Helen's church at Kelloe (DS)

A rural scene at Old Cassop (DS)

The tiny village of Town Kelloe (DS)

Hett village duckpond (DS)

Croxdale Mill (DS)

St. Bartholemew's church, Sunderland Bridge (DS)

The chapel at Croxdale Hall (DS)

The village of Sunderland Bridge (DS)

Old windmill near Ushaw College (DS)

Gothic developments also took place around the Georgian core of the college. Several buildings were erected by successive generations of the architecturally talented Pugin family, with others built by Joseph and Charles Hansom of Hansom cab fame.

Buildings erected in the period 1839 to 1893 included a library, infirmary, museum, kitchens, swimming pool, cloisters, oratory, playground and a number of chapels. The college library, modelled on Oxford and Cambridge was built to house 45,000 books of a mostly historical and theological nature while the college museum housed Ushaw's cherished collection of relics. Many relics had been purchased from a private individual in Naples, Italy and in May 1860 they were delivered in a large wagon under the supervision of a priest. The wagon's load included 20 relics of Jesus, 3 of the Virgin Mary and 860 relics relating to various saints.

Other relics in the college possession included those of the English martyrs in other words Catholics who had been executed for their faith. Also amongst the relics was an Anglo-Saxon fabric from St. Cuthbert's tomb in Durham

Cathedral and a ring acquired from some Parisian nuns. It was allegedly recovered from St. Cuthbert's tomb many centuries before.

At the eastern end of the college, the massive walls of the racket court remind us of the unique ball game called Cat or Katt that is undoubtedly one of this college's most fascinating features. This game incorporates aspects of baseball, squash and golf and originated in the college of Douai where it was played from at least as early as 1760.

It is a seven a side game played with a hard ball that is smaller than a tennis ball and larger than a golf ball. Each bat, made of Ash wood, has a shaft like a golf club and a flattened bottle-shaped head 4 inches long and 2 inches in diameter. The game is played on a wide-open field with a circular track 80 yards in circumference with seven holes, around which the batting team assembles.

When the ball is struck, members of the striking team run as far around the circular track as they can. Fielders in the opposing team attempt to return the ball into a hole before a member of the batting team touches the said hole.

When batters progress around the track two times, plus five additional holes, the batsman attempts to achieve what is called a 'cross'. Upon striking the ball, members of the batting team run to the centre of the pitch cross their bats and return to the holes before the fielders can pot the ball. It is these crosses that gain the points and if a striker fails on three attempts to achieve a cross the team is out.

Cat was an annual event played from St. Cuthbert's Day March twentieth to the end of May, but because of dwindling numbers at the college it is rarely played today except by former students who occasionally return to the college to indulge. This unique ball game is not the only aspect of college life affected by a fall in the number of students wishing to take up the vocation.

The Cat Pitch at Ushaw College (DS)

Ushaw College has had to increasingly adapt with the times. Building development continued at the college until as late as 1964 with the construction of a new eastern wing, but although the college continues to work as a seminary it has had to find new means of sustaining its livelihood. Today the new wing now serves as a conference centre and since 1968 the college has been an officially licensed hall of residence for Durham University.

The college has continuously developed strong links with Durham University and especially the Department of Theology. Theological courses for lay people have become increasingly important and Ushaw college is constantly considering new uses for its land and buildings including the possible development of part of the college into a hotel or the extension of a nine hole golf-course to eighteen holes. The future of this college now seems uncertain, but with a history dating back more than four hundred years it would be sad if Ushaw College lost all links with its rich and intriguing past.

The impressive chapel at Ushaw College (NE)

Esh Winning and Waterhouses

Esh Winning lies in the valley of the River Deerness four miles west of Durham. It is one of the larger communities in the valley and is a former mining village. Its nearest neighbours are Waterhouses and Hamilton Row, much smaller communities just along the valley to the west, but the histories of the three places are closely tied.

Hamilton Row is the most westerly of the three settlements and is virtually a western extension of Waterhouses. Its colliery was the last of the three to open and also the most short-lived. It was a small-scale drift mine called Ivesley Colliery and was just north of the village near Ivesley Farm.

Ivesley is the site of a deserted medieval village. It is said that an avenue of trees leading up to the farm was planted in the 1300s to commemorate plague victims in the village. Little is known of the early village of Ivesley.

It was in 1871 that John Kellet, a Weardale businessman, opened the neighbouring colliery and named his mining settlement Hamilton Town. The main street was also called Hamilton Row and both were named after the Hamilton-Russells of Brancepeth Castle who leased the land to Kellet. After Kellet's death the lease passed to Joseph Walton of Middlesbrough, but the mine was abandoned in 1896.

Esh Winning's story begins at Waterhouses, since the Waterhouses colliery preceded the colliery at Esh Winning and it was the same company that established both mines. The histories of the two places are connected in other ways and it is notable that prior to the colliery development both places had strong links with Roman Catholicism.

Waterhouses was originally a collection of three farmhouses but the original Waterhouse, now gone, was named because of its location near the River Deerness or an adjoining stream. The exact site is unknown but in Elizabethan times it belonged to the Claxtons who were retainers of the powerful Neville family of Brancepeth Castle. Like the Nevilles, the Claxtons remained staunchly and secretly Catholic long after Henry VIII's religious reforms.

Waterhouses village (DS)

The Waterhouse was a meeting place for local Catholic nobility where meetings were held in secret because of Catholic persecution. The place has strong links with a Roman Catholic martyr called John Boste who was executed at Dryburn in Durham City.

Boste was a Roman Catholic priest who was born at Appleby in Westmorland. As a young man he was a practising Catholic but fled abroad to escape religious persecution. In the 1580s he returned to England following an education in France and ordination at Rheims.

Boste entered England at great risk to his life. News of his activities reached the ears of the Protestant authorities but Boste managed to evade capture in Yorkshire. He performed mass at many places across the North, including several venues on the vast Brancepeth Castle estate. In the meantime, some of Boste's close friends and supporters were captured and during severe interrogation it was revealed that the Waterhouse was one of Boste's meeting places.

The building was watched and in 1593, after Boste performed mass in the house, Protestant searchers burst into the building and broke down its walls, revealing Boste hiding in a secret place. William, the head of the

Claxtons, was not there. He was already imprisoned for his Catholic activities, but his wife, Grace, was present along with Lady Margaret Neville. Both women were found guilty of treason, but escaped punishment. Grace was spared when it was proved she was pregnant, while Lady Margaret was pardoned after the Bishop of Durham rather dubiously claimed she had converted to Protestantism. Boste was not so lucky. He was transported to London and displayed before Queen Elizabeth who wished to see the 'insolent fellow'.

Boste was imprisoned and tortured in the Tower of London before returning to Durham for trial in 1594. Sentenced on the morning of 23 July, a crowd assembled for his execution at Dryburn on Durham's north western outskirts. Witnesses claimed the hanging, drawing and quartering took place with great speed and brutality and many in the crowd mourned his loss. Boste's bravery and determination was not forgotten and nearly 400 years later, in 1970, he was canonised by the Pope as St. John Boste.

Joseph Pease

Despite its early links with Catholicism, present day Waterhouses owes its origins to the enterprise of a family who were members of a quite different Christian faith. They were the Pease family, chief amongst the Quaker fraternity of Darlington. Edward Pease had funded the Stockton and Darlington Railway and his son Joseph Pease established the town and port of Middlesbrough on the banks of the River Tees. Joseph Pease and Partners also owned several collieries in the Billy Row area of the Wear Valley that were known collectively as Peases West.

Just north of the Peases West Collieries the Pease family leased several hundred acres of Deerness valley land from the owners of Brancepeth Castle and opened the first pit at Waterhouses Colliery in 1855. The pit was called Mary Pit after a member of the Pease family but the colliery was initially called Peases West Brandon Colliery. More importantly the Peases instigated a new railway line called the 'Dearness' Railway with what seems to have been a slightly erroneous spelling of the valley name.

The railway officially opened in 1858, commencing at Waterhouses. It ran east along the valley before linking up with the Bishop Auckland line at Relly near Langley Moor. South of Waterhouses an incline linked the line with the Peases West collieries. Today the Dearness Railway has gone but the railway's course can now be traced along the course of what is now the Deerness Valley walk.

The railway truly opened up the potential for coal mining in the Deerness Valley and the Peases followed up the opening of Waterhouses Colliery with the establishment of the colliery at Esh Winning in 1866.

Both collieries experienced some periods of difficulty in which production ceased. The colliery at Esh Winning (which was actually called Esh Colliery) was temporarily closed between 1930 and 1942 when villagers had to find work elsewhere. Waterhouses colliery closed in the

difficult economic period between 1927 and 1929. However after reopening both collieries continued to operate until the 1960s. Waterhouses closed in 1966 and Esh Colliery two years later in 1968.

Waterhouses Station was at Esh Winning (JK)

The Peases who owned Waterhouses and Esh Colliery were not typical colliery owners and had some interesting ideas regarding the development of colliery villages. They tried to develop Esh Winning and Waterhouses as model colliery settlements. The houses of miners in the villages were more substantial than those found in other places and rather unusually, each house had its own large garden for the growing of vegetables or the fattening of pigs.

Pease and Partners gave great attention to drainage and sanitary conditions and took much interest in the education and welfare of their workforce. Schools were built for youngsters, whilst a Miners' Institute near South Terrace provided reading rooms and recreational activities. However, this building was somewhat eclipsed by the remarkable Pease Memorial Hall that opened in neighbouring Brandon Road in 1923.

The memorial hall, a Grade II listed building, that now has an uncertain future, was built to commemorate miners who lost their lives in the Great War. Now boarded up, it once had its own cinema, concert hall, library and swimming bath. Built in Edwardian style with several rooms, it was perhaps a little too grand for a small community and experienced financial difficulties in the late 1920s. Nevertheless it continued to operate a cinema and ballroom for many decades to come.

Esh Winning Memorial Hall (DS)

Pease and Partners were a major source of funding for the hall's construction, contributing £3,000 to the total cost of £10,000. Local miners raised the rest through subscription. On the opening day, the prominent miners' leader Peter Lee unveiled a plaque, but the Peases, though invited, chose not to attend. It was a wise move, since the family were no longer so popular in Esh Winning.

Miners were angered by the Pease firm's attempts to increase working hours on top of poor wages during the economic depression of the 1920s. Things reached a head in the 1926 General Strike when the firm employed black leg workers and billeted police to evict striking miners from their homes. The Secretary and the Treasurer of the Memorial Hall were among those evicted. After clashes with police they were arrested and imprisoned in Durham Jail for a month.

Despite the higher quality of houses in Esh Winning and Waterhouses none of the nineteenth century terraces built by the Peases in these model villages survive. The site of Waterhouses Colliery village lies in empty woodland north of the Deerness Railway. The railway itself is now a walk but adjoining woodland paths mark the course of former streets like the unimaginatively named North, West and East Terrace. The colliery stood nearby.

Today Waterhouses is a small village, consisting of Station Street, that led to a small goods station and a main thoroughfare called Russell Street. This road continues west into the neighbouring settlement of Hamilton Row. Both streets are named after the Hamilton-Russells of Brancepeth Castle.

Esh Winning has seen the growth of new housing estates in recent years but much of the older colliery village has gone. Like Waterhouses, there was a North, West and East Terrace all located in what is now empty land north of Esh Winning Industrial Estate. The industrial estate occupies the site of the colliery.

South Terrace, a later addition, to the south of the colliery was built in the 1870s or 80s and still exists, while Lymington Terrace further to the south across the River Deerness formed a virtually separate hamlet.

Lymington Terrace was most probably named after Lady Lymington, the daughter of Edward Pease but its origins are uncertain. It may have housed workers of a neighbouring nineteenth century brickyard. The terrace has now gone, but lay near the present (but later) terraces of Woodland Place and West View. These still form an area of Esh Winning known as Lymington.

The three main roads in Esh Winning itself are Fair View, Durham Road and Newhouse Road. All date from the nineteenth century and intersect to form a triangle near

Esh Winning's centre. Durham Road and Newhouse Road join at Esh Winning's market place where the post office and Stag's Head pub have stood since the nineteenth century. A cinema called the Pavilion stood behind the pub in the early twentieth century.

The road called Station View leads south from the market place to the site of a railway station. Though situated in Esh Winning it was called Waterhouses Station and was a passenger station that should not to be confused with the smaller goods station that existed in Waterhouses itself. The passenger station closed in 1951.

The Roman Catholic Church of Our Lady Queen of Martyrs stands at the northern end of Esh Winning near the junction of Fair View and Newhouse Road. It is situated alongside a little stream called the Priest Burn, that serves as a reminder of the area's historic Catholic links.

Newhouse Catholic church at Esh Winning (DS)

The church is nineteenth century in origin, but may stand near the site of an earlier Catholic chapel called Newhouse that was established in the 1650s. It was probably disguised as a farmhouse. In times gone by the priests of Newhouse served many Catholic farms in the area, though mass was often held in secret. According to the records, one Newhouse Priest called Ferdinando Asmall who died in 1798, lived to the grand old age of 103.

In 1800, Newhouse chapel fell into ruin and its priest moved to a new chapel further north at Esh Laude near the little village of Esh.

Newhouse was without a priest until the middle or late nineteenth century when many Irish labourers came to work at Esh Winning. Our Lady Queen of Martyrs, which dates from 1881, was built in the Newhouse area of Esh Winning to serve the Irish settlers who were numerous here.

Workers seemed to come to Esh Winning from almost every county in the Emerald Isle, and included my great Grandfather from County Monaghan whose family settled in the village. However, we should note that as in most Durham mining villages most of the residents were indigenous miners from County Durham. Nevertheless immigrants to Waterhouses and Esh Winning came from many other parts of England including a significant number from non-mining areas like Suffolk. So not everyone was Roman Catholic and of course as is the case with most pit villages Methodist chapels were also built in the two villages. There was, however, no denying the area's strong Catholic links.

Esh Village and Esh Laude

Although most of the villages west of Durham City owe their origins to the mining era Esh Village or Old Esh as it is sometimes known dates back to Anglo-Saxon times. It developed as an agricultural settlement but is often confused with the much larger mining village of Esh Winning that developed in the 1850s a mile to the south. There is no direct road across the hills between Esh and Esh Winning and the little village's nearest

neighbours are actually Langley Park and Quebec. In fact as boundaries stand in 2006 Old Esh and Langley Park are located in the council district of Derwentside, whilst Esh Winning is in Durham City.

Esh cross, Esh village (DS)

Esh is an Anglo-Saxon name meaning Ash tree and the spelling reflects the old Northumbrian dialect that was once spoken throughout the north. There may have been a prominent ash tree here or extensive woodland but whatever the origin, Esh gave its name to a family called De Esh who resided here from medieval times up to the reign of Henry VIII. Family members included Simon De Esh, a High Sheriff and Bailiff of Durham in the 1300s. The Esh family's medieval residence is not known but Esh village church dedicated to St. Michael probably stands on the site of the family's private chapel dating from 1283.

On September 10, 1306, King Edward I visited this church and said mass before heading north to fight the Scots, leaving an offering of 7 shillings before his departure. The church was rebuilt in the 1770s with further restoration in the 1850s. Only the lower walls of the church are thought to be ancient but the church does

contain a medieval effigy of a costumed lady thought to be one of the De Eshes.

South of the church lies the walled village green with a solitary stone cross at its southern end inscribed with the letters I.H.S. and dated 1687. It may stand on the site of an earlier medieval structure.

Just south of the green is Esh Hall, erected by the Smythe family in the 1600s. The Smythes inherited Esh village and its surrounding land around 1560 when Margaret De Esh, daughter of Anthony De Esh (the last of the male line) married William Smythe, a member of a staunchly Roman Catholic family from Nunstainton near Sedgefield.

The Smythes actively encouraged Catholicism in and around Esh during the Tudor era when Catholics were suppressed. Although they lost their land for a time after 1569 it was later restored. A place of Catholic worship had been established by the Smythes a mile south of Esh at Newhouse to serve the surrounding farms and it operated in secret during periods of Catholic suppression.

Esh Hall near Esh village (DS)

The place of worship at Newhouse church continued in use until about 1798 when its last priest, Ferdinando Asmall died at the age of 103. Newhouse would later become the site of a Catholic Church serving the Irish community of the newly established colliery village of Esh Winning from 1871, but the original foundation had in the meantime moved to a new site.

The original Newhouse had fallen into ruin at about the time of Father Asmall's death and Sir Edward Smythe of Esh Hall wanted a new, more accessible foundation. A slackening of laws restricting Catholicism and the associated establishment of the Catholic Ushaw College on land provided by the Smythes gave the family a new sense of optimism. The Smythes wanted to establish a church in keeping with the neighbourhood's strong Catholic traditions. A new site was chosen half a mile along the road west of Esh Village and was named Esh Laude. Perhaps wary of past suppression or in emulation of previous Catholic places of worship, it was decided that the church should be built to resemble a farmhouse so as not to draw attention.

Esh Laude near Esh Village (DS)

Like its Anglican counterpart in Esh village, Esh Laude church was dedicated to St. Michael and the building

was constructed around a courtyard. Esh Laude is a very beautiful building and will take the passing motorist by surprise when it is seen for the first time. It opened in 1800 and is the oldest church in the Roman Catholic Diocese of Hexham and Newcastle. This diocese covers the whole of North East England north of the River Tees.

Despite their involvement in the establishment of Esh Laude and Ushaw College the Smythes increasingly came to favour residence at their property of Acton Burnell in Shropshire. The Durham historian Surtees writing in the 1820s described Esh Hall as deserted.

In the 1850s the Smythes leased Esh and its hall to Henry Smith, a Catholic of Drax Abbey, near Selby in Yorkshire for forty years and this had disastrous effects. Smith raised the rents of local farms, forcing many tenant farmers out. He replaced them with new tenants from Yorkshire but the Yorkshire farmers, finding the conditions difficult would later depart.

Smith's impact on Esh Hall had a much longer-lasting effect. By 1857 he had completely removed the old hall with its oak-panelled walls, great kitchen and welled staircase and replaced them with a new hall using some material from the old. A priest's hiding place – a priest hole – was discovered during the demolition complete with vestments and sacramental vessels. It was a reminder of the Catholic secrecy of times gone by.

Esh village is a rather tiny place that has seen very little growth in recent centuries compared to many Durham villages and it still retains a rural charm. In the nineteenth century there was only very small-scale mining near the village, but there were two smithies and a cartwright's shop.

The Cross Keys pub in Esh dates from the nineteenth century when it was notorious for cock fighting but it

stands on the site of an earlier thatched inn used by cattle drovers. The village saw slight growth along the road to the east in the late nineteenth century and further growth east and west of the green in the late twentieth century. In truth this expansion was so slight that it is barely worthy of note. The village has been served by two schools – Catholic and Anglican since the nineteenth century and in this respect it serves as a little centre for an extensive farming area just as it did in the days of old.

Quebec and Hamsteels

The former colliery village of Quebec is located along a front street a mile west of Esh village and to the north west of Esh Winning. A farm building just to the north gave its name to the village and was named after the famous Canadian city or province.

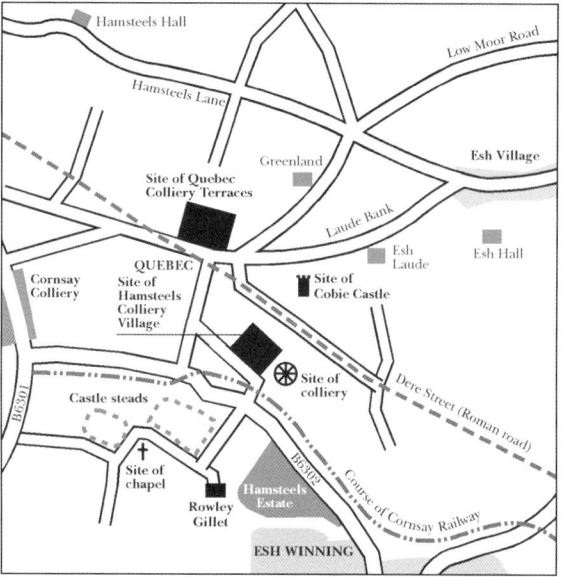

Map showing history of Quebec and Hamsteels (NE)

The fields were enclosed here in the mid-1700s when Britain was at war with the French Canadians and Quebec may have seemed a topical name. On the other hand it may simply have something to do with the perceived remoteness of the fields in this area of Durham. This would explain the name of a neighbouring farm called Greenland, half a mile to the north east.

Quebec is located on Hamsteels Common, where the fields were enclosed in the eighteenth century. Hamsteels Common is named after a little settlement called Hamsteels that lies a mile to the north west, half way between Quebec and Lanchester. Hamsteels' Anglo-Saxon name, 'Ham-Stigel' means the 'steep ascents by the homestead' but it is now only a small collection of buildings clustered around Hamsteels Hall. The hall dates from the 1700s and is now a Bed and Breakfast Guest House.

Hamsteels was also the name of a quite separate colliery village that came into being in the nineteenth century. This village has now gone but was located half a mile south of Quebec and had its own colliery located nearby. Most of the senior colliery staff resided at Hamsteels colliery village, but Quebec village housed the majority of the miners.

Hamsteels colliery came into being in 1867 and was initially called Taylor Pit. It was built on the site of the Esh Tile Works and probably used buildings from the old works. In 1861, most of the area was empty farmland but by 1871 there were 38 families at Hamsteels Colliery and 110 at Quebec.

The colliery owner, a Mr Johnson built houses along the main road that became Quebec's Front Street, with a further nine streets like Brockwell Street and Busty Street built at right angles to the main thoroughfare.

Historic view of Quebec village

At Hamsteels Colliery, Johnson built Office Street, High Street and South Street, each with their own garden plots. Although Hamsteels housed senior employees most of the village amenities were at Quebec including the school, a church and a miners' institute. Johnson, a brewery proprietor built two pubs at Quebec called Hamsteels Colliery Inn and Hamsteels New Inn, but the miners probably had mixed feelings about his ownership of their pubs.

Hamsteels Colliery continued to operate until its closure in the 1920s when Stanley Sadler, a Teesside industrialist acquired small drift mining interests here and apparently named them Clifford and Ethel after his son and daughter.

The mines operated under the name of Hamsteels Colliery until their closure in the 1950s. By this time Hamsteels Colliery and Quebec, like many other Durham villages were declared 'Category D' under the County Development Plan. Such communities were described as lacking in social facilities, situated in poor locations, with no source of employment and having properties in poor condition.

Investment in these places ceased and residents, despite their strong attachments were relocated to allow for demolition of the villages. All houses in Quebec except for Front Street and the farm were demolished in the 1950s and the residents were relocated to Langley Park and Esh.

At Hamsteels Colliery, the streets were not completely removed until the early 1970s. Only 17 families resided there by 1973 when residents included a retired African bishop. The National Coal Board carried out extensive open cast mining soon after the demolition of these last remaining houses. Hamsteels Colliery village is now an empty field, and there is virtually no trace of its existence.

A Hamsteels housing estate was created half a mile south of the old colliery on the outskirts of Esh Winning, partly to re-house former Hamsteels residents. In recent years the estate has occasionally been the subject of a boundary dispute, as it is the only part of Esh Winning situated in Derwentside district rather than Durham City as boundaries stand today.

A large area of land between the former colliery site and the new estate is of archaeological interest and demonstrates how depopulation of old settlements is nothing new.

Rowley Gillet and Rowley farmhouses lie immediately to the west of the Hamsteels estate and include several interesting archaeological remains. Rowley Gillet, sometimes spelled Gillot (arguably pronounced with a soft G) is named after a family called Gelet who owned land here in the 1200s. Earthwork traces of a large, rectangular fortified manor house called Castlesteads lie just to the east alongside the site of a medieval chapel. The whole area may have belonged to the De Esh family of Esh village, but nothing is known of its history. It was probably abandoned in the 1600s.

Several other earthworks can be found nearby and it is probable that the area was occupied from ancient times. All the sites are scheduled ancient monuments and are protected by law.

Historic view of Hamsteels Hall (HH)

A woodland area just north of Hamsteels Estate called Rotten Row Plantation, suggests further abandoned settlement. Dere Street, the most important Roman Road in the north runs through the heart of this area in between Quebec and the former colliery site and it is possible that the various archaeological sites have some connection with the road. A farmhouse called Cobie Castle stood on the northern side of Dere Street between Quebec and Esh Laude until the early twentieth century and may also occupy a site of antiquity.

It is interesting to contemplate that while there are extensive traces of deserted medieval settlements nothing at all remains of the more recent village of Hamsteels Colliery.

Chapter Eight

Bearpark, Witton Gilbert and Langley Park

The River Browney rises in the Pennines near Satley and flows east past Lanchester and then on towards Langley Park and Witton Gilbert where it makes a sudden detour to the south. Here it passes Bearpark before skirting the western suburbs of Durham City around Langley Moor and Neville's Cross. It eventually joins the River Wear at Croxdale.

Near Lanchester the Browney is a stream but it forms a substantial valley that has helped in determining its river status. The river broadens out as it reaches Durham City but although it is a more significant rivulet than the Deerness it is always nothing more than a very large stream. In this section of the book we are concerned with the villages of Bearpark, Witton Gilbert and Langley Park that dominate the middle part of the valley.

The former mining village of Bearpark is located on a hill between the valleys of the Deerness and Browney a mile west of Durham City. Only Deerness Valley Comprehensive School (now Durham Community Business College) now separates Bearpark from the neighbouring village of Ushaw Moor to the south.

Ushaw Moor and Bearpark have almost merged following continuous growth in the late twentieth century, but while Ushaw Moor's history belongs to the Deerness valley, Bearpark's story is firmly linked to the valley of the Browney.

Bearpark Colliery closed in 1984 and is now a woodland plantation, but the nearby terraces of the original colliery village were demolished much earlier in the 1950s and are now a field. Both colliery and village overlooked the countryside of the Browney valley that lay to their east.

Beau Repaire

Just across the river from the Bearpark colliery site on a slightly raised bluff can be seen the medieval ruins of Beau Repaire. It is here that the history of Bearpark really begins. Beau Repaire's name is French and means beautiful retreat. Here was a manor house and an adjoining park used by the priors and monks of Durham Cathedral. It may have housed up to forty monks at any one time.

Bertram of Middleton, Prior of Durham between 1244 and 1258, established a lodge and a chapel here dedicated to St. Edmund. The surrounding land encompassed both sides of the River Browney and already belonged to the Priory of Durham Cathedral who received it as a gift from Gilbert of Witton Gilbert in 1154.

Monks could walk to Beau Repaire from Durham via the Prior's Path that ran up from somewhere near Redhills Lane in Durham City. It then ran close to the present Toll House Road and along past Arbour House and Stotgate Farm. The names of these two places mean 'shelter house' and 'horse gate farm'. Arbour House stands on the top of a hill that played a major part in the Battle of Neville's Cross in 1346. You can read more about this battle in the accompanying book that features Durham City.

The ruins of Beau Repaire (DS)

A path still more or less follows the route of the Prior's Path to the Beau Repaire ruins on the eastern side of the River Browney. Alternatively, the ruins can be reached from the western side of the river along the course of an old railway that is now the Lanchester Valley Walk. A footbridge over the river links the railway walk to the ruins.

It was Hugh of Darlington, Durham Prior from 1285 who enclosed the surrounding land with a wall and palisade to create a hunting park for the retreat. In fact the name of Bearpark derives from a mispronunciation of Beau Repaire Park and there is no evidence that any bears were ever kept here.

In 1289 Hugh of Darlington was succeeded by Prior Richard of Hoton who became involved in a quarrel with Anthony Bek the Bishop of Durham. Bek encouraged his men to tear down the fences of the prior's park and drive out the deer.

Prior William of Tanfield succeeded Hoton in 1308 and Bishop Richard Kellaw succeeded Bek in 1311. These two men seem to have had a better relationship than their predecessors and Kellaw granted Tanfield a licence to increase the size of the park. Beau Repaire's estate included 14 farms and covered about 1,300 acres stretching as far to the west as where Ushaw College stands today and extending as far east as the outskirts of Neville's Cross. In the north the park reached as far as Witton Gilbert and a northern section of the park wall is recalled in the name of Wall Nook near Langley Park.

The Beau Repaire ruins lie close to the southern end of the old park and were once an extensive collection of buildings that included a hall, a large kitchen, an oven, a back room, a dormitory, courts, gardens and a chapel.

Successive rebuilding took place at Beau Repaire from early times, partly due to the constant encroachment of invading Scots who made Bearpark a prime target during their raids upon the Durham City area. In 1315 they managed to destroy and steal almost all the game and cattle in the park and caused great damage to the Beau Repaire buildings.

The prior, Geoffrey of Burdon seems to have escaped along with the monks, but several servants were left behind and taken by the Scots. In 1346, a Scottish army returned again under the leadership of King David Bruce who camped in the park overnight prior to the Battle of Neville's Cross.

Of course the English fought back whenever they could. King Edward I, II and III all stayed at Beau Repaire with their armies during English campaigns against the Scots. Edward III visited Beau Repaire three times in 1330, 1333 and 1335. Beau Repaire must have been suitable accommodation for a king and a survey undertaken in 1450 describes its rich furnishings.

From 1341 to 1374 Beau Repaire was the favourite residence of Prior John Fossor who may be responsible for constructing the buildings that remain today. Little else is known of Beau Repaire after Fossor's time until the reign

of Henry VIII, who closed down Durham Cathedral Priory. The king gave the manor and park of Beau Repaire to the cathedral's Deanery that was established in the priory's place.

In 1641 and 1644 during the period of the English Civil War a final blow was delivered to Beau Repaire and it was the Scots who were responsible once again. A Scottish army occupied Durham in these years and caused severe damage to Beau Repaire's buildings. In truth it may have already fallen into serious disrepair before the Scots arrived, but whatever the cause of its demise, Beau Repaire never seems to have recovered. By 1684 the buildings were described as dilapidated.

Today, the roofing has long since gone and few walls remain, but there are plenty of features to explore. Since the closure of Bearpark colliery in 1984 it is now much easier to imagine how Beau Repaire and its park would have appeared in medieval times.

Bearpark Village

Bearpark Colliery and the first terraces of the mining village of Bearpark were located on the hill, a quarter of a mile south west of the Beau Repaire ruins. These early terraces have now gone and the heart of Bearpark village is now situated alongside the main road from Durham, a further quarter of a mile south of the original terraces.

The area along the main road that now effectively forms the front street of Bearpark was once a separate hamlet called Auton Stile that was itself an extension of another hamlet to the east called Aldin Grange. Both places originated in medieval times.

Aldin Grange is still a farm and hamlet and was originally called Aldingrig meaning Alda's ridge. Early spellings of Auton Stile suggest that Auton Stile was originally Alda's

'tun' or enclosure, but who Alda was is not known. Stile suggests there was a gate or steps across a roadway.

Aldin Grange manor belonged to the Bishops of Durham until the twelfth century but passed to the monks of Baxter Wood near Neville's Cross and then later to Finchale Priory. From the 1600s, Aldin Grange's land and its H-shaped manor house belonged to a series of farming families before passing in the nineteenth century to the Cochrane family who owned New Brancepeth Colliery. When the Cochranes moved to Eshwood Hall sometime after 1874, Aldin Grange Hall, as it had become known, was broken up into a number of smaller cottages.

Mining had been carried out in the Bearpark area since the 1300s when it was recorded that the Prior of Durham had pit workings at Beau Repaire. The Prior agreed to be supplied with coal from a neighbouring mine at Broom (Broompark), providing that the Broom workings did not damage those of Beau Repaire.

Such medieval mining was on a small scale and although a drift was mentioned at Bearpark in 1854, the mining possibilities were not fully realised until the North Eastern Railway opened the Lanchester Valley Railway through the Browney valley in 1862. Ten years later in 1872 Bearpark Colliery was opened and its underground workings encompassed most of the old Beau Repaire estate.

The Bearpark Coal and Coke Company owned the colliery and was headed by a Quaker called Theodore Fry. He was a Darlington ironmaster who later became that town's mayor and its MP. Fry's directors included several Teesside and south Durham industrialists who were attracted by Bearpark's high quality coking coal.

Signpost to the site of Bearpark Colliery (DS)

Bearpark coke was ideally suited to their industrial purposes and came to be internationally recognised as a quality standard. The coke was produced at a coke works next to the colliery until the works closed in 1960. The works used coal produced at the colliery as well as coal from Burnhope Colliery near Lanchester. Coal was brought from Burnhope by means of a five-mile long aerial ropeway.

Chemical by-products produced at Bearpark colliery like tar, crude benzole, napthalene and sulphate of ammonia were also important and it was significant that Samuel Sadler the founder of Teesside's Chemical industry was a Bearpark director from 1877.

The original colliery village came into being in 1872 and had eight terraces, each with 30 miners' houses. Six of the terraces were named after colliery directors. These were Fry Street, Bouch Street, Dodds Street, Dyson Street, Thompson Street and Swan Street. The other two terraces called Edmund Street and Catherine Street were named

after chapels at Broom and Beau Repaire. All these streets have since been demolished and are now an empty field, but the nearby Bearpark Colliery Road more or less marks the site of an even earlier colliery terrace called Sinkers Row that housed the men who first sunk the colliery.

A school was built near the terraces in 1877 for 400 pupils and is now a primary school. Three Methodist chapels opened near the school in the 1880s and 1890s, although one was replaced by a new building in 1908. All gradually fell out of use and were replaced by a new chapel in the Auton Stile area of Bearpark in 1969.

Auton Stile is home to Bearpark's parish church that opened in 1879 and like the old chapel at Beau Repaire, it is dedicated to St. Edmund. In the 1850s there were few buildings in Auton except for three houses called Auton Field, Auton House and Auto Stile. There was also a coaching inn called the Sportsman but this was renamed the Dog and Gun before the end of the nineteenth century and still exists today.

Former Methodist chapel at Bearpark Colliery (DS)

Some housing developments associated with industrial growth took place along the main road at Aldin Grange Terrace in Auton Stile before or during the 1890s, but Aldin Grange itself retained its rural setting and still does today.

At Aldin Grange the bridge over the Browney is famed as the place where David King of Scots was allegedly found hiding after the Battle of Neville's Cross in 1346.

Bearpark railway station opened in 1883 half way between Auton Stile and Aldin Grange but the North Eastern Railway originally called it Aldin Grange Station. The Bearpark residents protested and it was rather cumbersomely renamed 'Aldin Grange for Bearpark'. The name was eventually simplified to Bearpark in 1927 but was only used for another twelve years as the station closed in 1939. The railway itself closed in 1966 and is now Lanchester Valley Walk.

Urban growth in the early years of the twentieth century took place mainly along Victor Terrace and South View Terrace near the main road. There was also considerable development in the fifties and sixties between these streets. It was spurred on by re-housing that resulted from the demolition of the old colliery terraces that lay to the north. Newly constructed streets like Kingston and Ritson Avenues were amongst the first of many.

Despite the changes in the village, the actual colliery at Bearpark continued to operate and did not finally close until 1984. The colliery land has been reclaimed since then and is now a woodland plantation looking out towards the ancient ruins of Beau Repaire.

Witton Gilbert

Witton Gilbert can trace its history back to prehistoric times and this is clearly demonstrated by the ancient stones that are occasionally uncovered in the area. In North Eastern England, only north Northumberland and parts of Teesdale can match Witton Gilbert for its carved Bronze Age rocks.

Several rocks with simple cup-like features have been found throughout the area including two prominent slabs with mysterious cup and ring markings. One of these was found on land belonging to Witton Hall Farm and another found in 1995 on a field belonging to Fulforth Farm. The markings date from approximately 1700 BC.

Subsequent excavation of the Fulforth field revealed that the slab covered one of two burial cists that once housed the cremated remains of prehistoric men. Nearby were carved stones and cobbles, possibly used in the formation of a cairn above the burial chambers.

Ancient carving from Witton Gilbert (FM)

Despite its prehistory Witton Gilbert did not come into being as a settlement until Anglo-Saxon times about two and a half thousand years later. Like other places called Witton it was originally Widu-ton meaning wood settlement, implying that it relied on the felling of wood for its livelihood. The addition of Gilbert to the name came after the Norman Conquest when French was the language of prominent landowners. Witton Gilbert is still pronounced Jilbert with a soft G and the French origin explains the pronunciation, but who exactly was Gilbert?

The Gilbert in question could be either Gilbert de la Leia who owned Witton in the 1100s or Gilbert De Layton who held land here in the following century. The first of these Gilberts played a significant part in the history of Witton Gilbert. He was the owner of the vast Witton estate which in those early days stretched from the River Browney as far north as Beamish, Stanley and Tanfield Lea. In fact the last of these places was once called Tanfield De La Leia after Gilbert's family.

The Bishop of Durham granted this tract of land to Gilbert around 1154 and in a location called Witton Field near the Browney, Gilbert established a leper hospital. It was dedicated to St. Mary Magdalene and was a religious establishment founded for the upkeep of five lepers under the jurisdiction of an almoner.

At least two Norman chapels were built nearby and one, connected with the hospital, may have stood at St. John's Green near the Browney close to where a sewage plant now stands. The other chapel can still be seen, as it is now Witton Gilbert's parish church of St. Michael and All Angels. It was substantially rebuilt in the 1860s but some rounded Norman windows betray its earlier origins. Originally a local chapel belonging to St. Oswald's parish in Durham City, it became a parish church in 1423 following a petition by William Batmanson and other Witton Gilbert residents.

Witton Hall Farm stands close to the church. It looks like a late eighteenth century farmhouse but incorporates masonry from the leper hospital that stood here. The most obvious remnant of the hospital is a pointed window head dating from the late twelfth or early thirteenth century.

Witton Gilbert church (DS)

The church and Witton Hall make up the oldest part of Witton Gilbert village and are situated along a short road (called the Coach Road) that runs south towards the River Browney. This part of the village predates the rest of Witton Gilbert including the village Front Street from which it is now separated by a bypass road. Part of the Coach Road crosses over the bypass by means of a bridge that links the two parts of the village.

The Coach Road area ceased to be the focal point of Witton Gilbert many centuries ago and the old leper hospital probably closed during the dissolution of the monasteries in the 1500s if not earlier. For most of Witton Gilbert's history up until the twentieth century the majority of the village population seems to have lived in Front Street.

Front Street was built in an east to west direction north of the Coach Road and the two roads joined at a T-junction. Precisely when Front Street came into being is uncertain but its construction brought about a complete change in the orientation and focus of Witton Gilbert village.

Witton Hall, a former leper hospital at Witton Gilbert (DS)

Front Street is certainly of considerable age. Some buildings in the street date to the early 1600s, but the street may have come into being long before that time in the medieval period. It is certainly much older than the front streets of most of the colliery villages that surround Durham City.

By the 1700s Front Street was part of a busy turnpike road and a tollgate was erected at the western end where Norburn Lane climbs up towards the summit of Charlaw Fell.

Witton Gilbert was very much an agricultural village in origin and even in the late nineteenth and early twentieth century there was still a predominance of rural trades in the village. There were farmers and farm labourers, masons, carpenters, cartwrights, shoe makers, weavers, a hatter and a tailor.

Much of Front Street still retains the feel of the pre-industrial age and this is especially noticeable at the western end of the street where we find Snook Acres Farm, a lovely stone building dating from 1620.

Snook is an Anglo-Saxon word that can refer to a pointed piece of land or a snake. Either way, the reference is to the winding course of the River Browney which lies to the rear of the farm. It is known that the course of the Browney here was once much more snake-like than it is today.

Next door to Snook Acres Farm is another attractive old building that was formerly a blacksmith's shop. Now a listed building, it was still in use during the early twentieth century and during the First World War horseshoes were forged here for use by the army. Bicycles were also occasionally made. The building is a charming reminder of Witton Gilbert's rural past.

Towards the eastern end of Front Street is an area called the Fold that was once the site of a market where coals and rural produce was traded. It was seemingly in existence before the 1800s and continued trading until the early part of the twentieth century.

In 1801 the population of Witton Gilbert Township was 369 and most people in the area lived in the village itself. By 1861 when the population of the township had risen to 2,098, this was no longer the case as the growth was largely due to the birth of Sacriston, a colliery village that lay within the township.

The growth of neighbouring mining villages also had an effect on the population of Witton Gilbert village itself. Some Witton Gilbert residents swapped their traditional rural employment to work in the mines where wages were often better. Agricultural labourers in particular would have found coal mining a more desirable form of employment, in financial terms at least.

Despite its rural origins many miners came to live in Witton Gilbert. Langley Park Colliery and Charlaw Colliery at Sacriston rented houses for miners in Witton Gilbert, while the Bearpark Colliery owners built four

streets in the village specifically for Bearpark miners. These were located just east of Front Street at the bottom of the Clink Bank, where a playing field now stands alongside the village bypass. This area was named from an earlier association with gypsies who regularly camped there. Clink was an allusion to tin items that gypsies sold from door to door.

The four Bearpark miners' streets on the Clink were demolished after the First World War owing to subsidence and some residents relocated to Bearpark. Others moved into new estates or into what were then overcrowded yards like Best's Yard adjoining Front Street. Bearpark Colliery had operated a small drift to the east of the four streets and they operated another across the Browney slightly nearer to Bearpark. Another drift managed by Langley Park Colliery operated at Kaysburn just west of Witton, but apart from a colliery at Sacriston called Witton pit, there was no actual Witton Gilbert colliery.

Snook Acres Farm, Witton Gilbert (DS)

Pubs, schools and churches were essential services for expanding villages and Witton's Front Street pubs were the Three Tuns, Witton Gilbert Hotel, Oddfellows Arms, Black Lion, Travellers Rest and Glendenning (or Glendinning) Arms. Only the last two of these remain.

Brickwork at the gable end of the Travellers Rest suggests this building was an expansion of an earlier structure as the inner bricks have an Elizabethan type appearance.

Further west, the Glendenning Arms takes its name from a nineteenth century proprietor and it seems that the pub was once a thatched building. The thatched roof was blown off in a gale during the nineteenth century and the dislodged chimney apparently added a sooty flavour to the puddings that Mrs Glendenning calmly served to her guests.

Religion had come to Witton in Norman times but in the nineteenth century new churches were needed for the expanding population. Two Methodist Chapels opened in Front Street in the 1800s but other religious orders were probably represented in the village before that time. These may have included Roman Catholics, although Canon Peter Smarte, the staunch Protestant curate of Witton in the 1620s had fiercely opposed Catholics in the neighbourhood.

Quakers were well established in Witton Gilbert by the 1700s when a family of Quaker farmers called Mason resided in the village and established a Quaker burial ground. It stood on the north side of Front Street across from Snook Acres Farm and headstones could still be seen during the twentieth century.

A little school existed in Witton Gilbert from around 1730, followed by a larger National School built in 1845. The National School was on the south side of the Durham to Lanchester road, east of Front Street near Clink Bank and was extremely overcrowded.

In 1895 a larger school was built close by. Unfortunately like the nearby streets, it suffered subsidence and in 1918 was replaced by a hut in the Coach Road. The hut and a small Wesleyan schoolroom at the western end of Front Street served the community's needs until the 1930s when a new school was built in Sacriston Lane. In 1965, a fire largely destroyed the Sacriston Lane School, forcing pupils to resort to the hut while the damage was repaired. The present Witton Gilbert Primary School still incorporates parts of the 1930s building that survived the blaze.

One other school that should be mentioned in connection with Witton Gilbert was Earls House Industrial School for Boys. Now Earls House Hospital, it was built in 1885 along the main road just south of Witton Gilbert and was originally a kind of remand centre for 150 boys who were educated under strict guidelines. It became a sanatorium in the 1920s and a hospital in 1953. Earls House was once the name of a farmhouse occupying land that is said to have belonged to the Earl of Angus back in the fifteenth century, but the name goes back to at least 1382 when it was mentioned in Bishop Hatfield's survey as Erlehouse. Erle may have been someone's surname.

Today most people in Witton Gilbert live in the private and council housing estates in the northern part of the village. At the end of the nineteenth century there were only two isolated houses in this part of Witton Gilbert. One was Witton Cottage and the other was the White House. Both could be reached from Witton Front Street by a quiet country lane called Back Lane running towards Sacriston. This lane is now a built up road called Sacriston Lane and along with Front Street forms part of the B6312.

The northward expansion of Witton Gilbert began in the early 1900s with the erection of buildings along Back Lane. Some of the earliest buildings included Tile Shed Cottages that can still be seen. They recall a brick and roof-tile factory that stood nearby. Housing estates now dominate Witton Gilbert on either side of the lane.

Other developments occurred from around 1919 with the building of streets at Fair View, Chester Gardens and Hillside that extended northwards towards Rose Lea and the Crescent. They still form the most northerly edge of the village. In the 1960s and 1970s estates developed at Norburn Park in the west and in the Whitehouse Farm area just above Front Street where a private estate has developed with street names like Brookside, Glebeside and Burnside.

However it is Sacriston Lane that links the older and new parts of the village and this street has now more or less replaced Front Street as the focal point of the village. Sacriston Lane is the home of the village shop, school and a modern pub. The street clearly represents the most recent stage of Witton Gilbert's growth and development.

One of the biggest changes in Witton Gilbert's development came in 1996 with the construction of the long-awaited Witton Gilbert bypass road. Throughout the twentieth century traffic had become a major hazard in Witton Gilbert's Front Street as the street was part of the busy A691 Durham to Consett road. Villagers campaigned for a bypass for many years, though not everyone was happy with the eventual chosen route. The bypass cuts off Front Street from the old Coach Road, slicing the village and its farms into two. A quiet road bridge over the bypass now links the Coach Road with the Front Street. The parish church and old leper hospital are now rather isolated from the rest of the village although in fairness few people live in Coach Road today. Fortunately despite the division of the village, the busy bypass road is barely visible and Front Street is now a much safer place to explore.

Langley Park

In the 1850s the valley now occupied by Langley Park consisted of empty fields and scattered farmhouses south of the River Browney. A mile to the east lay Witton Gilbert, tracing its origins back to Norman times and nearby, the village of Sacriston, then only about ten years old.

There was not yet a village called Langley Park, but alongside the River Browney, the small hamlet or village of Wall Nook was already in existence. Wall Nook is thought to be named after a wall at the northern corner of Beau Repaire Park which was one of a number of parks that existed in the area. Wall Nook Mill, dating to at least 1720, was the village's main feature and became a farmhouse after the First World War.

Wall Nook village (DS)

Another place that existed before Langley Park, was Hill Top village that stands, not surprisingly, on a hilltop just south of the village. Here there are superb views of the Langley Park terraces nestling in the valley bottom at the foot of the hill. Hill Top is reached from Langley Park by two rapidly ascending roads that approach it from both the east and the west in two hair pin bends.

The gradient is too steep for Langley Park and Hill Top to be linked directly by a straight road, but a direct uphill route can be taken on foot via the so-called Silly Steps. These emerge rather rewardingly near Hill Top's Board Inn pub. It is said that you cannot be a true Langley Park local until you have climbed the Silly Steps.

Hill Top, known historically as Esh Hill Top owes its origins partly to drift mining that took place here from the nineteenth century. More significantly it seems to have developed as a kind of service village for the Catholic seminary of Ushaw College that lies just to its south. In the 1850s the Durham historian Fordyce described Hill Top as principally occupied by tailors and tradesmen employed by the Ushaw College students.

Returning to the valley bottom, the farmhouses of Blackburn and Biggen House have a long history and lie in open country just west of Langley Park's housing. Furthest to the west is Biggen House, near Quebec and Hamsteels Hall. It looks north across the Browney towards Burnhope hill and in the 1600s 'Biggin' was home to a family called Burnup who took their name from the neighbouring hill. Blackburn farm lies further east closer to Langley Park and in the 1300s was the property of a man called Robert Carlisle.

The Carlisles owned Blackburn and a neighbouring farm called Mauldunderside until about 1488 when the property was sold to the Thirkelds. Mauldunderside is thought to have been named after a tenant called Maud, but by the nineteenth century the farm was simply called Underside and lay beneath the Hill Top slopes called Groove Bank. The last remnants of the farm and two neighbouring farms called Finings and High Finings were demolished in the second half of the twentieth century.

The Finings belonged in the 1850s to the Hedley and Wigham families.

All of these aforementioned farms stood close to a nursing home that was formerly an infectious disease hospital. It stands on the southern edge of Langley Park.

One other farming settlement that should be mentioned in connection with Langley Park was Low Side. This was a small collection of farm buildings and a pond that was just to the north east of Underside. It was swallowed up by Langley Park's expansion in the early twentieth century and became part of the village's Woodside Terrace.

All of these farms were within easy reach of two adjoining muddy country lanes that crossed this low-lying valley on the south side of the Browney. One lane with two little streams flowing along either edge would later become Langley Park's Front Street. The adjoining lane, leading west to Quebec Farm, would become Langley Park's other major thoroughfare that is now called Quebec Street.

The land on the northern side of the Browney had long been known as Langley and is demonstrated by place-names like Langley Mill and Langley House. Langley is an Anglo-Saxon name meaning the long woodland clearing and in later centuries much of this area's history was concentrated in and around the historic Langley Hall.

Langley hall, now in a ruinous and sadly inaccessible state is a fortified Tudor house, almost on the scale of a castle and lies hidden amongst woodland on a lane ascending the slopes that form the fells of Burnhope and Charlaw. This was the Langley of historic times and belonged in the 1100s to Arco, a steward of the Bishop of Durham. Other subsequent owners included the Lisle family of Wynyard, the Percys, and from the 1300s, the Scropes. It was Henry Scrope (the name is pronounced Scroop) that built the huge fortified hall complete with a moat during the reign of Henry VIII.

The ruins of Langley Hall (DS)

Scropes's descendants held the estate up until the 1750s but the hall had fallen into ruin by that time. It is currently included on English Heritage's Buildings at Risk register and it may not be long before it crumbles to the ground.

Climbing to the top of the hill above Langley Hall we find some excellent views. We can clearly see Durham Cathedral and on the horizon, a further twenty miles away, the distant Cleveland Hills. These hills are part of Langley Park's history because it was a railway link from Consett to Cleveland that really brought about the birth of the mining village.

Nineteenth century illustration of the Langley Hall ruins

Ironworks were established at Consett in 1841 but in the 1860s Consett needed better access to the iron town of Middlesbrough and the ironstone of the Cleveland Hills. There were some circuitous rail links between the two towns but a direct route was needed. The Browney valley provided the ideal setting for such a line.

Old doorway, Langley Hall (DS)

In February 1861 construction of the North Eastern Railway Lanchester branch commenced and this line was officially opened the following year. It was initially a single-track line with stations at Consett, Knitsley, Lanchester and Witton Gilbert.

Witton Gilbert station opened in 1862 and the building can still be seen today. It was not located in Witton Gilbert, but at Wall Nook on the edge of what is now Langley Park. Witton Gilbert's name was adopted for the station because Witton Gilbert was the nearest place of significance in 1862. Langley Park simply didn't exist then.

Witton Gilbert Station near Langley Park (MR)

Now a privately owned building, the old station has a rugged stone-built exterior, remarkably similar to another former station at Lanchester that was of course the next station on the line. Witton Gilbert station closed to goods in 1963 and last served passengers in 1939. The line closed in 1966 and is now Lanchester Valley Walk. A railway bridge that crossed Langley Park's Front Street at the entrance to the village was removed along with the line.

It was the railway that caused Langley Park's birth because it opened up mining possibilities in the Browney valley.

Big collieries needed good transport facilities and the railway provided the answer.

In 1870, Lord Lambton, who owned land in the valley accepted an application to search for coal and the following year it was found. The North Eastern Railway doubled the track in anticipation of colliery demand and collieries opened along the line at Bearpark, Malton, Lanchester and Langley Park.

Though Langley Park was originally farmland some small drift mines had already existed at Hill Top village before the arrival of the railway. These mines were incorporated into Mr S.A. Sadler's Malton Colliery that opened in 1870 about two and a half miles west along the Browney near Lanchester. During the twentieth century the drifts at Hill Top were linked to Malton by an aerial ropeway.

Langley Park Colliery came into being in 1874 at the bottom of the valley on the northern side of the river. An unknown person first sank a shaft here in 1871, but it was abandoned due to flooding and incorporated into the colliery at a later date.

In 1874 the sinking of Langley Park colliery was taken over by the Consett Iron Company. The establishment of the mine was fraught with problems and internal flooding almost drowned the workers employed in its construction. It forced a complete upgrade of water pumps used in the process and the seam was not reached until April 1875. Coke ovens were erected south of the river and the construction of Langley Park village also commenced on this bank of the Browney.

Front Street and Quebec Street developed from country lanes, but the first houses were not built in these streets. That honour fell to North Street and South Streets that have since been demolished. They consisted of temporary houses of wood and stone that housed the sinkers

employed in the colliery's construction. Other early streets in Langley Park were East and West Cross Streets, Langley Street, Durham Street and Railway Street. The last of these was built alongside a mass of railway sidings that served the colliery coke works. Housing development also took place at the northern end of Front Street and along Quebec Street and these would become a focus for shops, pubs and other services.

Consett Iron Company built Langley Park's earliest houses in stone using material from a quarry at Hill Top that had also supplied stone for the construction of Ushaw College. Brick was only used in Langley Park houses after the 1880s. It is the stone terraces at the heart of the village that make Langley Park visually appealing despite its industrial origins.

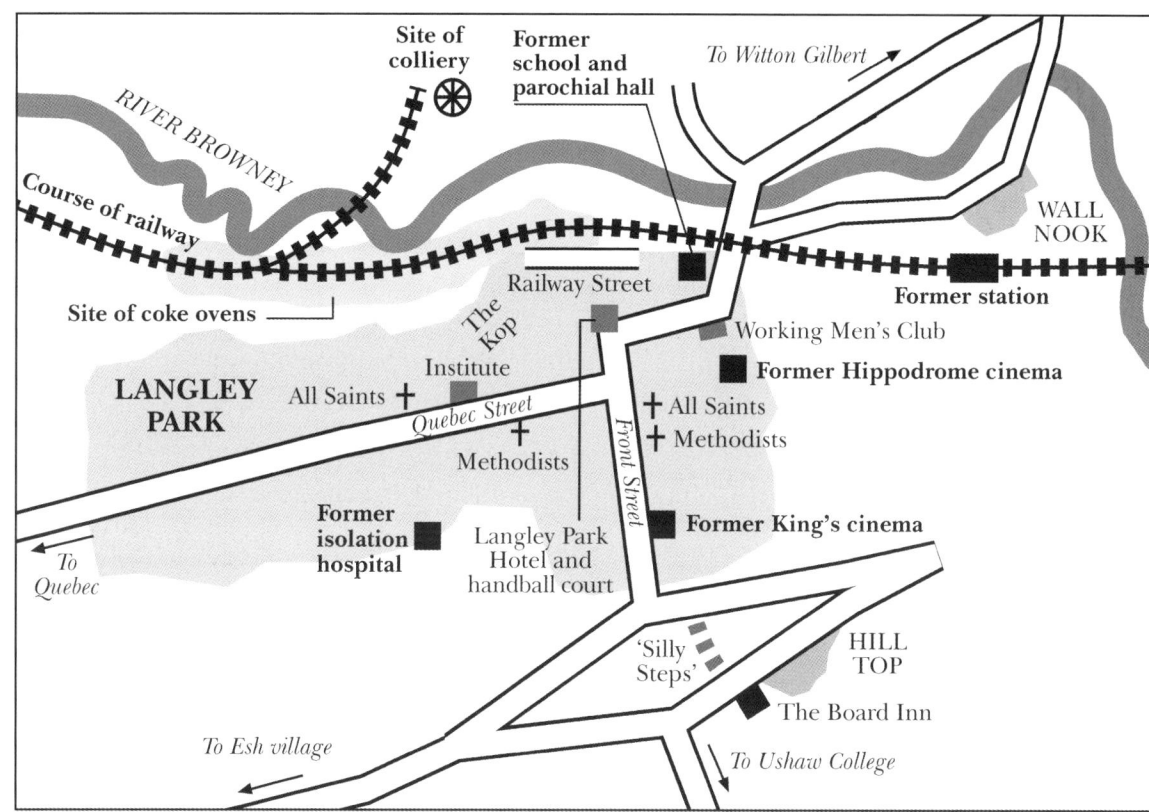

Map showing history of Langley Park (NE)

It is said that only a select breed of men were allowed to work at Langley Park in the early days. The first manager, William Logan an employee of Consett Iron Company was in charge at Langley Park for twenty years and it is said he was very particular about selecting his workers, apparently only choosing those attending interviews with a collar and tie. Those who made the grade included some Cornish tin miners and some former lead miners from Weardale. The new workers required houses, shops, churches, schools and pubs and we now turn our attention to these important features of the village.

Langley Park's most historic pub is the Langley Park Hotel in Front Street. It dates from July 1875 and is built of stone. The pub was built and managed by Consett Iron Company, but in 1909 Newcastle Breweries took it over and through an association with the company logo, it has long been known as the Blue Star Pub.

The pub's most remarkable feature is the old handball court to the rear. Consisting of high walls enclosing a yard it is a listed building protected by law. Handball, also called Fives is an energetic game resembling squash but is played with bare hands rather than a racket. It is still played across the world today but players normally wear gloves. In Durham, where miners' hands were toughened from work at the coal face, they were quite happy to use their bare palms.

For many years the Langley Park Hotel was the only drinking establishment in Langley Park, but the fittest villagers could climb the silly steps to the Board Inn at Hill Top village or head east to the Station Hotel at Wall Nook.

The Board Inn was in existence long before neighbouring Ushaw College was built and may partly date to the 1500s. In the 1800s it was a meeting point for huntsmen as hunting was a significant part of life in this area in times gone by. It continued to be so in the early twentieth century. No less a person than King George V was a guest of Lord Lambton in a shooting trip at Langley Park in 1912, but this particular hunt was held at Kaysburn Wood, just north of Wall Nook.

Handball court, Langley Park Hotel (DS)

Wall Nook was the home of yet another drinking establishment that served the Langley Park area. This was the Station Hotel that served villagers and rail passengers alike. In later years it was called the Gay Tavern until 1974 when it was renamed by its new proprietor, an army major, who called it the Centurion Inn after a Centurion Tank. The hotel served the community until quite recently but is now a private house.

Drinking places in Langley Park today include the Workingmen's Club in Front Street and the Ram's Head in Quebec Street. The Ram's Head was formerly a Butchers Shop established by a family called Coates in 1909 but incorporated an off-licence with its own snug. It officially became a pub in 1951.

Langley Park colliery had only opened in 1874, but by the 1890s the population of the village had risen from about a dozen farming families to 2,000 people, mostly employed in mining. By 1914 the population was 5,000. Education was an important requirement for such an expanding population and Langley Park's first school, called the British School opened north of Front Street in March 1878 with support from the Consett Iron Company.

The village population continued to expand and in 1907 a separate infant school was built further to the south in Wood View followed in 1910 by yet another school (the present primary school) in the south of the village behind Front Street.

Langley Park's first school was no longer suitable and was closed. It was used as a parochial hall for many years and became a youth centre in 1964. The Wood View school is now a Community Centre.

Around 22 shops and trades were in place at Langley Park by the 1890s rising to 37 in 1910. One of the first shops was the Co-operative store but other features of the village built around the turn of the century included the Literary Institute and Library near All Saints Church in Quebec Street. Also not far to the south was the isolation hospital for infectious diseases. This was erected in 1895 in a location that was then slightly away from the village, but is now a nursing home well within the built up area of Langley Park.

From the 1880s Langley Park was well served by churches. All Saints Anglican church in Quebec Street dates from 1887, but probably replaced an earlier, temporary church. Two Methodist chapels were also in place by this time. The Wesleyan Methodist chapel in Front Street was built in 1881 and the Primitive Methodists in Quebec Street in 1883. The two merged in 1977 and now both use the Front Street chapel. Also near here is a Baptist Church of 1895.

The church at Esh Laude near Esh village initially served the spiritual needs of Roman Catholics in Langley Park but before the 1930s and up until the construction of St. Joseph's Church in the 1960s they used St. Joseph's Hall near the former Hippodrome Cinema.

During Langley Park's period of expansion from 1895 to 1920 around thirty new streets had been built in the village. Between 1901 and 1905 an estate called the Kop was built west of Railway Street consisting of Lambton, Darcy and Dale Streets. Kop may be a reference to a Boer War battle or perhaps to German designed coke ovens called Koppers erected at the nearby coke works in 1915.

In 1908 Logan and George Streets were built straight through the gardens of the earlier Railway and Durham Streets and by 1909 streets with names like Ash, Oak and Elm Street were built east of Front Street in a development called New Town.

A Variety Theatre was built in New Town in 1911 that became the Hippodrome Cinema in 1920. It closed in 1960 after 40 years of films in the village and became a bingo hall for a time. It is now in a rather dilapidated condition and its future is uncertain.

After the Second World War, the rival King's Cinema opened in Front Street but in 1953, a fire closed it down. It served as a dance hall and wrestling venue before it too became a bingo hall. Now the headquarters for the coaches of Bob Smith Travel, it is perhaps Langley Park's most prominent building.

Buses and coaches are an important aspect of Langley Park's history and a garage now used by Maddrell's coaches just up from the old cinema was once home to Langley Park's Gypsy Queen service.

Willy Benton, a Langley Park off-licence owner, started this business in the village around 1920. For years he delivered goods to villagers with his horse and cart until the army confiscated the horse during the First World War. In its place Willy bought a car and then in 1920 purchased a charabanc or open-topped bus with a retractable canvas hood. Benton called his fledgling bus service Gypsy Queen, after a horse that unexpectedly won him £3,000 in the Irish Sweepstakes after the race leader and favourite fell at the final fence. Benton acquired newer buses as the business grew but it was eventually bought by Go-Ahead Northern in 1989.

Former King's Cinema, Langley Park (DS)

In the First World War, 73 Langley Park servicemen lost their lives and are commemorated on the War Memorial at the junction of Front Street and Quebec Street. The Second World War claimed the lives of a further 27 men from the village and their names were added to the memorial.

However, Langley Park's most intriguing memorial to the war lies further west along Quebec Street in the graveyard of All Saints church. In May 1942 an elderly Langley Park couple called Mr and Mrs Bolton received sad news from the army notifying them of the death of their son, Private William (Billy) Bolton. His body was returned with full honours and on 21 May his funeral was held and attended by many Langley Park residents. Imagine the shock when two weeks later, Mrs Bolton heard a motorcycle pull up outside her door and Billy walked in. The body of the soldier buried in the graveyard has never been identified but in 1978 the grave was adopted by the Fellowship of the Services who provided a new headstone dedicated with the inscription 'A soldier of the 1939-45 war. Known Unto God'. It is reputedly the only Tomb of the Unknown Soldier in England apart from the one at Westminster Abbey.

Housing developments continued in Langley Park after the war when temporary prefabricated houses opened in Kingsway. They gave way to permanent old peoples' homes in the 1970s in a decade that also saw the building of the Hilltop View estate on the slopes climbing towards Hill Top village. Since 1998 the estate has been the subject of a regeneration project and many houses are currently empty.

Langley Park fell on hard times following the closure of its colliery in 1975 but the colliery site on the north side of the Browney is now Langley Park Industrial Estate. South of the river, the coke works closed back in 1961 and is now the Riverside Industrial Estate. The industrial estates brought new jobs to the village with one of the most unusual enterprises being the popular Diggerland theme park that opened on the Riverside Estate in 2001. Here children operate diggers and other construction vehicles under supervision.

Tourism is not an obvious industry for a former mining village, but the Browney valley and neighbouring Ushaw College are potential attractions of a kind. Langley Park's appealing terraces often attract TV and film crews and have featured in TV shows like the Fast Show and Ripping Yarns. A TV drama about a football team starring Dennis Waterman and Tim Healy, entitled The World Cup a Captain's Tale, was filmed in Railway Street as well as at the Langley Park Hotel. A Langley Park boy played the captain's son. The drama captured the story of a football team from the south Durham village of West Auckland that won the World Cup in the early 1900s.

Aerial view of Langley Park from the north (NE)

Langley Park Hotel (DS)

Langley Park's fame has some unexpected aspects and the village has even featured in the name of a successful late

1980s pop album entitled 'From Langley Park to Memphis' recorded by a local band called Prefab Sprout.

Returning to football, Langley Park has close links with the former England and Newcastle United football manager, Sir Bobby Robson. He was born in nearby Sacriston in 1933 but Robson's family moved to Langley Park when he was still a baby. Robson spent his formative years playing football with Langley Park Juniors before signing for Fulham in 1950 at the beginning of a long and eventful career. As a boy, Robson was taught the bugle by a member of the colliery band and on a day of remembrance at the age of seven, young Robson was honoured to play The Last Post at the grave of Langley Park's Unknown Soldier. There are it seems many aspects to Langley Park's history. It is certainly a place with lots of character and a great deal of community spirit.

Chapter Nine

Satley, Cornsay, Lanchester and Burnhope

In its upper reaches the River Browney, though always a small river peters out into a trickling stream. Near Satley in the south west its valley takes on a typical Pennine appearance and to the north is Lanchester one of the most attractive villages around.

Satley and Old Cornsay are much smaller villages than Lanchester and can be reached on quiet back roads from Durham or from Lanchester itself. It is around here that the typical Pennnine scenery of rolling hills and dry stone walls replace the slightly more urbanised scenery of the colliery districts around Durham.

Satley and Cornsay were little affected by the coal mining that was so prevalent to the east near Durham City and it was rural industries that dominated both of these places

Satley is the most westerly of the two and is about eight and a half miles west of Durham City. It is situated alongside the B6296 in the ravine formed by the Steeley Burn half way between Tow Law and Lanchester. This stream feeds the source of the little River Browney about a mile to the north where the river begins its winding journey towards Durham.

In the nineteenth century Satley included a smithy, a cobbler and a miller and although there was also some stone quarrying most Satley inhabitants worked in farming. Most buildings in Satley are farmhouses and there is one notable barn just outside the village that incorporates the tomb of a notorious livestock thief or mosstrooper called Thomas Raw who died in 1714.

The family called Greenwell owned Satley in the 1300s but later owners included the Marleys and Heswells. Satley was of some importance to the surrounding area, as it was the site of a medieval chapel, but this was a dependent church of Lanchester parish. Satley's present church dates from the nineteenth century.

Satley village (DS)

Satley's most prominent building is however the Punch Bowl Inn which has served the village since the nineteenth century. It has long been popular with travellers and farmers from miles around.

Old Cornsay and Cornsay Colliery

Old Cornsay lies about a mile and a half nearer to Durham than Satley and is situated on a minor road that is off the beaten track. The village dates from Anglo-Saxon times when it was called Cornesho meaning hill

spur of the crane. Strangely, such a bird is rarely found in Britain today and then found only in lowland fens. However if the explanation of the place-name is to be believed it seems that at least one crane found its way north to these Pennine foothills many centuries ago.

Cornsay is a rather scattered collection of stone houses clustered around a large undulating green. In the Boldon Buke, Durham's Domesday Book of 1183, the village belonged to Walter the Chamberlain who annually transported wine, 12 oxen and 2 ropes to the Bishop of Durham's hunting expeditions as payment for the land.

A 200-year-old coaching inn called the Black Horse is a major feature of the village. Built on a road that brought goods and mail from Weardale, it is claimed that a ghost called Mavis haunts the pub cellar and toilets.

Another interesting feature of the village is the stone superstructure built on the green in 1743 to cover the village well. It now incorporates a post box and must cause nervous moments for residents who listen for their post to hit the bottom.

Post Box at Old Cornsay (DS)

The Black Horse pub at Old Cornsay (DS)

Old Cornsay is more correctly just Cornsay but we need to distinguish it from Cornsay Colliery, another village a mile and a half to the east. Cornsay Colliery is on the western edge of the coalfield and its nearest neighbours are old mining villages like Quebec and Esh Winning. Another nearby village called Wilk's Hill between Quebec and Cornsay Colliery was once important for quarrying.

Whilst Old Cornsay and Satley are typical Pennine farming settlements Cornsay Colliery is a more typical mining village. As with neighbouring Quebec, only houses in the main street survive. This street is called Commercial Street and is part of the B6301.

The village's most prominent building is the Royal Oak pub, built with the rest of the village on empty fields and woodland in the nineteenth century. Most of the colliery streets in the village have now gone but stood in the fields across the road from the pub.

Ferens and Love opened the colliery at Cornsay Colliery in 1868 and employed 700 men at the mine and its associated drifts. Some land was leased from Ushaw

College and some streets in the village like Gillow Street were named after the college priests. However, the village was not wholly Catholic and the only church was a Methodist New Connexion Chapel built by Mr Love, the staunchly Methodist coal owner.

Two schools, (one Catholic) were situated at the northern end of the village along with a Temperance Hall that was later a cinema called The Victory. Most of Cornsay Colliery's terraced rows were removed by the mid-1970s and some residents were relocated to Esh Winning's Hamsteels estate.

Cornsay Colliery village (DS)

Cornsay colliery's actual colliery stood at the southern end of the village on the western side of the main road but of almost equal importance to coal mining was the extraction of fire clay that seems to have been particularly abundant at this locality.

Mr Love established a works alongside the colliery specifically for the manufacture of bricks and sanitary pipes using fire clay extracted from the mine. The brick works operated for some time after the closure of the colliery in 1953. The Cornsay Railway of the 1860s linked Cornsay Colliery to the Deerness Railway and ran

along the valleys of the Priest Burn and Hedleyhope Burn from Esh Winning.

A number of outlying drifts operated by Cornsay Colliery were linked to the main works by smaller wagonways. One drift, a mile and a half to the west was situated on the eastern outskirts of Old Cornsay village while another was located at Hollinside near Lanchester about two miles to the north.

The picturesque hamlet of Hollinside south of Lanchester housed Cornsay miners from Colepike drift. It consists of a single row of eighteen houses of which number one and number eighteen are larger than the rest. It was built by Ferens and Love in 1892.

Lanchester

Longovicium was Lanchester's Roman name and although the Roman meaning of the name is open to dispute, later settlers called it 'Lang Chester', meaning long Roman fort. It was certainly a large fort covering six acres and the remains can still be seen today. The site of the fort is just outside Lanchester village on the south side of the B6296 Satley road about a quarter of a mile south west of Lanchester village.

The ancient Roman road of Dere Street crosses the Satley road at right angles making its way north from York to Scotland but the course of this road is hard to find amongst the fields. Longovicium is easier to locate and is situated on private farmland half way between Lanchester and the little hamlet of Hollinside.

Three Roman aqueducts collected water from the hills west of Longovicium and provided water to the fort. They seem to have converged at a point close to where Hollinside now stands. The aqueducts curled their way round the foot of the nearby Humber Hill and it has been suggested that the hill was the site of a Roman signal station that enabled Lanchester to communicate with the neighbouring fort at Ebchester on the River Derwent.

Only very slight traces of the Roman aqueducts can be found, most notably near Hollinside, where a row of trees now grows along its course. In the hills three miles to the west are the slight remains of a semi-circular Roman dam located in the valley of a little stream near Castleside. This dam maintained the correct level of water in one of the aqueducts to ensure a constant supply of water to the fort.

Water at the fort was stored in a number of wells and a reservoir seems to have been located in the south west corner. It was used for drinking and bathing, as a bathhouse is known to have existed at the fort.

Dere Street was built around AD 80 during Roman military campaigns into Caledonia and predates Hadrian's Wall by approximately forty years. Longovicium was built approximately twenty years after the road was completed. The fort was built later than the neighbouring Dere Street forts at Ebchester near Consett and at Binchester near Bishop Auckland. Longovicium appears to have superseded both of these forts in importance and served as an important military garrison on Dere Street. It protected the road's crossing of the River Browney and the neighbouring tributaries of the Alderdene and Smallhope Burns.

There is no public access to Longovicium fort but the local family called Greenwell, who have owned the land since 1633 take every care to protect the site. It is possible to get very close to the fort and a small car park is provided with a helpful information board giving details of the site's history. The information board stands near the north western corner of the fort, but Dere Street itself ran along the fort's eastern flank.

Longovicium was of course a military establishment, but there is evidence of a significant civilian settlement in Roman times just outside the fort to the north and south. Traders, merchants, retired soldiers and Roman soldiers' wives would have resided in such a settlement, but they were not allowed to take up residence in the fort itself. The present Lanchester village site was probably not occupied at the time, but there would be native settlements in the surrounding hills.

Roman soldiers are often perceived as being Italian in origin, but this was rarely the case in Britain. For many years the soldiers garrisoned at Longovicium were Lingones of Gaulish origin, originating from what is now France. During another era soldiers called Suebi (Swabians) of German origin who served in the Roman army were garrisoned at the fort. The fort was occupied for around three hundred years and it is interesting to speculate that some of the fort's descendants may still live in Lanchester.

There is some evidence that Longovicium fell out of use during the first half of the third century but it underwent some restoration in the fourth century when it appears to have come back into use. Although little can be seen on the ground today, the fort is known to have had walls standing 15 feet tall.

Dr A. K. Steer undertook the last major archaeological excavation of the fort in 1937, but in the early 1990s a magnetic survey was undertaken at the fort that provided a very useful insight into the layout of Longovicium. The fort included a headquarters building and a commandant's house along with several other buildings, but there are very few surface traces to be seen.

Two hundred years ago, features remaining at the fort were probably more visible and it is believed that local acts of enclosure in 1773 forced many people to plunder the Roman site for its stone for use in the construction of local farms and walls.

Altar commemorating Garmangabis, Lanchester

Lanchester's parish church and many of the older stone houses in Lanchester village are thought to incorporate stones from the old fort. Some inscribed Roman stones from Lanchester can be seen in Durham University's archaeological museum housed in the riverside fulling mill, beneath the towers of Durham Cathedral while others can be seen at Newcastle's Museum of Antiquities.

One of the most impressive Roman finds from Lanchester is an altar dedicated to the Swabian goddess Garmangabis that can be seen in the village church. It was found in farmland outside the fort and may have been situated in a temple to her honour.

Remains of Lanchester Roman fort (DS)

Little is known of Lanchester's transition from a Roman fort to a medieval village. The fort at Longovicium had fallen out of use by AD 400 when most Romans returned to the continent. Anglo-Saxons from northern Europe arrived in their place establishing Lanchester village north east of the fort.

Initially pagan, the Anglo-Saxons adopted Christianity and may have built a church in the village. It probably stood at the heart of an important Anglo-Saxon estate. Symeon of Durham, a later Norman historian claimed that monks carrying St. Cuthbert's tomb rested one night at Lanchester during the Anglo-Saxon era and this might partly account for Lanchester's continuing importance.

Despite the numerous Anglo-Saxon place-names throughout England, archaeological finds of Anglo-Saxon origin are comparatively rare but Lanchester was the site of one very important find. In 1861 a hoard of 18

Anglo-Saxon iron objects including a sword, knife, blades and tools were discovered by an angler buried in the Smallhope Burn, a mile and a half west of Lanchester near the hamlet of Hurbuck. Dating from the 9th or 10th century, the finds can be seen in London's British Museum and are one of Britain's most important Dark Age hoards.

More is known of Lanchester after the Norman Conquest. In 1183 it was mentioned in the Bishop of Durham's Boldon Buke when Ulf, Meldred, Ulkil and the wife of Galfrid Personis were Lanchester's principal landowners.

Lanchester's beautiful parish church was built in 1147 and is one of the finest medieval churches in the county. It is dedicated to All Saints, but until the late nineteenth century it was the church of St. Mary the Virgin. A white-faced clock on the Norman tower dates from 1902 and replaced an earlier black-faced clock of 1716. Wooden pews by the Yorkshire wood carver Robert 'Mouseman' Thompson were added to the church in 1939.

Lanchester was one of the largest medieval parishes in Durham, encompassing extensive lands between the Rivers Derwent and Deerness. Parish administration and management was undertaken by a Dean based at the Deanery near the church. However, by the nineteenth century, population growth in Durham caused Lanchester parish to be broken up into several new parishes.

For centuries Lanchester village was a quiet rural oasis with trickling burns and mills surrounded by what was then well-wooded countryside and rolling hills. There were of course occasional disruptions. In the early 1300s Edward I and Edward II punctured the peace when they marched with their armies through the village during their Scottish campaigns.

Lanchester village green (DS)

More worryingly, in 1346, David the Scottish King came this way with his army prior to his defeat at the Battle of Neville's Cross. Lanchester residents may have kept well away but there was no escape from the ravages of the plague that hit the village two years later. It would visit again in 1500, 1579 and 1665.

Lanchester village (DS)

Lanchester's Manor House called Maydenstanhall stood half a mile south west of the village centre where Manor House Farm stands today. In Medieval times it belonged to the Prior of Hexham, but later passed to the Hodgsons and Stevensons. For a time it belonged to a London banker called David Bevan but had already been demolished and replaced with Manor Farm when Surtees, the Durham historian, mentioned it in the early nineteenth century. Manor House Farm was not a true manor house and only came to be called a manor after it was acquired by the manor of East Greenwich in London in the late 1500s.

The River Browney meanders its way towards Durham half a mile south of the village, but Lanchester is really located in the valley of the Browney tributary called the Smallhope Burn. A hump-backed bridge once crossed this stream on the edge of the village green in the centre of Lanchester linking Lanchester's Front Street with the road to Durham City. Near this bridge, a smaller stream called Alderdene Burn joined the Smallhope after rather inconveniently flowing along the length of Front Street.

Lanchester village scene (DS)

In times gone by, the two streams were the most significant natural features in the village, but it is easy to miss them today. Both now flow in culverts beneath the village. A culvert was built for the Alderdene Burn in 1904 and culverts for the Smallhope Burn were added in 1937. The Smallhope Burn had cut through the western side of the village green but was diverted to the east and the old course filled in, thus increasing the size of the green. The old humped-back bridge and two other rustic looking bridges have also long since gone.

The village green has long been a feature of Lanchester's landscape. In 1575 it was recorded as the site of the village stocks that were a constant reminder to misbehaving locals. The stocks were still there in 1758 when 1s 2d was paid for their repair. In centuries past the green may have sheltered livestock but in 1898 there was much amusement when a sign was erected declaring 'No donkeys allowed on green except for parish councillors'.

The main road from Durham to Shotley Bridge did not come to pass through Lanchester until 1810 when a turnpike road was built through the Lanchester valley replacing what Surtees described as 'a circuitous route through the heights'. The new road followed the course of what is now the A691 from Durham until reaching Lanchester where it formed a track straight through the centre of the village green. It then continued straight up Lanchester's Front Street.

All this changed in the early 1970s with the construction of a new bypass road that takes the A691 along the western edge of the green. The old road across the green ran close to where the war memorial now stands and its removal made the green even bigger than ever. The creation of the bypass also made Front Street a much safer and more pleasing place to walk.

Most buildings in Lanchester's historic heart predate the industrial age but like many other places in County Durham, Lanchester saw the greatest changes in the nineteenth and twentieth century.

Lanchester workhouse when it was a hospital (NE)

If you glance at old maps or photos of Lanchester you soon notice the imposing Victorian buildings of Lanchester Union Workhouse. Erected in 1839 and extended later in the century these buildings dominated the western side of the village between Front Street and the railway line.

Managed by a board of 28 guardians, the workhouse provided accommodation for the poor and needy in return for the carrying out of menial tasks. Housing around 150 inmates, the workhouse served the population of North West Durham (the Union) but in the census of 1881 a third of the inmates gave their birthplace as Ireland. Most inmates were either older than 50 or less than 16 years of age. Intriguingly, one fourteen-year-old inmate of 1881 was a scholar called Margaret Lanchester. Her birthplace was recorded as unknown.

Old postcard showing Lanchester

The workhouse became Lee Hill Hospital around 1939 and operated until closure and eventual demolition in 1980. A street called Lee Hill Court now occupies the site but the workhouse boardroom survives. For a time this served as a courthouse and police station and has housed Lanchester library since 1973.

The Lanchester Valley Railway opened in 1862 and ran along the western flank of the workhouse. It linked Consett iron works with Cleveland's iron supplies and joined the main line along with the Dearness Railway at Relly near Langley Moor. The Lanchester Valley Railway was dismantled in 1965 and is now the Lanchester Valley Walk.

Lanchester's railway crossed the Smallhope Burn by an iron bridge south of the village before crossing it again via a wooden viaduct a mile and a half to the west at Hurbuck. An embankment now stands on the site of the viaduct. Railway bridges also crossed Newbiggin Lane and Station Road but were demolished in 1972.

North of Station Road, Lanchester's former railway station of 1862 closed to passengers in 1939 and is now a private house in a little park alongside the Lanchester Valley Walk. Day-trippers from Consett and Tyneside once alighted from trains at this station for picnics on Lanchester green and throngs of miners would assemble here on miners' gala day before their journey to Durham City.

Lanchester has far too many pre-industrial buildings of a rural nature for it to be described as a pit village, but it did have its share of mines. Lanchester Colliery was situated on the south side of the railway near a house called Lizards just north west of the village. The colliery owners were Ferens and Love and later Mr S.A. Sadler but the mine was disused by the end of the nineteenth century. Several drifts also existed in and around the village including Fenhall Drift that closed in 1963. At Peth Bank just east of the village, a substance called Witherite was mined between 1930 and 1958. It could be used in the manufacture of paper, glass and paint.

Just south of Lanchester was Malton Colliery, operated by Love, Sadler and later the NCB. It opened in 1870 and from 1890 held the distinction of providing gas for lighting Lanchester village. Malton Colliery closed in 1961 and the site is now more or less occupied by a pretty picnic spot incorporating Lanchester Valley Walk and the little River Browney.

Schools and places of worship are always important in village history and although Lanchester church was built in 1147 the first school was apparently not established until 1748. In 1804 a 25 year old man called John Hodgson (1779-1945) became schoolmaster at Lanchester before he became Curate of Satley and Esh. Later he became the Reverend Hodgson and was famous as the foremost historian of Northumberland.

In 1819 a little Methodist chapel was erected on Lanchester green by public subscription that served as a school on weekdays.

Two new Methodist chapels – Primitive and Wesleyan – were built in 1868 and 1884. They superseded the earlier chapel and the old building became a blacksmith's shop. The congregations of the two new chapels were united in 1945 and one chapel then served for a time as the village hall.

A new school opened on the corner of Newbiggin Road and Front Street but closed in 1964 when pupils were transferred to a new school across the road. The old school became Lanchester Community Centre, taking over this role from the village hall.

A Catholic church and small convent opened in the village in 1901 but was succeeded in 1925 by a new Catholic church of Bavarian design in Kitswell Road.

For a time, nuns from the convent taught children at a Roman Catholic mixed school erected in 1905 but they later returned to the Catholic establishment at Esh Laude. The most important educational development of recent times was St. Bede's Roman Catholic Secondary School. It opened in 1966 and dominates the northern edge of Lanchester.

Former Lanchester railway station (DS)

There are a number of interesting old halls and houses located in and around Lanchester that enhance the desirability of the village and its surrounding countryside. Some halls have since been demolished, but others remain as private residences. However, before we recall Lanchester's historic private homes we should mention that Lanchester also has its share of public houses.

Front Street pubs include the Black Bull and Lanchester Arms that were once posting houses and also the Queen's Head, but the village's most imposing pub is the King's Head. Known to be a hotel by 1900, its date of origin is uncertain as it was previously the site of a private house belonging to an ornithologist called John Hutchinson. In 1840 Hutchinson published a book called Birds of Durham.

The King's Head Lanchester (DS)

Other cultural developments in Lanchester include the Memorial Hall opened near Kitswell Road in 1922. It became the Labour Exchange and Empress cinema and is now the site of a block of flats for the elderly.

In fact housing development has been the most prominent feature of Lanchester's recent history. The village population of 700 or so souls grew very little between 1801 and 1850 and although some growth occurred in the later 1800s, the biggest changes came in the twentieth century.

A council housing estate was erected along Durham Road after the Seond World War and between 1959-1969 the village population doubled with new brick houses supplementing the stone dwellings of the village core. Lanchester is increasingly seen as a desirable place to live and large new housing estates sprung up to the east and west of the village in the 1970s and 80s. By 1988 Lanchester was a home to 4,000 residents, but fortunately despite its growth it still manages to retain its rural charm.

Historic view of Greencroft Hall near Lanchester

Prominent town houses in Lanchester include a late Georgian house called the Lodge near the village bypass. Standing near a 1930s school that is now a college, the Lodge belonged to the Ormesby family who lived in Lanchester from at least the 1500s. In 1798 they built Ornsby Hill House, north east of the village incorporating wells within its grounds. A funeral chute inside the house was used for moving deceased residents downstairs from their deathbeds.

Historic view of Greencroft Tower

At Ornsby Hill, a back road leads a mile north to the site of Greencroft Hall. A Greencroft manor was first mentioned here back in 1183 when the land was shared between the Roughhead and Kellaw families. The Roughhead share passed to the Hall family in 1468 and by this time the Kellaw's share had passed to the Claxtons.

The Claxtons had their land confiscated after the family supported Brancepeth Castle's Earl of Westmorland in the Catholic rebellion of 1569, but the Hall family retained their land despite their Catholic sympathies. After the rebellion Katherine Gray, Westmorland's daughter, took refuge with the Halls at Greencroft. She had been hotly pursued for supporting and assisting banned Catholic priests like John Boste who was executed at Dryburn near Durham City in 1594.

Katherine was captured at Greencroft by a supporter of Toby Matthew, the Protestant Bishop of Durham and imprisoned at Durham Castle. In a letter to the High Treasurer of England, Matthew speculated that Katherine had been illegally married in a Catholic ceremony to one of the Hodgsons of Lanchester Manor.

The Hall family survived the rebellion but during the Civil War, they supported the losing Royalist side and this led them into financial difficulties, forcing them to sell Greencroft in 1670 to the Clavering family of Blaydon.

Allegedly descended from a Norman Knight called Sergo De Burgh, the Claverings built a grand and spacious mansion with gardens, ponds, summerhouses and a deer park. From 1794, Sir Thomas Clavering held the estate but was captured and imprisoned in France by Napoleon's troops and held for four years. After release he preferred to reside with his French wife at Cheltenham.

Sir William Clavering succeeded Thomas, but around 1872 William's illegitimate son, John, became the last male Clavering heir. John's two daughters married some Belgian barons and although their descendants owned the property until the 1930s Greencroft was leased to the Cochranes and then to the Johnsons of Hamsteels.

In 1939 the army acquired Greencroft Hall but it fell into disrepair and was finally demolished in 1960. An impressive Gothic tower in the grounds had been demolished five years earlier.

Returning to Lanchester, part of the village opposite the Ornsby Hill road is called Fen Hall. Tenants here in the 1300s included one John Fenhall, but the Priors of Hexham were its owners in the 1400s. An L-shaped hall once stood in the area incorporating the arms of the Greenwell family.

The Greenwells purchased Fenhall in the early 1600s along with some land at Greencroft but also acquired a place called Ford near the River Browney, half a mile south of Lanchester. The place was subsequently renamed Greenwell Ford. Greenwells have lived near Lanchester (initially in the Satley area) since the 1300s and are still important landowners hereabouts.

Canon William Greenwell who was born at Ford in 1820 was undoubtedly the most famous member of the Greenwell family. Educated at Durham School and Durham University, he was vicar of St. Mary's Church in the North Bailey of Durham City from 1865 and eventually became canon and librarian of Durham Cathedral.

The Greenwell's Glory fishing fly

More significantly Greenwell was an accomplished antiquarian, noted for excavations of ancient barrows and cairns across Britain. Locally, he was President of the Architectural and Archaeological Society of Northumberland and Durham and his translation of ancient documents like the Boldon Buke made County Durham history so much more accessible.

In his spare time Greenwell was a keen angler and learned to fish in the River Browney. He is most famously

remembered as the inventor of the Greenwell's Glory fishing fly. Greenwell Ford house has an eighteenth century facade and lies north of the Browney but a road called Bargate Bank leads south across the river to the hamlet of Bargate. A pub called the Greyhound Inn stood here until 1965 and a tollgate existed nearby.

Greenwell Farm and Colepike Mill are a little further upstream and on the B6296, a mile to the west is Colepike Hall. This area was called Coldpigg, Cowpigg and Colpit in medieval times when it belonged to the sacrist of Durham Cathedral.

The hall later passed to the Scotts, Cooksons, Bowlbys and Robinson-Stoveys and by the nineteenth century was the home of Edward Taylor-Smith who built the present Regency style hall in 1859. Taylor-Smith also built Broadwood Hall a mile to the west, but this was sold to the Penman family in 1888 and they held it until 1958. In 1960 it was sold to Tom Cowie and was replaced with an executive style house.

The original Broadwood Hall near Lanchester

Burnhope and Maiden Law

Maiden Law stands on top of a hill a mile north east of Lanchester where a crossroads leads to Leadgate, Durham and Annfield Plain. It was a hamlet in the nineteenth century and though it grew in the early 1900s it is still very small.

Until 1914 a windmill stood north of the village, but most early buildings were farms. Stone quarrying was important here and collieries were located nearby at Annfield Plain, South Moor and Burnhope. Maiden Law Hospital care home is the most familiar landmark in the village today but it is actually down the bank near Lanchester's Ornsby Hill.

Maiden Law's name is a mystery but one place-name expert has suggested that it was frequented by maidens in ancient times seeking love and fertility from a yet to be discovered fertility stone. Such a stone may have been located on the hill or 'Law'. Interestingly, Lanchester 'manor', at the foot of Burnhope Hill was once called Maiden-stan-hall (Maidenstone Hall) and may be connected with the site. It only came to be called a manor after it was acquired by the manor of East Greenwich in the late 1500s.

Take the Durham road south from Maiden Law and in a mile you reach Burnhope in blustery surroundings on top of a hill 800 feet above sea level. Burnhope's name could mean broomy valley or stream valley but is most likely named from the River Browney that lies at the foot of the hill. This river is rather like a burn or larger stream and was known in times gone by as the Brune.

Burnhope is a much bigger place than Maiden Law and the village is best known as the site of the 750 feet high TV mast that can be seen from miles around. Located alongside the road south west of the village, the mast was built in 1959, the year Tyne Tees Television began its broadcasts to the region.

Just to south of the mast on the Durham road are a couple of houses that once formed a hamlet variously known as Try 'em All, Spite of All and Jaw Blades. The last name commemorates the arch of a whale's jawbone that once stood, quite inexplicably, nearby. Until 1968 the hamlet had its own pub called the Black Horse Inn. Nearby, a little further east was a farm called Stand Against All that was demolished in 1970 following a murder.

Burnhopeside Hall was the home of William Hedley

Burnhope village is situated along the road running north east from the mast towards Holmside and Edmondsley. Housing developments took place at the western end of the village throughout the twentieth century and have continued to expand to within a stone's throw of the mast. However the oldest parts of the village are at the eastern end.

Burnhope developed in the 1840s on empty upland fields after the land was linked by wagonway to areas further north at Craghead and South Moor. The mine and wagonway was developed by the famous industrialist William Hedley who built the Puffing Billy locomotive at Wylam Colliery in 1813.

Hedley lived his later life at Burnhopeside Hall overlooking the River Browney at the foot of Burnhope hill. The Hall dates from 1800 and was acquired by the Hedleys through marriage. Hedley died there in 1843, aged 63 and his four sons continued Burnhope colliery's developments after his death.

At first Burnhope Colliery was called Ibbotson's Sike Pit after a nearby stream but was renamed the Fortune Pit. The village itself seems to have been initially called the Sikes.

In 1845 a stationary engine was erected north of the village on the wagonway where it hauled and simultaneously lowered wagons to and from Craghead. The wagonway at Craghead joined a railway further north at Pelton and this subsequently joined the main line near Chester-le-Street.

The Hedleys built Burnhope village north of the colliery and the village's first school, now demolished, was opened in 1855. A church dedicated to St. John was built close by in 1865 for a new parish called Holmside. Burnhope's church served Craghead, South Moor and Holmside as well as Burnhope itself.

The Annie Pit and Fell Pit opened at Burnhope colliery in 1868 along with a short-lived pit at Jaw Blades, but other mines followed at the colliery in subsequent decades including several nearby drifts.

At some stage the colliery passed to new owners and then changed hands again but the dates are uncertain. We know however that in 1881 the mine was sold to a man called Utrick Ritson. Ritson resided at Muggleswick and was a JP and Deputy Lieutenant of Durham.

The Burnhope war memorial (DS)

The memorial may be Burnhope's most extraordinary monument but the most remarkable event in Burnhope's history undoubtedly took place in 1926 during the General Strike when Burnhope became the only place other than Durham City to host the Durham Miners' Gala.

It was in 1926 that the organisers of the annual Durham event decided that few people would attend the gala that year because of a public transport strike and they cancelled the event altogether. Miners at Burnhope had a different idea and set about organising the gala in their own village. On 23 July, 1926, approximately 40,000 miners from throughout County Durham climbed the hill to Burnhope to be addressed by their leader, A. J. Cook. It was Burnhope's proudest moment.

The church at Burnhope (DS)

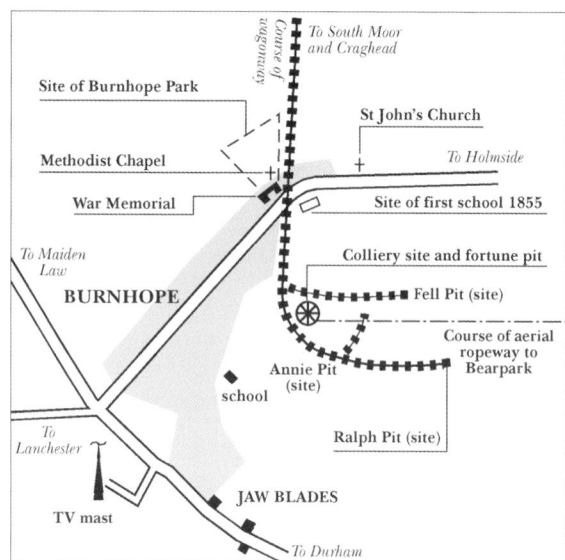

Map showing history of Burnhope (NE)

Noted for his philanthropic gestures, Ritson gave Burnhope a reading room, cricket field and a polo pitch, but the massive and rather striking war memorial is the most remarkable legacy of his time. Built of stylish little red bricks enclosing a memorial garden on three sides, it dates from 1919. Eight recesses incorporate park benches with a gateway at the centre dedicated 'To the Glorious Dead'. The memorial formed the entrance to a park complete with a lake but these have now gone. A Methodist chapel dating from the 1880s stands just within the former park behind the memorial entrance.

Burnhope Colliery remained in the hands of Utrick Ritson's successors until 1939 when Bearpark Coal and Coke Company acquired the mine. A five-mile aerial ropeway was built from Burnhope to Bearpark enabling the movement of Burnhope coal to the Bearpark coke works. Sadly, Burnhope Colliery closed in 1949 shortly after it was acquired by the National Coal Board.

Chapter Ten

Sacriston, Edmondsley and Plawsworth

To the north of Durham City lie the villages of Holmside, Edmondsley, Sacriston, Kimblesworth, Nettlesworth and Plawsworth. These places come in a great variety of shapes and sizes with the town-like settlement of Sacriston at the centre being the largest.

In the east stands the village of Plawsworth near to which lies the lush and sparsely settled farmland along the banks of the River Wear. Here are little known farms like Harbour House, Southill, Nag's Fold and at the southern fringe are the beautiful ruins of Finchale Priory. Across the river to the east lie Great Lumley, Cocken and the Raintons.

The scenery around Plawsworth is in marked contrast to that around Sacriston to the west. After crossing the Great North Road that splits Plawsworth from its near neighbour at Kimblesworth the land gradually rises. Much of the area around Sacriston is dominated by moorland and this becomes especially apparent as we climb to the summit of the hill called Charlaw Fell on Sacriston's western flank. Here the views stretch for miles

as they do at neighbouring Burnhope to the west or at Waldridge Fell to the north near Chester-le-Street.

Attractive woodland intersects the landscape here and there and this is most notable between Burnhope and Charlaw but it is also very apparent on the western edge of Sacriston. There are numerous little-known but richly wooded valleys formed by tiny streams, especially around the villages of Holmside and Edmondsley on the northern edge of Charlaw.

Holmside

Holmside is a pretty little village in a tiny valley formed by the Wardles Burn half way between Burnhope and Edmondsley. Not to be confused with Hollinside near Lanchester, Holmside developed in the late nineteenth century and was inhabited mostly by coal miners who worked at neighbouring collieries like Craghead, Edmondsley and Sacriston. In fact the mine at Craghead, was often called Holmside Colliery.

Holmside village (DS)

There is no church in Holmside village because Holmside's parish church, built in 1869, is actually

situated in the village of Burnhope two miles to the west. An inconvenience perhaps, but before this time Holmside was part of the parish of Lanchester when people had a much longer journey to make.

Scenery at Warland Green (DS)

There seems to have been a school at the northern edge of Holmside village from 1844 but this unfortunately closed before the end of the nineteenth century. Nevertheless, despite the distant church and lack of school, Holmside saw some further growth in the early twentieth century. It is still nevertheless a very small place by Durham village standards.

Holmside village did not come into being until the late nineteenth century, but the southern part of the village encompasses an earlier hamlet called Warland Green. This was first mentioned under the name Warlandes back in 1311 and the medieval name means taxable land, belonging to a villein or feudal tenant.

Warland Green was already well-developed by the 1850s when its buildings were clustered around the Wardles Bridge Inn, a pub that still exists today. Wardle probably comes from the name of the Wardel family who owned nearby Edmondsley in the seventeenth and eighteenth centuries. West Edmondsley Cottage and West Edmondsley Farm formed part of the Warland hamlet.

The Wardles Bridge Inn (DS)

The Eller Burn and Whiteside Burns meet at Warland where they become the Wardles Burn. Half a mile to the east the stream becomes the Cong Burn after further streams feed it from Holmside Hall and Wheatley Green. Cong Burn is an historically important rivulet that joins the River Wear at Chester-le-Street. It most famously gave its name to Concangis, the Roman fort of Chester-le-Street.

Just north of Holmside is a house called Wheatley Green, that was part of a farm described by Surtees, the nineteenth century Durham historian as a village of neat tenements. It is situated on Wheatley Green Burn, a tributary of the Cong. Known as Whitley and Whetlay in earlier times, the manor was held by the Umfravilles in the 1300s, and later belonged to the Earls of Westmorland. In the early 1900s some relatives of mine called Littlefair farmed here, but only a private house remains today.

A quarter of a mile to the north of here, the road from Wheatley Green joins the Edmondsley-Craghead road or Black House Lane as it is known. A Black House Inn is shown at this junction on the 1850s map where we now find the Charlaw Inn.

A hamlet of houses called Blackhouse clusters around the inn but Blackhouse was also the name for a village of a hundred or so houses that stood in what is now an empty field near Edmondsley a little further east.

This older Blackhouse village was established in 1925 and consisted of 164 houses. Part of the village was called Claytonville after an early twentieth century headmaster at Edmondsley School. The whole village was demolished in 1978 owing to persistent problems with dampness. Residents were re-housed in new homes at Edmondsley's Jubilee Close.

The now demolished village of Blackhouse (NE)

The historic Holmside Hall lies in the countryside to the west of Holmside village and further west is yet another old mansion called Little Holmside Hall. Little Holmside is of the greater architectural importance but much of Holmside's early history is centred upon the other Holmside Hall. Both halls are Grade 2 listed buildings and are now private properties.

Little Holmside Hall (DS)

Holmside Hall was first recorded in the Boldon Buke of 1183 as Holneset and is thought to mean Holly fold or Holly Stable. Perhaps its name is associated with Holm Oak trees that have holly-like leaves.

Early Lords of Holmside took the surname Holmside, but the family seem to have died out. By the late 1300s Holmside belonged to the Umfravilles, a powerful northern family of Norman origin who may have built the hall. It was built as a defended manor and this fact is betrayed by the slight remains of a medieval moat. The moat surrounded the whole collection of buildings including a chapel that stood nearby.

Holmside Hall was probably built around a courtyard but underwent many alterations in the seventeenth, eighteenth and nineteenth centuries. Unfortunately little of medieval origin remains today. The hall passed through marriage from the Umfravilles to the Tempest family but was seized from the Tempests after 1569 following their involvement in a Catholic rising.

Holmside was home to Sir Henry Gate in 1573, but he was only the tenant of the new owner, the Manor of East Greenwich. In 1595 the property passed to Henry Jackman and then to Sir Timothy Whittingham in 1613. The estate was divided up during ownership by Sir Timothy's grandson, who was also called Timothy and the division resulted in the building of Little Holmside Hall in the later 1600s.

The older hall passed to the Spearmans and as a result of a Spearman marriage became the property of Thomas Wilkinson of Witton Castle who owned it in the early nineteenth century.

Little Holmside Hall, built around 1668, was initially the property of John Hunter of the Hermitage. It was described in the 1950s as 'one of County Durham's best small country houses', by the architectural historian Nikolaus Pevsner but Pevsner also commented on the building's pitiful state of decay.

Fortunately a local solicitor acquired the hall in the late 1980s. He received a Durham County Council Environment Award for what was described as an 'heroic restoration of the property.'

Edmondsley and Daisy Hill

The village of Edmondsley, north of Sacriston dates to Anglo-Saxon times but is first mentioned in Durham's Boldon Buke of 1183. A decade later it also receives a mention in a medieval manuscript about the Life of St. Godric of Finchale. A short chapter describes the miraculous cure of a woman called Eda of Edemannesleye.

Early spellings of Edmondsley suggest it was the 'ley' or clearing of a shepherd. It seems that Edeman was an old word for a herder of sheep. However there was also a possibility that Edmondsley was named after Eda's man – the husband of the aforementioned Eda.

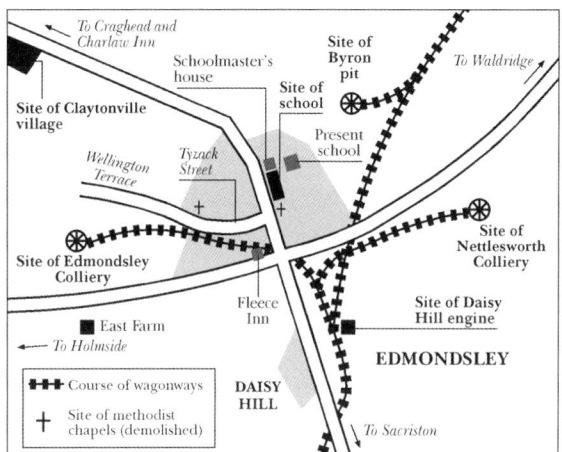

Map showing history of Edmondsley (NE)

Edmondsley is situated on Edmondsley Fell, a moorland location between the fells of Waldridge and Charlaw and the three fells provide good views of distant Tyneside and the Durham countryside to the north and east. Robert Surtees, Durham's early nineteenth century historian, described Edmondsley as a medieval manor carved out of the wastes of Chester-le-Street.

Edmondsley probably didn't exist as a village in medieval times. Early references to the place really concern farms and associated land along the south side of the Cong Burn between the present village and the settlement of Holmside to the west. Early recorded owners of Edmondsley included William de Edmansley who died in 1362 and John Killinghall in the later 1300s. The Sacrist of Durham Cathedral also held Edmondsley land around this time. Other Edmondsley owners in the late fourteenth century included the Umfravilles and Nevilles.

During the fifteenth century Edmondsley belonged to John Herdwick but had passed to the Tempests and Claxtons by the 1500s. Their lands were confiscated after their involvement in a Catholic rebellion and Edmondsley became the property of a Berwick sea captain and a London goldsmith.

Edmondsley 1966 (NE)

John Heath of Kepier (near Durham) purchased Edmondsley in 1573 but the Heaths granted it to the Wardel family of Easington in 1632. The Wardels held East Edmondsley Farm (near the present village) until 1757 when it passed through marriage to the Reed family. However, West Edmondsley Farm near Holmside village remained a Wardel property and the family is still remembered there in the name of Wardles Bridge.

Edmondsley pit village did not really come into being until 1840 with the opening of Edmondsley colliery. Who started the colliery is not clear, but coal had been mined on a small scale in the neighbouring Charlaw area since medieval times. The establishment of a larger colliery enterprise was a natural progression. It is known that Edmondsley Colliery was initially called 'Wellington Pit' and was owned by a Mr Tyzack of Sunderland in the 1850s. He gave his name to Tyzack Street (pronounced Tissack) in the village. However by the 1890s, Edmondsley Coal Company owned the mine. Edmondsley Colliery continued to operate under this company until the colliery's eventual closure in 1921.

At the western end of Tyzack Street a lane leads off slightly to the north following the course of an old colliery street called Wellington Terrace. This terrace existed before Tyzack Street and appears on the 1850s Ordnance Survey map but only a few of its houses remain.

Edmondsley colliery stood close by and a wagonway ran from the colliery along part of the terrace and then diagonally through the village centre. Two pubs were located on either side of the wagonway. One pub, the Fleece Inn, still remains and you can see that a corner of the pub was chamfered to allow coal wagons to pass by smoothly at a tight angle. At Daisy Hill, a quarter of a mile south of Edmondsley, the wagonway joined the wagonway from Sacriston.

Daisy Hill developed later in the nineteenth century than either Edmondsley or Sacriston and is the smallest of the three places. A large co-operative store existed here as did a pub called the Crown Inn, but there was no Daisy Hill colliery. There was however a stationary engine north of Daisy Hill that hauled wagons up the hill from Sacriston Colliery and under Daisy Hill's main road.

The engine then lowered the wagons downhill to Waldridge Fell, past a short-lived Victorian mine called Byron Pit. This pit was linked to the wagonway a quarter of a mile north east of Edmondsley. A pit close to this site was once blown up by a French film crew for the recreation of a mine explosion.

Old school house at Edmondsley (DS)

From Waldridge the wagonway from Edmondsley joined a railway at Pelton where coal was transported to the Tyne. Wagons from Edmondsley and those from another short-lived nineteenth century mine called Nettlesworth Colliery were also hauled by the Daisy Hill engine towards Waldridge.

Edmondsley, though larger than Daisy Hill, was always smaller than Sacriston and never had a parish church. There were however two Methodist chapels and a school. Edmondsley's Wesleyan Methodist chapel of 1881 was located near Wellington Terrace and was demolished in the early 1970s. In 1875, the Primitive Methodist Chapel and an adjoining school had been built on the east side of the main road from Durham. This section of road was called Hunters Terrace after the Nettlesworth Colliery owners. Sadly, the terrace, school and chapel were all demolished in the 1960s. Only the schoolmaster's house of 1881 remains with a more recent school tucked behind.

Sacriston

Sacriston is a former mining village located two miles north west of Durham City. It developed in the middle of the nineteenth century on empty moorland, although a medieval manor house stood nearby.

Evidence of Bronze Age occupation has been found at nearby Witton Gilbert and settlers of the Iron Age and Roman period probably knew the Sacriston area too. It is also notable that Edmondsley, just north of Sacriston, is almost exactly half way, as the crow flies, between the Roman forts of Lanchester and Chester-le-Street.

Anglo-Saxons succeeded the Romans in the north and their presence is demonstrated by Anglo-Saxon place-names like Plawsworth, Findon, Fulforth, Witton and Edmondsley. In truth Anglo-Saxon place-names are found everywhere and it is actual Anglo-Saxon finds that are quite rare. It may be significant that a gold Anglo-Saxon pendant of the seventh century AD was found at Daisy Hill between Sacriston and Edmondsley in 1991. Somewhat mysteriously, the design of this pendant does not seem to originate in northern England. Now part of the collection of the Bowes Museum the pendant was found on a building site, and may have arrived in Sacriston as the result of landfill.

Anglo-Saxon pendant found near Sacriston (BM)

Charlaw Fell rises to the west of Sacriston with a densely wooded ridge at its base that makes a definite ninety-degree turn at Edmondsley. This wooded slope skirts the western fringe of Daisy Hill and Sacriston. The Anglo-Saxons called the sharp bend a Cerr, although they may equally have referred to the steep ascent. Pronounced chare, the word gave rise to the name of Charlaw or Cherlawe, as the hill was still called in the 1200s. Charlaw could literally mean bending hill.

Sacriston's history is focused upon the wooded base of the hill as it runs south from Sacriston Wood to Fulforth Wood. The land just below the wood was the site of the two collieries that brought about Sacriston's growth. A hill spur called the heugh (pronounced yuff) formed by the wood was also the home of the medieval manor house that gave Sacriston its name.

Hugh Pudsey, a Bishop of Durham gave the hill spur and its surrounding land to the Sacrist of Durham Cathedral monastery in the 1100s. Revenue from farming this land was used for financing the sacrist's work and a manor house was built for the sacrist in the thirteenth century.

Sacrists were senior monks responsible for sacred relics, vessels, vestments, lighting, heating, sweeping and cleaning the monastery. Also called sextons or sacristans, their title derived from segrestein, a medieval English word of French origin.

In the 1300s the Sacrist's manor at Sacriston was called Segrestaynheugh and was farmed by the Durham monks. The estate, but not the manor house, was let to some Durham City merchants in the 1400s but in the 1500s the house was home to a retired soldier called Leonard Temperley. Following the dissolution of the monasteries in the later 1500s the house and estate passed to Durham Cathedral's Dean and Chapter.

On a 1576 map the manor is called Segerston Heugh but was sometimes called Sacristan Heugh. When the mining village developed in the nineteenth century it adopted the name Sacriston rather than Sacristan possibly because it looks more like a village name. However, it is notable that many locals still use the old pronunciation Segerston.

Remnants of the medieval manor house survived in Heugh House, a farm building on a cleared area above the wood at Sacriston Heugh. Unfortunately, this building was demolished in the 1950s owing to mine subsidence, but the site can still be reached by a footpath.

Agriculture was the main activity at Segerston Heugh, Fulforth and Findon in times past, but small-scale mining had taken place in the area since medieval times. When larger collieries developed at Sacriston in the nineteenth century, traces of medieval workings were occasionally uncovered.

Although Sacriston's mining village came into being in the mid-1800s, one of the two collieries that stimulated the birth and growth of Sacriston had been operating as early as the 1700s. Records show that in 1733, Charlaw Colliery, on the edge of the wood was leased to a certain Ralph Ferry for a period of 21 years.

Old photograph showing the now demolished Heugh House at Sacriston (GN)

A little later, in 1740 a pit at nearby Findon Hill was also mentioned in a 21 year lease to a man called John Richardson. These were however tiny mines employing small numbers of people and brought no major population changes to the district.

It was a century later in 1839, that the Charlaw mine reopened as a larger enterprise. At around the same time a colliery also opened further north along the woodland edge below Segerston Heugh. It was these two mines that brought about the birth and growth of Sacriston.

In 1800 the site of Sacriston village was empty moorland that was broken up into fields by acts of enclosure in 1809. There were scattered remnants of coal workings throughout the area, dating in some cases to medieval times, but there was no mining village.

At Sacriston Heugh, thick woodland separated the land that was to become the village, from the higher ground of Charlaw Fell to the west. There was no village but there were several farmhouses including the old manor house of the Durham sacrist at Sacriston Heugh. Other farm buildings included Nettlesworth West House, Fulforth Farm near Witton Gilbert, Acorn Close on a lane ascending Charlaw Fell and two farmhouses at Findon Hill.

Until the 1830s the only village in the area was Witton Gilbert, then a little agricultural village to the south. The Sacriston crossroads, at the heart of the area, was no more than a meeting of dirt tracks from Plawsworth, Witton Gilbert and Durham. Further north on the western side of the track that became Front Street stood Lingy House Farm. This was one of the oldest houses in Sacriston but was demolished in recent times. It was replaced by modern houses in St. Cuthbert's Drive.

Sacriston village really came into being in 1839 when a colliery called Victoria Pit opened below the woodland of the Heugh. At about the same time Charlaw Colliery reopened only a quarter of a mile to the south. Coal from the two collieries was transported using the newly constructed Sacriston wagonway. A stationary engine at Daisy Hill hauled wagons along this wagonway to Waldridge Fell from where a railway transported coal to the Tyne for shipment.

Edward Richardson of West Hendon and Joseph Hunter of Walbottle owned Charlaw Colliery in 1839. They may have also owned Victoria Pit, but the ownership of this pit is unclear and changed frequently in the early days.

One unusual change of ownership took place in April 1851 when a remaining two-year lease of the Victoria Pit was sold at auction. The working stock had already been sold and the sale of this short lease attracted little interest at the auction. Eventually, after a solemn pause, a humble grey-haired miner called Peter Strong plucked up the courage to shout to the auctioneer 'I'll gie ye a farden sir'. It caused amusement and laughter amongst those attending, but the auctioneer requested a coin of higher value. The same miner and a colliery viewer then simultaneously offered a shilling, but the bid was rejected because they had shouted together. Finally, Peter made a brave offer of 2 shillings and this was accepted. One of his colleagues remarked 'Peter, thoo's been a poor pitman lang enough, but thoo's a greet coal owner noo!'

Sacriston in 1904

How Peter made use of his purchase is not recorded but the mine passed later to a Mr Bell. It then passed to William Hunter and George Elliot who became owners of Charlaw, Kimblesworth and Nettlesworth Collieries. The mines amalgamated in 1890 as the Charlaw and Sacriston Colliery Company.

Charlaw Colliery had closed six years earlier in 1884, but in 1859 its owners had sunk a new mine called Witton Pit, a little to its south and this continued operating after 1884.

Victoria and Witton Pits were by then a single colliery called Sacriston Victoria and their workings were linked. A colliery coke works opened in between the two pits in 1891. Six years later a new mine called Shield Row drift opened behind the coke works as part of the colliery. Other drift mines opened at Sacriston Colliery in the 1930s and 40s (see map on page 122).

Early housing in Sacriston was centred upon the village crossroads on the south side of Witton Road and adjoining parts of the Durham Road. There was initially less development on other parts of the crossroads, but Plawsworth Road was the site of a smithy.

North of the crossroads, a series of colliery terraces called the Cross Streets, clustered along the eastern side of Sacriston Front Street consisting of five basic streets of ten back-to-back terraces with narrow alleyways in between. Cross Street inhabitants included a significant number of Irish families. Indeed a doctor visiting Sacriston in the 1860s remarked upon black-shawled Irish women squatting at doors smoking clay pipes. However, Sacriston's Irish population, though significant, was probably no greater than most other Durham pit villages.

A school opened across the road from the Cross Streets around 1844 but Sacriston parish church did not open until 1866. Pubs called the Boot and Shoe (later the Queen's Head), Colliery Inn (replaced by a building of the same name in 1902) and George and Dragon served the community and are on the 1850s map.

Later nineteenth century developments included the construction of the Staffordshire Streets on the western side of Front Street. These were really one very wide street of two rows. The Staffordshire Streets were probably built around 1860 and commemorated an influx of miners from the south Staffordshire coalfield. Down the centre of the street were outhouses dividing it into two parts.

Where the street joined Front Street, the terraces were divided by a Wesleyan Methodist chapel, but after the First World War the Sacriston Memorial Institute was built on the site.

St. Peter's church and vicarage, Sacriston (DS)

Other developments took place behind the Cross Streets where Elliott, Hunter and Blackett Streets were built as part of an area called New Town, while Church Street was built to its north. The Cross Streets were demolished around 1939 and the inhabitants moved to new housing south of Plawsworth Road. The Staffordshire Streets were also demolished, as were many streets in the New Town development. In fact little now remains of Sacriston's early streets.

By the 1890s Sacriston was virtually a town. It was a thriving mining community of hard working miners with a good share of drinking places to quench the miners' thirsts. Pubs like the Robin Hood were established in the village by the end of the nineteenth century and from the 1920s this pub and another called the Colliery Inn were also satisfying the pitmen's passions for gambling and

sport. Handball courts were built at the rear of the two pubs, where miners played the squash-like game, called Fives using their hands. Gambling was an important feature of these games and miners liked to bet on the result.

Back in the nineteenth century Sacriston had a bit of a reputation for drinking, gambling and occasional lawlessness. Fortunately there were several religious institutions keeping things in order. By the end of the

nineteenth century, there was one Anglican church, one Roman Catholic church and three Methodist chapels.

As in many Durham villages Methodism was represented by the Wesleyan, Primitive and New Connexion sects. Methodist chapels were built in several different locations in Sacriston during the nineteenth century but St. John's, the prominent Methodist Chapel on the western side of Front Street came quite late and only dates from 1898.

A Sacriston scene (NE)

Sacriston's Church of England parish was created in 1863 from parts of the parishes of Chester-le-Street and Witton Gilbert. It initially encompassed Sacriston, Findon Hill, Daisy Hill, Edmondsley, Nettlesworth and Plawsworth Gate.

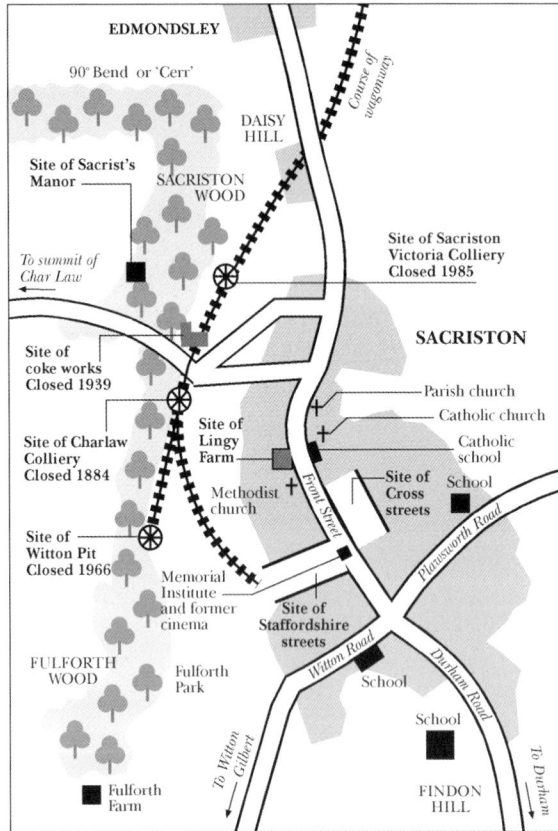

Map showing history of Sacriston (NE)

A mission church served the area, until St. Peter's parish church opened in 1866. The vicarage was built behind this church in 1868. The church and vicarage were built in what was then open countryside north of Sacriston on the road to Edmondsley.

Sacriston was only slightly bigger than Edmondsley in those days and since Edmondsley was part of the parish, the midway location of the church suited both places. Daisy Hill (in between Sacriston and Edmondsley) would not develop as a settlement until the later nineteenth century.

In the 1890s a field still separated Sacriston's parish church from the rest of Sacriston village. South of the field, on the northern edge of the village stood St. Bede's Roman Catholic church of 1881 and St. Bede's Catholic school in nearby Front Street. St. Bede's church and school still serve Sacriston today, but housing along Front Street now occupies the once empty land that separated the Catholic and Anglican churches. The catholic school once overlooked Lingy House Farm (now demolished) on the opposite side of Front Street and was one of a number of schools serving Sacriston by the 1920s. Two schools had opened on Witton Road near Sacriston crossroads around 1912 and are now Sacriston Junior and Infant Schools.

There were also Sunday Schools in Front Street but Fyndoune Community College and Plawsworth Road Infant School came much later in the century.

Sacriston's educational and religious needs were supplemented by a choice of recreational facilities. In 1932 part of Fulforth Wood opened as a public park called Fulforth Dene, tucked away behind a series of allotment gardens. For those preferring indoor entertainment dance halls and cinemas were an important feature of Sacriston life from 1900 to 1960.

A concert hall called Club Hall was built near Front Street in the early 1900s and dance venues included the Store Hall in Plawsworth Road and Drill Hall in Charlaw Lane.

Sacriston's first two cinemas were the Victoria Picture Hall and the Theatre Royal, both established in 1921. Victoria Picture Hall burned down in 1941, but stood behind the Post Office on the eastern side of Front Street north of the crossroads. It had been built as a concert hall in 1897. The Theatre Royal cinema in Church Street closed in 1931 but reopened for a short time in the 1950s.

The two cinemas were known as Top and Bottom Pictures but were supplemented in 1924 by a 'Middle Pictures' called the Institute Pictures. This cinema occupied the upper floor of Sacriston Memorial Institute, a building opened after the First World War on the site of a Methodist chapel. The Institute's lower floor included a billiard room and reading room. In 1961 the whole building was severely damaged by fire and hastily rebuilt. It was reopened as a community centre in a ceremony performed by the Sacriston born actress, Wendy Craig.

In 1937 the management of the Institute supported the construction of yet another cinema in Sacriston but this did not come into being until 1957 when a purpose built cinema was built next door. This was a short-lived enterprise and was used as a bingo hall from 1962. Now a furniture store, the canopy over the pavement betrays its original purpose.

Historic view of Witton Pit at Sacriston

Of course Sacriston's lifeblood was always the colliery on the wooded western fringe of the village. Dating to 1839, developments had taken place at the colliery in the 1920s and 30s with the opening of new drifts, but the coke works of 1891 closed down in 1939, in the colliery's 100th year. The following year Sacriston was shocked by further sad news when five of its miners were killed by a roof fall at the pit. Sacriston's Witton Pit closed in 1966, and in 1981 the remaining Victoria Pit was listed for closure. Despite a reprieve and the long miners' strike of 1985, Sacriston colliery finally closed on 15 November, 1985. It was a sad end to an important chapter in Sacriston's history but was by no means an end to Sacriston's history. Sacriston lives on and is here to stay.

Aerial view of Sacriston (NE)

Kimblesworth and Nettlesworth

Nettlesworth and Kimblesworth are former mining villages on the western side of the Great North Road between Chester-le-Street and Durham. On the 1850s map Nettlesworth was called Broadmires and consisted of terraced rows. Nearby, south east of the village was a tiny settlement called Tan Hill where Kimblesworth and Nettlesworth now meet. Kimblesworth does not seem to

appear on this map but closer examination reveals a little cluster of farmhouses and cottages called Kimblesworth, half a mile south of today's village. Later maps call this particular settlement Kimblesworth Farm or Kimblesworth Grange and it still exists today.

Kimblesworth was first mentioned in the 1220s, but dates to Anglo-Saxon times when it was Cymel's enclosure. Surtees, the Durham historian, writing around 1820 describes Kimblesworth as a village of two or three farmhouses and a few cottages to the left of the Great North Road. Since the present Kimblesworth didn't exist in his day, Surtees must have been referring to Kimblesworth Grange. In the 1850s, another Durham historian called Fordyce referred to the same place as having eight houses and two farms. The population in 1851 was only 36.

In a field south of Kimblesworth Grange there once stood a church. Nothing can be seen on the ground, but aerial photographs reveal the outline of a little building with an apse. This was Kimblesworth church and had already fallen into ruin by 1593 when parishioners transferred to Witton Gilbert.

After describing the foundations of the old Kimblesworth church, Surtees mentions very evident embankments north east of Kimblesworth on the edge of the Great North Road. He reveals that these formed the 'Vivarium de Kimblesworth', an artificially created fishpond, mentioned in a charter of Bishop Pudsey in the 1100s. The pond is still recalled in the name of Stank Lane, an old farm track leading up to Kimblesworth Grange from Pity Me garden nursery, half a mile to the south. A Stank was a fishpond or dam. The pond may have somehow been linked to, or was perhaps the larger version of a mere or lake that is sometimes thought to have given rise to the name of Pity Me. This often-discussed place name is sometimes said to derive from Petit Mere meaning little lake.

In the 1400s Kimblesworth belonged to the Eure family and passed to the Tempests of Holmside, who forfeited the land after the 1569 rebellion. Elizabeth I then gave Kimblesworth to the trustees of Robert Bowes from whom it passed to the Sandford family.

Cottages at Kimblesworth Grange (DS)

On 8 September, 1675, Richard Sandford of Kimblesworth was murdered in London and his land passed to his son, Richard, who was born, it is said, on the hour of his father's death. This Richard died without an heir and Kimblesworth passed to the Honeywoods and then to the Lambtons.

Nettlesworth, meaning enclosure of nettles, is mentioned in 1286 and although there are early records of its ownership, its original location is unclear. Surtees and a sixteenth century map of dubious accuracy place Nettlesworth south west of Plawsworth, but in 1894 Whellan's Directory of Durham places it to the north west. This was certainly the site of Nettlesworth Hall that stood until recent times on a pathway between Nettlesworth and Edmondsley. The hall was probably at the heart of Nettlesworth manor that belonged to a family called Gategang in the 1300s.

In later years Nettlesworth passed to the Hagthorpes, Wessingtons and by the early nineteenth century to the Askews. The Askews also acquired two smaller properties nearby. One property called Holemyers had once belonged to Kepier Hospital (in Durham City), the other called Broadmires lay slightly to the east.

In the 1850s Nettlesworth Colliery opened up near Edmondsley and I believe the now demolished terraces of Front Street and Back Street near Broadmires' Ugly Lane were built to accommodate the miners.

The actual street called Broadmires Terrace including the Black Bull Inn came later in the century. Broadmires village was presumably renamed Nettlesworth through an association with Nettlesworth colliery. In fact three mines called Nettlesworth existed in the area at one stage or another.

Nettlesworth's first colliery owner was Sir George Elliot of Houghton Hall who in partnership with William Hunter of Sandhoe, Northumberland, also opened Kimblesworth Colliery in 1873.

The now demolished Kimblesworth viaduct (NE)

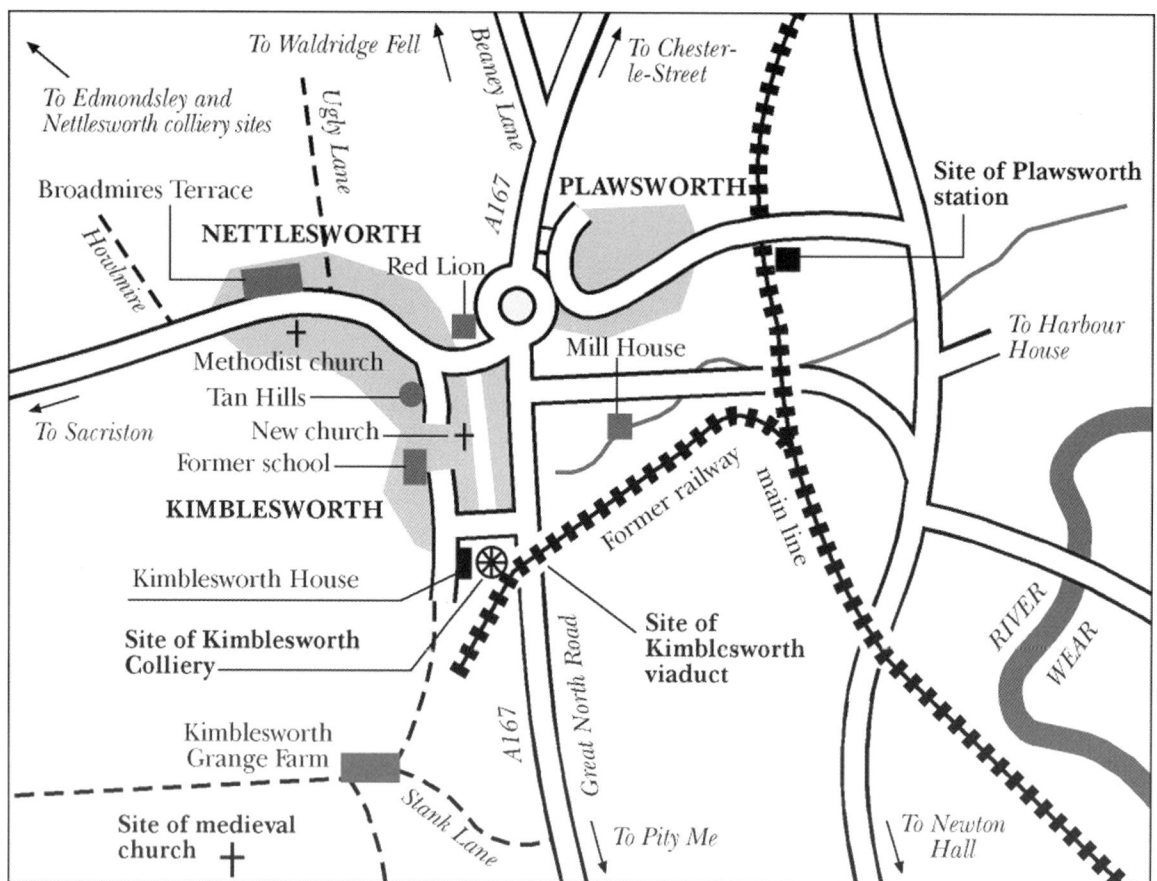

Map showing history of Kimblesworth and Plawsworth (NE)

Kimblesworth colliery had its own railway that crossed the Great North Road (now the A167) by a viaduct before joining the main line near Plawsworth. The colliery closed in 1967 and the viaduct was demolished in 1972. Kimblesworth mining village developed north of Kimblesworth colliery absorbing Tan Hill or Tan Hills as it had come to be known. The colliery village consisted of terraced streets like Charles Street, William Street and George Street. In 1897 streets called Jubilee Terrace and Victoria Terrace were also built at Pity Me by the Kimblesworth Colliery owners to house miners from the colliery. Pity Me served a dual purpose as a mining village for both Kimblesworth Colliery and Framwellgate Moor Colliery but it did not have a colliery of its own.

In the 1950s and 60s the terraces in Kimblesworth were no longer suitable for habitation and were gradually demolished and replaced with the council houses and bungalows that stand in the village today.

Some better-built terraces formerly occupied by colliery officials escaped demolition, as did Kimblesworth House, a larger building at the south end of the village. Once the colliery manager's house, this still overlooks the old colliery buildings and stands near a lane leading to Kimblesworth Grange.

Kimblesworth's colliery owners established a school at Kimblesworth in 1878 but this is now a home for old people. Nettlesworth also had a Victorian school but this has gone. The present school further to the east dates from 1928.

Although the original Kimblesworth church fell into ruin in medieval times, new places of worship sprung up in the mining village during the Victorian era. Wesleyan, Primitive and New Connexion Methodist chapels were built respectively at Kimblesworth, Tan Hills and Nettlesworth, but only Nettlesworth's chapel survives, combining the three denominations.

Nettlesworth's New Connexion worshippers were originally based next to the Black Bull Inn, but they were uncomfortable with their close proximity to a pub and moved down the road later in the century.

Kimblesworth's present parish church dedicated to St. Philip and St. James dates from 1893 and started life as a mission church. It may have superseded an earlier mission house in Plawsworth's Mill Lane. The new Kimblesworth church incorporates a font rescued from the medieval church at Kimblesworth Grange. Rather appropriately it gives the Kimblesworth of today a spiritual link with the Kimblesworth of the past.

Plawsworth

The village of Plawsworth, is separated from Kimblesworth and Nettlesworth by the dual carriageway of the A167, or Great North Road as it was historically known. Unlike Kimblesworth and Nettlesworth, Plawsworth probably still occupies its original site. It also differs from the other two in that it can't really be called a former pit village. There was no great nineteenth century colliery at Plawsworth and the village has the feel of a more rural age.

A Plawsworth Colliery is mentioned in 1647, but this was a small-scale enterprise compared with the standards of later centuries. Today, several houses in Plawsworth are apartments or self-catering cottages developed in the late 1990s, but many buildings betray their earlier, rural origins and the overall effect is quite picturesque.

Plawsworth Hall Farm (DS)

Plawsworth's name dates to Anglo-Saxon times, but is first recorded in 1135. Intriguingly, the name signifies an enclosure for sports, games or amusements, but the nature of the play (plaw) area is unknown. We know, however that 'worth' was an Anglo-Saxon word for an enclosure.

A Plawsworth scene (DS)

In the 1100s Plawsworth belonged to Simon Vitulus who provided greyhounds for the hunting expeditions of Durham's Prince Bishops. In fact the family of one Prince Bishop called Richard Kellaw, held land at Plawsworth in medieval times. Other medieval landowners included a family called Plawsworth who were named after the village.

Plawsworth's land was divided into four parts in medieval times, making the history of its ownership rather complex. Various landholders included the Dalden, Bowes, Claxton, Lindley and Read families but after 1627 two separate segments of Plawsworth came into the hands of Barnaby Hutchinson, a proctor of Durham. His daughter and only heir married a South Shields man called Rowe and the Rowes gradually purchased additional portions of Plawsworth land.

Plawsworth Township covered approximately 1,244 acres in the 1850s and was the site of 58 homes. There were 6 farms, 2 pubs, a corn mill and a gentleman's house called Plawsworth Cottage. The cottage stood until quite recent times half a mile north of Plawsworth, but was well across the western side of the A167 near Beaney Lane.

Most of Plawsworth is located along Wheatley Well Lane off the eastern side of the A167. Unfortunately for Plawsworth, the village pub, the Red Lion Inn, is inconveniently located on the west side of the dual carriageway. A former coaching inn, the Red Lion appears on the 1850s map, in the days when crossing the road was much less of a problem. The inn was a much smaller cottage-like building in those days.

The 1850s map also shows that another coaching inn called the Highland Laddie stood slightly further south on the same side of the road. The Highland Laddie was part of a roadside hamlet called Sunnyside that merged with a later row of nineteenth century houses called Plawsworth Gate. Once inhabited by miners, only two Plawsworth Gate houses remain. Highlander farm, the former Highland Laddie Inn can still be seen.

Former Highland Laddie Inn on Great North Road (DS)

Directly opposite, across the A167 is Mill Lane that leads off towards Leamside and Durham's Newton Hall estate. A tollgate once stood near here from which Plawsworth Gate took its name. Mill Lane proceeds east past the site of Plawsworth corn mill. The nearby house called Mill House only dates from the early 1900s, but there was a mill before then. The old mill was connected to a millrace fed by a stream that flows alongside the lane.

Further east, a little railway viaduct carries the main London-Edinburgh railway line over both the lane and the valley of a little wooded burn. Proceeding along the lane we find an area of quiet lowland roads, wooded copses and scattered farmhouses.

We have now entered the sparsely populated area that is sandwiched between the A167 and the River Wear. In fact the river is never more than a mile and a half to the east. A Roman road runs through this area, but its course is uncertain. Rather mysteriously it can be traced through Shincliffe and Sedgefield to the south and even through built-up Chester-le-Street and Gateshead to the north. Its exact course through Durham City and Plawsworth is unknown.

Farmhouses in this secluded area east of Plawsworth include the eighteenth century Bishop's Grange Farm near Finchale Training College and a farmhouse called Nag's Fold. One private road leads to Harbour House Farm, an eighteenth century property built on the site of a medieval manor. It is located very close to the river but was not a riverside dock. It apparently takes its name from an old word Herberwe meaning lodgings.

In medieval times Harbour House belonged to the same Kellaws who owned Plawsworth before passing to the Forcers who owned it until the 1780s. A medieval chapel dating from 1432 once stood nearby and just south of the farm was a little coal mine that had fallen out of use

by the 1890s. In the nineteenth century Harbour House belonged to Thomas Fenwick, a Newcastle banker who also owned Southill Hall just to the west, a little nearer Plawsworth. The Fenwicks also owned a brewery in Chester-le-Street. Dating from the eighteenth century, Southill Hall was substantially rebuilt for Fenwick by the Newcastle architect John Dobson in 1821.

Wheatley Well Lane, the road from Plawsworth crosses the main railway line just north of Southill Hall. Plawsworth Railway Station stood south of the lane on the eastern side of the railway. The line and station opened in 1868 but the station closed in 1963. The station was demolished later in decade but the line is still the main route from London to Edinburgh.

The now demolished Plawsworth Station (NE)

Chapter Eleven

Cocken, Great Lumley and the Raintons

Cocken

Cocken lies on the eastern and northern side of the River Wear. It is on the opposite bank of the river to the Plawsworth area which lies to the west while Finchale Priory stands in a little nook to the south.

The name Cocken derives from Cocca's Ea and is thought to describe a stretch of river where fishing rights belonged to someone called Cocca. The riverside is densely wooded here and forms a beautiful gorge. At the top of the riverbank the scenery stretches out into swathes of attractive farmland wedged between Great Lumley in the north and West Rainton beyond the motorway to the east.

There is no village called Cocken but the Wear forms a rather striking meander that encircles Low Cocken Farm near Cocken Bridge. This iron bridge of 1886 links Cocken to the open countryside surrounding Plawsworth and Newton Hall housing estate on the western bank.

Raised land at the neck of Cocken meander was the site of a stately seventeenth century mansion called Cocken Hall. At one time or another it was home to a Mayor of Newcastle, a convent of nuns and a champion pugilist.

Nothing is known of the Anglo-Saxon Cocca who owned Cocken in the earliest times, but in 1133 a priest called Ellafus gave Cocken to the Priory of Durham. In agreement with Roger of Kibblesworth (sic) the priory exchanged Cocken for lands at Wolviston, but Roger's daughter and heir, Petronilla sold Cocken to Finchale Priory.

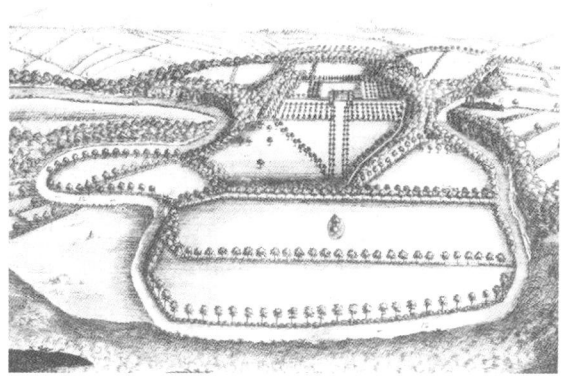

Illustration showing the grounds of Cocken Hall

After the dissolution of the monasteries Henry VIII gave Cocken to John Hilton of Newcastle, whose wife, Isabel, was previously married to Ralph Carr, a Newcastle mayor. After Hilton's death she married another Newcastle man, John Frankleyn but her grandson from the first marriage (another Ralph Carr) inherited Cocken in the late 1500s. Cocken then passed through this line until 1642 when a separate branch of the Carrs purchased the estate.

A later member of this branch was yet another Ralph Carr who was a Mayor of Newcastle in 1676, 1693 and 1705 and also an MP. In around 1671 the Carrs of Cocken acquired additional land at High Grange near Gilesgate Moor in Durham City, and their estate stretched as far as the north side of what is now Carrville High Street. This nineteenth century colliery village may well be named from the family.

Although the Carrs remained owners of the property, Cocken Hall became a convent for a group of Teresian (Carmelite) nuns in the early 1800s. The nuns had been expelled from England during the Reformation and had taken refuge at Lierre in Belgium. The French Revolution forced them to return to what was by then a more Catholic tolerant England in 1795. The nuns found accommodation in County Durham at St. Helen's Hall, a Carr property in St. Helen Auckland but the Carrs brought the nuns to Cocken in 1804.

The convent consisted of 16 choir nuns, 6 lay sisters and a Prioress called Dame Jessop. They remained at Cocken until around 1830 when the opening of a nearby coal mine is said to have forced them to seek a new site. They moved to Field House in what was then open countryside near Darlington. Now absorbed by the urban growth of Darlington the convent still exists in the Nunnery Lane area of that town.

In the meantime the Carrs remained owners of Cocken and in 1812, William Carr of Cocken inherited some Cheshire lands and a new title that made him William Standish Standish of Duxbury Hall.

In his later years William resided at Cocken, where he died in 1856. He was buried in an old hillside quarry that had been consecrated at Houghton-le-Spring. The churchyard of Houghton parish (which included Cocken) was apparently too full of bodies from the Sunderland cholera epidemic and William was one of many people to be buried there. Some local people claim Standish-Standish committed suicide by riding his horse off the neighbouring cliff and his ghost is said to haunt the site.

Sometime after the departure of William, (although the exact date is uncertain), the famous champion pugilist turned coal owner, John Gully came to live at the hall. Gully who came from Bath was once defeated in a 59 round bare knuckle boxing bout but later became a champion and invested his winnings in racehorses and Durham mines like Thornley, Ludworth and Wingate.

From Cocken, Gully later moved to 7 North Bailey in Durham City where he died aged 80 in 1863 leaving behind 24 children from two successive marriages.

The now demolished Cocken Hall (MR)

At the end of the nineteenth century Cocken Hall was home to the Sunderland shipbuilder Samuel Austin, but in July 1914 *The Northern Echo* reported that the house had been without a tenant for eight years. Its last occupant was a ship owner called Hudson but in succeeding years the house, by then a property of the Earl of Durham, remained empty and was looked after by a caretaker called Herdman.

Bridge over the River Wear at Cocken (DS)

When Herdman routinely arrived at the house at 7.30 on the morning of 14 July, 1914 he found the exterior of the house strewn with literature plastered with the words 'Votes for Women' and 'this is the work of militants'. He found a drawing room window open and inside there was much evidence of an elaborate preparation to start a fire. Thankfully, the staircase though saturated with oil, was only smouldering and Herdman was able to prevent the spread of fire.

An alarm clock fitted with a fuse that stopped at 12.25 was also found, along with a bag of oil and resin but there had been no explosion. Local farmers witnessed a car in the area around midnight that had returned half an hour later. *The Northern Echo* concluded that the hall was singled out as a target for suffragettes because of its uninhabited and isolated situation.

Later, in 1914 a service battalion of the Durham Light Infantry occupied the house and many photographs exist showing the soldiers training outside the hall. Sadly, sometime after the war, so-called builders flattened the empty house and nothing was built in its place. Today

Cocken, though undoubtedly a beautiful spot exists only as a collection of scattered farmhouses.

Great Lumley

Great Lumley was a rather rural looking little place until the later decades of the twentieth century, when housing estates were developed that more than quadrupled the area covered by the village.

Today Great Lumley has a population of around 5,000, but back in 1801 it was home to no more than 696 souls. Mining developments increased this population to 1,730 in 1851 and by 1891 it had risen to 1,927.

The village is located on a hill at the northern end of a lane from Cocken and Finchale that overlooks the valley of the River Wear to the west. West Rainton and Leamside lie across the motorway to the south east and also across the motorway, to the north east, is the village of Fencehouses.

The place-name Lumley means clearing of the pools as 'lum' seems to have been an old name for a deep pool in a river bend. The Lumley family took their name from this place but their name is most closely associated with Lumley Castle that lies a mile north of Great Lumley in a nook formed by the confluence of the Lumley Park Burn and River Wear at Chester-le-Street.

Lumley Castle is situated in a location that was once called Little Lumley and it seems that Great Lumley and Little Lumley were associated with two separate branches of the Lumley family from an early period.

Liulf of Lumley was the first known member of the Lumley family. He was murdered by an officer of the first Norman Bishop of Durham called William Walcher, in 1080 but he probably hailed from Little Lumley rather than Great Lumley. Liulf's murder was a significant event that ultimately resulted in the murder of the bishop at Gateshead by an angry mob.

Later in the Medieval period an elder line of the Lumley family retained Lumley Parva (Little Lumley) while Lumley Magna or Great Lumley became the estate of a younger line headed by Matthew de Lumley.

Rural scene at Great Lumley early 1900s (GN)

Matthew seems to have been the father of another Matthew who gave 2 acres of land in Lumley to the monks of Finchale Priory. However, it was the elder branch of the Lumleys that rose to power. They built a mansion during the reign of Edward I that would later develop into Lumley Castle. However the Lumleys of Great Lumley still seem to have been a family of importance. A Henry Lumley is mentioned in connection with Great Lumley in the 1200s and was seemingly the father of Waleran Lumley a Mayor of Newcastle.

Unfortunately the Lumleys of Great Lumley had a succession of female heirs so the family's connection with Great Lumley gradually disappeared. For a time a family called Laton held land hereabouts but they seem to have inherited their property through the Brackenburys – one of whom had married a daughter of Waleran Lumley.

From the Latons, Great Lumley passed to the Tylliols and then the Moresbys, Colvylles, Knivitts and Musgraves.

From the 1400s the estate of Great Lumley was divided into two parts called East Hall and West Hall. The old house called East Hall lay in ruins at the beginning of the nineteenth century. It was said to have been the seat of Liulf and the Lumley family before Lumley Castle was built but it was probably only the seat of the younger Lumley branch.

One of the most curious features of Great Lumley that can unfortunately no longer be seen was Duck's Hospital founded in 1686 by John Duck, a mayor of Durham City. He was otherwise known as Durham's Dick Whittington.

Along with John Potts, a yeoman of Great Lumley, Duck bought land in the village from William Clarke of Newcastle and erected the hospital here. It was a kind of almshouse built for the relief of 'poor, old and impotent people' of the district.

Rather like Sherburn Hospital it was built around a quadrangle and over the door was written an inscription in Latin with the date MDCLXXXVI.

Duck owned a large mansion house at neighbouring West Rainton but died in August 1696. His Great Lumley estate passed to his wife Dame Anne Duck and included fisheries and mills.

From Dame Duck it passed to Richard Wharton and then James Nicholson of Rainton who died in 1727. Nicholson's estate passed to three daughters including Jane who married an Earl of Strathmore and Anne who married Patrick Lyon. They were ancestors of the present Royal family and through them the land passed to John, Lord Glamis who became the 9th Earl of Strathmore.

The estate was later acquired by John George Lambton, the Earl of Durham.

Duck's Hospital stood in what are now empty fields on the west side of Great Lumley. The fields are overlooked by Back Lane – the main road to Lumley Castle. The hospital consisted of 12 apartments and a small chapel and looked after 12 inmates. There was a communal water pump and the apartments were lit with oil lamps. Residents of the hospital had to obey a daily curfew as the gates closed every evening after which there was no admittance.

During the nineteenth century the Earl of Durham kept the building under repair but most of the hospital was demolished in the early 1950s. Part of the hospital was still standing in 1960 when its last occupant was re-housed in a council flat. This last tumbledown remnant of the hospital may have been the hospital chapel which had later served as an additional apartment. Demolished in March 1960 it had been standing for 274 years.

Remnant of Duck's Hospital at Great Lumley in 1960 (NE)

North of Great Lumley towards Lumley Park Burn is an old house called Lumley Thicks that was restored in the nineteenth century. It was once thought to have had its own private chapel. The Thicks in Lumley Thicks refers to a thicket and the place is thought to have been synonymous with a medieval estate called Wodeshend that once belonged to the Kellaw family.

Just north of Lumley Thicks is the wooded valley of the Lumley Park Burn beyond which lies Bournmoor village and the extensive grounds of Lambton Park. The families of Lumley and Lambton dominated the history of this area for many centuries but their stories belong to the Chester-le-Street area.

Coal mining has a very long history in the Great Lumley area. As early as 1776 two pits were sunk at Lumley Park but others soon followed. By 1791 there was a 'fifth pit' at Lumley and then by 1841 there was a ninth. Tragedy visited these Lumley pits from time to time during this early period when colliery explosions seem to have been frequent. Thirty-one lives were lost in a Lumley mine on 11 April, 1797 and 39 were killed on 11 October, 1799. A further 13 died at the Lumley George Pit on 9 October, 1819 and then 14 were killed five years later on 25 October, 1824.

Lumley's ninth pit opened in 1841 when the Lumley collieries seem to have been operated by Stobart, Bell and Company. Whellan's Directory of 1894 mentions activity at the Sixth Pit (at Fencehouses) and by this time the collieries were worked by Lambton, the Earl of Durham who employed around 500 men and boys at Lumley.

By the 1850s Great Lumley included a police station, a few shops and seven public houses like the Dun Cow and Dog and Gun. There were two Methodist chapels, one now standing on the western edge of the village overlooking fields. It has been converted into a private house.

Former Methodist chapel at Great Lumley (DS)

Early streets in the village included Paradise Row and Love's Row adjoining Front Street and there was a National School at the west end of the village.

The school stood in what is now a field overlooked by Back Lane. When the Reverend D. J. Stewart visited this school in June 1853, 69 boys and girls attended. Stewart filed a report on conditions in the school that give a good insight into a typical school of the time. It reads as follows:

> 'Buildings: good sized room used for Divine Service, no class room; all the walls are cracked from a 'creep' in the pit below. Furniture: four loose desks; pulpit, clock, book closets. Playground: part of it laid out as a garden. Books: good. Apparatus: two blackboards, 2 easels, map stand. Methods: discipline and instruction fair. Organisation; standard of classification: reading and arithmetic. Four classes for all subjects, under master with certificate of merit and one pupil teacher; one division for scripture and geography

lessons; two groups for arithmetic in first and second class. The pupil-teacher is confined to one class for one week.'

Another school followed at the east end of the village later in the century but this building is now a snooker club. It stands close to Christ Church of 1859 that serves the parish of Great Lumley. A vicarage was built at this eastern end of the old village and can still be seen. It was erected near the site of a sawmill that existed here in the early nineteenth century.

Little remains of the original Great Lumley village that was clustered along the Front Street. Today Great Lumley has the appearance of a former mining village with additional housing estates.

Great Lumley has an intriguing ghost story relating to a rather unconventional form of criminal justice. In 1632 a young girl in the village called Annie Walker became pregnant, possibly by her uncle for whom she was acting as a housekeeper. Later, she went missing and when the curious members of the village enquired about her whereabouts it was said she was away visiting relatives.

Some months later a miller called James Graham was working alone late at night grinding corn at his mill two miles from Lumley. Here he was confronted by the apparition of a wild-eyed young lady who said she was Annie Walker and had been murdered by a local miner called Mark Sharp with the encouragement of her uncle.

She explained her uncle had told her that Sharp would transport her to the safety of a relative some distance away so that she could give birth away from the prying eyes of local people.

Instead, according to Miss Walker, or at least according to the miller's story, Sharp took Annie to a nearby moor and smashed her skull five times in the head with a colliery pick.

The miller claimed that the ghost had five bloody wounds to her head around which her bedraggled hair was hung in a fearsome manner. She was seemingly a very helpful ghost and gave the miller details of the precise spot on which the murder took place and the location of a neighbouring pit shaft down which her body was thrown.

Initially the miller took no action, but the ghost was persistent and made visits to the mill over and over again. Occasionally she would bolt the doors behind her or tug on the miller's bed clothes as he slept, but always she pleaded with him to inform local magistrates about the incident.

Eventually, he gave in to her pleas as he feared for his life and reported his sighting to the authorities. These were superstitious times and the magistrates, far from being suspicious of Graham, took the report very seriously and investigated the moor and associated pit that he had described.

Sure enough the unfortunate girl's body was found with evidence of five severe blows to the head. The location of the murder weapon and some bloodied clothes were also found nearby following a further tip off from the miller based on information supplied by the ghost.

Sharp, a local miner originating from Blackburn, Lancashire was arrested along with the uncle of the ghost. Neither would confess, so the two were tried in the assizes court that then stood on Durham City's Palace Green. During the trial it was said that the apparition appeared again, this time to the judge and also to the foreman of the jury. If this wasn't conclusive evidence enough one witness that said they thought they saw the likeness of a child appear upon the shoulders of Annie's uncle. In the minds of the seventeenth century jury all evidence pointed in one direction. Sharp and the girl's uncle were found guilty of the crime and upon the alledged evidence of the ghost, both were hanged.

West Rainton and Leamside

Rainton was originally 'Raegnwald's tun', a farming settlement established by Raegnwald, the son of Franco. Franco was one of the seven monks who escorted St. Cuthbert's coffin from Lindisfarne to Chester-le-Street in the ninth century AD, about a hundred years before it was brought to Durham City. Over the centuries, villages called West and East Rainton developed as separate 'townships' on Raegnwald's ancient estate and in recent decades, their history has become a 'tale of two cities'. East Rainton is now in the City of Sunderland while West Rainton, half a mile to the west, is in the City of Durham.

The Raintons were already noted for mining in medieval times but in the nineteenth century they became one of the busiest colliery areas in the county. Here was a complex network of railways and wagonways and at least 10 local mines owned by the Marquess of Londonderry.

Aerial view of West Rainton (NE)

The monks of Finchale and Durham were Rainton's first mine owners and records show that their mining activity at Rainton went back as far as 1347. At Moorhouse just south of Rainton they were the first in the region to mine below the level of free drainage, using elaborate and often costly pumps.

Although miners numbered amongst Rainton's population in early times, the Raintons were for most of their history predominantly farming communities. Indeed, West Rainton still has a strong rural feel about it today.

Back in the 1300s much of Rainton was parkland belonging to the Priory of Durham and we know a park keeper was appointed here in 1338. The park was called Rainton Parke and survives only in the name of Rainton Park Wood, a National Trust woodland on the banks of the River Wear between Belmont and West Rainton. This managed woodland is joined by another, called Malygill Wood, that runs along the course of a little stream down towards the Wear.

There are several traces of early mining in Malygill Wood, but it was probably outcrops of exposed coal on the river bank that saw the earliest activity. Intriguingly, the bed of Mallygill stream is paved and marked with wheels. Once thought to be a Roman road, this is in fact another remnant of mining activity. Also close by and south of Malygill is a stream called Winch Gill that possibly refers to the winching of coal from the river bank in times past. The gill passes under the Al (M) motorway and joins the Wear as it twists its way south towards Kepier Wood and Durham. The related history of Kepier Wood is featured in the accompanying book on Durham City.

In the 1600s a man called John Duck leased mines at Rainton from the cathedral's Dean and Chapter and successfully won a seam of coal that came to be known as Old Duck's Main. Duck was known as 'Durham's Dick Whittington' and built the now demolished Rainton Hall that was once the most prominent building in West Rainton.

Duck was a Yorkshireman who came to Durham to seek his fortune but was sacked as a butcher's apprentice in the city, on suspicion of being a Scot. As he wandered despondently along Durham's river banks, a raven dropped a gold coin at his feet and using this coin Duck went on to make his fortune.

He became a Mayor of Durham in 1680, founded the hospital at Great Lumley in 1686 and was made a Baronet by James II in 1687. Titled Sir John Duck of Haswell on the Hill, (where he had bought the manor) Duck built the mansion at Rainton in 1688 but didn't reside there long. When he died in 1691, aged 59, he was at home in his Durham City mansion in Silver Street.

In the late nineteenth century Duck's Rainton Hall, which has long since gone, fell into disrepair and became a collection of dilapidated tenements occupied by miners and labourers. West Rainton's Hall Lane gives a clue to its site. The hall stood at the lane's junction with South Street.

West Rainton's most prominent building today is the church of St. Mary that stands in a green oasis at the village centre. It only dates from 1864, but an earlier chapel affiliated to Houghton-le-Spring stood here from 1825 and became the parish church in 1846. This chapel was probably built on the site of a twelfth century chantry dedicated to the Virgin Mary that was demolished in the 1500s. West Rainton church was built by E. R. Robson in 1864, two years before the parish church of St. Cuthbert was built at East Rainton. The impressive spire of West Rainton church can be seen from miles around but was a later addition erected in 1877 by Sir George Elliot.

Elliot was chief viewer of the Marquess of Londonderry's Rainton Collieries and was a remarkable man whose story, like Duck's, was one of rags to riches. He started life as a trapper boy at a Penshaw colliery aged ten, but was keen

to learn. He studied surveying and mine engineering and eventually acquired mine interests in Wales. He became a pioneering manufacturer of transatlantic telegraph cables, an MP for North Durham in 1868 and a Baronet by 1874. Elliot was a favourite of Disraeli and held much political influence, becoming the financial adviser to the Khedive, or ruler of Egypt.

Sir George Elliot

The spire at Rainton was built in memory of Elliot's daughter and inside, within the north wall of the spire is a granite stone from the great pyramid of Ghizeh. It was brought over by Elliot with the permission of the Egyptian Khedive, Ismail Pash. Inscribed with the name

of the donor it was a mark of thanks for Elliot's safe return from Egypt.

Historic view of South Street, West Rainton (GH)

In 1876 Elliot had installed a similar tablet, from the pyramid of Cheops, at All Saints church in Penshaw. It is extraordinary to think that stones from these ancient pyramids that long predate the days of Christianity, can be found inside these two Victorian churches.

West Rainton church (DS)

Although coal mining took place around the Raintons from medieval times, it was the arrival of the railways in the nineteenth century that really stimulated colliery growth. Mines served by local colliery railways included the Adventure and Resolution Pits of 1816, the Plain Pit of 1817, the Hazard Pit of 1818 and the Meadows Pit of 1824 (see map on page 135).

East Rainton's Hazard Pit was presumably a hazardous place to work, but it was Plain Pit that suffered the worst disasters. Explosions there in 1817 and 1823 claimed 27 and 55 lives. Most Rainton mines belonged to the Marquess of Londonderry, officially under the ownership of his wife, Lady Frances Anne Vane. The Hazard Pit at East Rainton and the North Hetton Pit (founded in 1821) at Low Moorsley were operated in the 1850s by the North Hetton Colliery Company. Proprietors included the Earl of Durham.

One of the first wagonways in the area was a wooden one called the Londonderry Railway that connected the Londonderry mines with coal staithes on the River Wear at Penshaw. This terminated at the Adventure Pit but had already been removed by the time of the 1857 Ordnance Survey map.

During the 1830s, three new colliery railways came to Rainton. One was the Rainton and Seaham Railway of 1831 that linked the Londonderry mines to Seaham Harbour, passing Rainton Bridge with branches to pits at Moorsley as well as the Hunter's House, Meadows, Dun Well and Nicholson Pits. A brickworks operated near the last of these pits during the later nineteenth century.

The mid-1830s saw two further railways at Rainton. From the north came the Earl of Durham's Lambton Railway, linked to Staithes on the Wear. It had branches to Pittington, Sherburn, Littletown, Frankland, Brasside, Lumley and Cocken. In 1836, the Durham and Sunderland Railway (from Sunderland to Shincliffe) came through the area serving Lady Seaham Colliery at

Pittington and the nearby Belmont Colliery – but by the far the most important railway through Rainton was George Hudson's Newcastle and Durham Junction Railway of 1844.

Historic view of Station Road, Rainton (GH)

This railway was later the North Eastern Railway's London to Newcastle line and, although it has not served that particular purpose since the 1870s, it still exists today. Now named after a little village on the western fringe of West Rainton, it is known today as the Leamside line.

When John Wesley - the founder of Methodism – preached at Rainton in April 1747, he noted that there were already many collieries and an abundance of people here. But in truth, the real growth and industrial development came with the railways in the nineteenth century. From 1801 to 1821, West Rainton's population rose from 435 to 1,160.

Similar growth occurred at East Rainton, where the population increased from 294 to 671. In between the two villages, a small mining hamlet called Middle Rainton came into being in 1820.

It was only in 1822 that the Raintons received their first place of worship when a Wesleyan Methodist Chapel opened up off West Rainton's Hall Lane. Other chapels were built later by the Primitive and New Connexion Methodists at Leamside and at Rainton Gate in 1867 and 1874.

West Rainton had two Victorian schools. One was the now-demolished St. Godric's National School of 1861 that stood in the village churchyard. The other was the earlier Londonderry School of 1850, founded by the Marchioness of Londonderry. Now a private house, the building still has an inscription on the wall that rather vainly declares: 'This edifice erected in 1850 by Frances Anne Vane, Marchioness of Londonderry, as an encouragement to the colliers to promote the moral and religious education of their children and as a lasting memorial of the interest she takes in their welfare.'

Former National School, West Rainton (DS)

A National School was also built at Leamside in 1865 – but all of these Victorian schools were superseded by a new establishment in 1927 that is now the West Rainton Primary School.

As well as promoting local education, the Londonderrys were keen to encourage participation in local regiments and built a drill hall in West Rainton for the Second Durham Artillery Volunteers. This building is now the West Rainton Jubilee Hall and can still be seen at the north end of the village. Close by is West Rainton's present day school, on the corner of Station Road, that links Leamside to Rainton Gate on the western fringe of the village.

Rainton Gate, now split in two by the A690, was once a separate settlement, but was virtually swallowed up by West Rainton in the mid-twentieth century.

Hinge of the old gate at Rainton Gate (DS)

Rainton Gate is named from a toll gate that stood at the junction of Station Road and what was once the main Durham to Sunderland road. The hinge of the old toll gate can still be seen on the wall of a newsagent. Just opposite the newsagent is the former Rainton Gate Co-operative store and nearby along the old road to Sunderland is the Mason's Arms.

Between this pub and the shop is a house that was formerly the Three Tuns Inn. It was one of several pubs dotted along the Durham to Sunderland road ready to quench the thirsts of miners and travellers in times gone by. At Rainton, they included the Nag's Head, just south of the village, and The Oak Tree, on the main road to the north.

In West Rainton itself, there was a pub called the Lord Seaham, at the east end of the main street, and there were at least three other pubs in this village. Pubs could also be found at East Rainton, while at Moorsley there were six and, at Leamside, five. These were the Robin Hood, Bonnie Pit Lad, Highland Laddie, Railway Hotel and Leamside Hotel. The last of these, demolished very recently, stood close to Leamside Railway Station, but the station itself has long since gone.

The now demolished Leamside Station on the Leamside railway (GH)

As we draw to a close I note that we have mentioned Moorsley briefly. Moorsley consisted of two places called Low Moorsley and High Moorsley. Here, however we have left Durham City's administrative district behind and entered the outskirts of what is officially the City of Sunderland. The two Moorsleys lie on a hill and straddle a road running from Low Pittington to Hetton-le-Hole.

First mentioned in the 1100s the name of Moorsley derives from Morulf's law meaning the hill belonging to Morulf. High Moorsley is the smaller, more westerly of the two settlements and includes a farm. It stands on a magnesian limestone hill that is slightly higher than Pittington Hill, its neighbour to the immediate south. A colliery called the Alexandrina or Letch Pit stood at the foot of the hill to its north and here was also the site of Rainton Station. Close by is the village of Low Pittington and neighbouring Elemore Hall that brings us full circle in our tour around the surrounds of Durham. Also nearby are the mining village of Easington Lane and the tiny settlements of Elemore Vale and Hetton-le-Hill, both in Sunderland. The last of these is a rural looking hamlet of magnesian limestone cottages and should not be confused with the much larger neighbouring town of Hetton-le-Hole.

Low Moorsley is High Moorsley's more easterly neighbour and was the site of the North Hetton pit. Today the village has become a virtual suburb of the town of Hetton-le-Hole. Hetton as Hetton-le-Hole is known for short is now also within the City of Sunderland but was once the site of Hetton Colliery. This was one of the most famous collieries in the Durham coafield. It was here in 1822 that George Stephenson developed his Hetton Colliery Railway. It was operated with locomotives and was then the largest railway in the world.

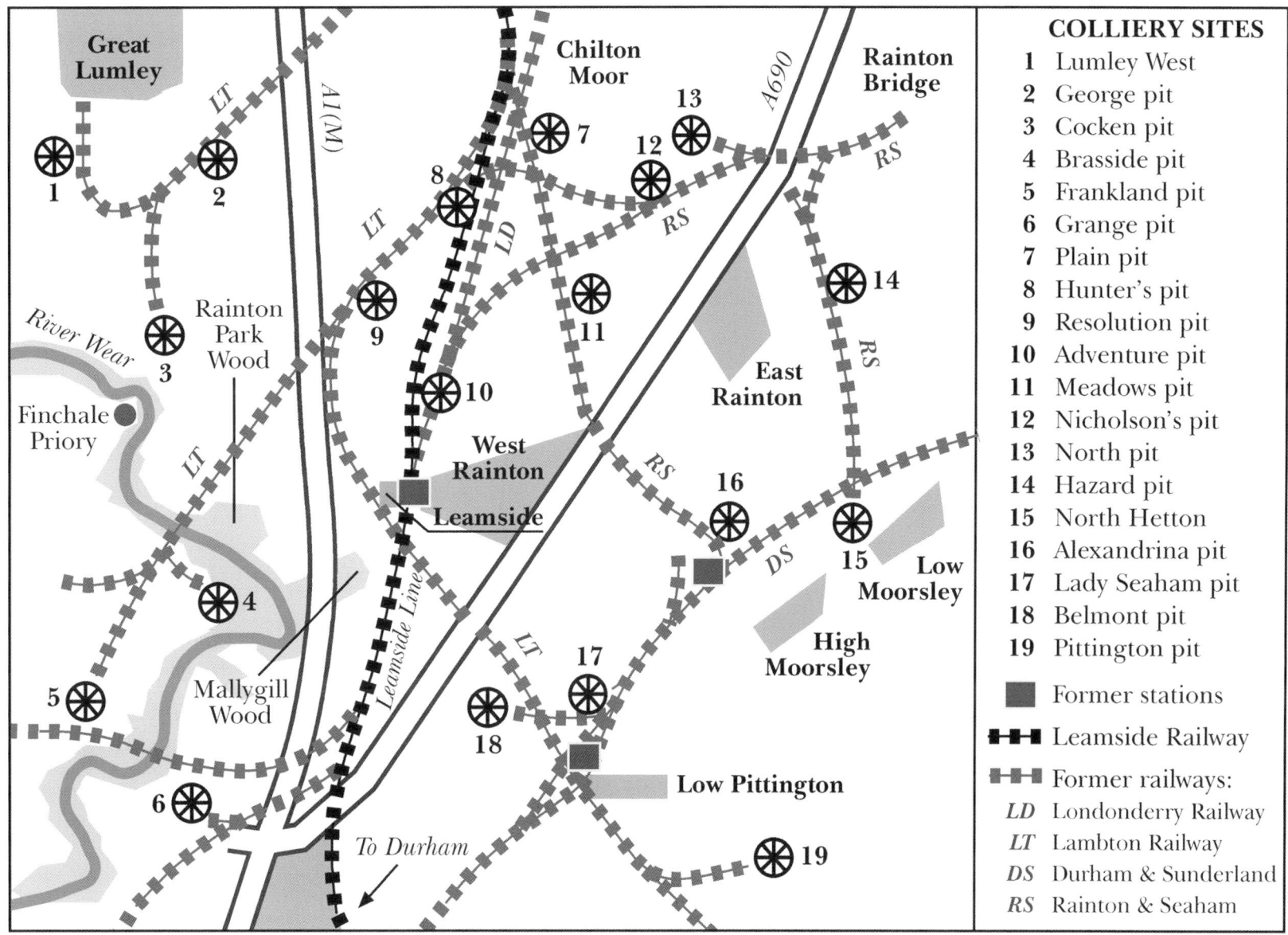

COLLIERY SITES

1 Lumley West
2 George pit
3 Cocken pit
4 Brasside pit
5 Frankland pit
6 Grange pit
7 Plain pit
8 Hunter's pit
9 Resolution pit
10 Adventure pit
11 Meadows pit
12 Nicholson's pit
13 North pit
14 Hazard pit
15 North Hetton
16 Alexandrina pit
17 Lady Seaham pit
18 Belmont pit
19 Pittington pit

■ Former stations

▬▬ Leamside Railway

▬▬ Former railways:
LD Londonderry Railway
LT Lambton Railway
DS Durham & Sunderland
RS Rainton & Seaham

Map showing colliery sites and former railways of Rainton area (NE)

View across the City of Durham from Brandon Hill looking towards Pittington Hill (DS)

Index

Durham City
by David Simpson
ISBN 978 1 901888 50 8
Price: £12.95

Durham City is based on the 'Durham Memories' column that appears in *The Northern Echo* and features the history of Durham City and its surrounding suburbs. It includes the historic city centre with all its wonderful buildings and wealth of history but also visits the city's outer reaches, where Framwellgate Moor, Pity Me, Crossgate Moor, Neville's Cross, Gilesgate Moor and Carrville and many places besides, are explored.

Whether you are a visitor, a local or an exile, it is hoped that you will enjoy this journey through the history of Durham City.

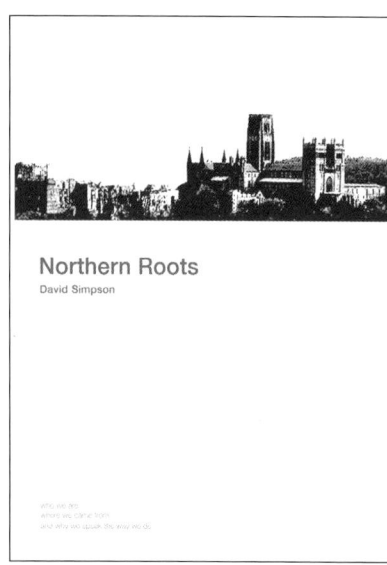

Northern Roots: who we are, where we come from and why we speak the way we do   *by David Simpson*

ISBN 1 901888 35 5   Price: £7.95

Northerners speak with distinct local dialects and have their very own sense of history. In the guise of Yorkshiremen, Cumbrians, Geordies, Scousers, Lancastrians or Northumbrians, all have contributed to the rich culture of Britain.

But who are these Northerners and where did they come from?
What clues exist in history to the ancient and more recent origins of Northerners and their speech? This book traces the languages and origins of various people who have settled in the North over two thousand years to give it the distinct character it has today.

North East England: places, history, people and legends   *by David Simpson*

ISBN 1 901888 37 1   Price: £8.95

Stretching from the River Tees to the River Tweed the North East of England was the ancient heartland of the Kingdom of Northumbria. It was the birthplace of the railways, the 'borderland zone' of the Scottish raids and the quiet retreat of the ancient Celtic saints. It is a region steeped in history and a home to wonderful sites like Durham Cathedral, Hadrian's Wall and the bustling Quayside of Newcastle upon Tyne. Travelling across the region from Durham to Teesside to England's northernmost county of Northumberland, this book explores the places, history, people and legends of this remarkable northern region.

Millennium History of North East England   *by David Simpson*

ISBN 09536984 3 2   Price: £7.50

North East England has a strong sense of identity that sets it apart from other areas of England. The roots of this identity lie in two thousand years of distinct history that have made the region what it is today. From the Roman frontier zone of Hadrian's Wall, to the powerful Christian Kingdom of Northumbria, through the gloomy days of Border warfare up to the great age of coal mining and railways, each era has played its part. This unique, 336 page, beautifully illustrated hardback book explores the events, people and places that have shaped the region's history over the last two thousand years.